The Politics of Alcoholism

The Politics of Alcoholism

Building an Arena Around a Social Problem

Carolyn L. Wiener

Transaction Books
New Brunswick (U.S.A.) and London (U.K.)

Library of Congress Catalog Number: 79-66450
ISBN: 0-87855-379-7   -
Printed in the United States of America

Library of Congress Cataloging in Publication Data

Wiener, Carolyn L 1930-
   The politics of alcoholism.

   Includes bibliographical references and index.
   1. Liquor problem. 2. Social problems 3. Political sociology. I. Title.
HV5035.W36   363.4'1   79-66450
ISBN 0-87855-379-7

Contents

v

vi   Contents

*For Mayer Licht and Aaron Mathew Wiener,
my links to the past and the future.*

Preface

The Politics of Alcoholism can be read on one level as a fascinating history of the evolving politics of what this country is doing about "the problem of alcoholism." Not so long ago that problem was scarcely larger than a human hand against the horizon, but now it makes good, regular newspaper copy. A few years ago the federal government entered the picture. Its interest and funding precipitated a rapid explosion of activity and organization-building in this general area. Each year brings more groups, organizations, and representatives of scientific, therapeutic, and other movements into competition, conflict and cooperation over a variety of issues: What is alcoholism? What is an alcoholic? Where does alcoholism begin and ordinary drinking end? Should anything be done about alcoholism per se, or only about individual alcoholics? Should this be treated as an illness, a moral problem, or something else? What therapies are most effective? What researchers are most valuable? (The ideologies about all those questions are abundant.)

But no political scientist or sociologist will read Wiener's account as pure history, nor has she meant it to be read primarily in that way. The book, I predict, will be one of the important monographs of the year because it addresses successfully two outstanding theoretical issues. First, it follows through on the much-raised question of how a social problem becomes defined as a large scale problem, when the same phenomenon now labeled as "a problem" was not so named before. What is offered here is a direct attack on the rise into public visibility of something previously the concern of a relatively small number of people and groups, and which gets defined along the way as a problem for the whole nation.

The second issue addressed is closer to the political scientist's traditional interest, namely the politics of handling public issues: research and theorizing here usually focus on interest groups, lobbying, public debate, legislative rights, constituencies, and so on. Using concepts like social worlds and arena, Wiener has sketched out the numerous social worlds and sub-worlds and their representative organizations, which have entered this alcoholism arena, their relationships to each other, their ideologies and predominant directions of action, their relationships to governmental agencies, and of course the debates over prevailing issues in the arena. Since a principal feature of this particular arena has been its quick rise to public visibility, the framework of her book is largely organized around the evolution of this public visibility: the heart of the book consists of a number of processes and sub-processes linked with that evolution.

This process-oriented, basically interactionist approach is very successful: it builds good substantive theory, and it also offers a clear path through the jungle of events that appear everywhere on the pages of the book. This kind of "arena analysis" has great potential for research in many other areas other than alcoholism.

—ANSELM STRAUSS
University of California at
San Francisco, 1979

Acknowledgments

As a college "drop-out" and "re-entry woman" before either of these terms had gained currency, I owe many debts for the support and encouragement that made this book possible.

I am deeply grateful to my husband, Stanley Wiener, who first suggested that I take a course or two, and then steadfastly suffered through thirteen years of papers, examinations, and the agonies of research. His estimation of me has always surpassed my own and has made me reach beyond what I had deemed attainable. To my mother, Sarah Licht, go thanks for always providing a fund of uncritical love. I offer my appreciation to her and to my children, Joel, Gary, and Fredie Wiener, for understanding when I was too busy being a researcher to remember I was also a daughter and mother.

I owe a special debt to Anselm Strauss for first encouraging me to consider a career in sociology, and for teaching me to *see* with a sociological eye and to *do* sociology with the requisite skills. The balance of patience and prodding which he exhibited in the course of my development could only have come from a faculty advisor who is a sensitive friend.

I wish to thank Barney Glaser, whose instruction in a six-quarter seminar on qualitative analysis was invaluable in sharpening my ability to practice the art of sociology. Gratitude is also extended to the rest of the faculty of the Graduate Program in Sociology at the University of California, San Francisco—especially Leonard Schatzman—for the guidance I received while becoming a sociologist, and to Fred Davis, who, in the brief period when I was under his tutelage, broadened my sociological vision.

I am indebted to Don Cahalan, director of the training program that funded my research, for providing not only financial support but the total independence necessary for a research endeavor to flourish. I am grateful to the staff of the Social Research Group in Berkeley, especially Andrea Mitchell, who assisted my literature search, Ronald Roizen, who offered stimulating criticism of the early draft of this book (as a dissertation) and most especially Robin Room, who generously shared his time and ideas, extending assistance without interference.

Finally, I wish to express my appreciation to the people who cordially received me and shared their feelings about their involvement in, and perceptions of, the alcohol-use arena. I hope I have faithfully portrayed the composite picture of their interviews.

Part I

Introduction and Approach to the Problem

1.

Introduction

In 1970, the year of publication of *Precarious Politics: Alcoholism and Public Policy*,[1] the main obstacle to public support for alcoholism programs (as seen by its author, Dan Beauchamp) lay in demonstrating an invisible problem. By December, 1974, former Senator Harold Hughes, father of the 1970 Comprehensive Alcohol Abuse and Alcoholism Prevention Treatment and Rehabilitation Act, was expressing the distress of a Dr. Frankenstein:

> We have, in effect, a new civilian army that has now become institutionalized. The alcohol and drug industrial complex is not as powerful as its military-industrial counterpart, but nonetheless there are some striking similarities.[2]

Five years after the passage of the above act, Hughes could point to counsellors, scientists, "think-tank" personnel, administrators, government funding agencies, lobbyists, associations, consultants, evaluators, technical assistants. Eight years after passage, this arena had grown from an "invisible" state to a federal budget appropriation of $161,467,000.[3] What had happened in the intervening years to make such growth possible?

Obviously, considerable awareness of alcohol-related problems existed prior to 1970. Prohibition could not have come about without such

3

awareness. But the drive for alcoholism programs was based on belief in the existence of a *hidden* alcoholism problem—one that was far larger than was publicly recognized. Beauchamp's study took place in the District of Columbia, described as a community largely unaware of the situation with which it was supposed to cope. Alcoholism lay buried, with the individual alcoholic only surfacing in some aspect of the community control network—in the emergency room, in the doctor's office, on the policeman's beat, at the mental hospital. It is Beauchamp's thesis that the failure of Prohibition and Repeal forced people who were concerned with alcohol-related problems to search for appeals which did not attack the drinking behavior of a large number of the general public. Furthermore, "even though alcoholics could not happen without alcohol, the sheer and uncontrovertible evidence of millions of normal drinkers was seen as *prima facie* evidence that alcohol or drinking did not cause alcoholism." [4] Therefore, two distinct populations of drinkers were presented as "public facts": one, diseased, suffering from "loss of control," or addiction; and the other constituting a group of "social drinkers." Herein lay the impediment to building a public policy: "the alcoholic is identified by his compulsion or addiction (invisible cues) but not by his public behavior (visible cues)"; [5] and since "the alcoholic shares collectively legitimate behavior with all other drinkers (alcohol, drinking, intoxication). . . . there is no simple sign for alcoholism that can be used to represent the problem in policy communications." [6] Beauchamp could see this invisibility as working against a basic public policy precept—that of building a base of support around a valuable and tangible set of benefits. And he saw the clientele as highly unlikely to organize itself into a policy constituency.

What then had happened to bring about a mushrooming of Hughes' "civilian army"? To answer that question, we first have to look at the larger picture of the *emergence of a social problem*. Traditional sociological attention to social problems—crime, poverty, family disorganization, illegitimacy, alcohol, and drug use—was based on the assumption that the phenomenon under examination was inherently undesirable. It was taken as a given that social problems emerged because groups held opposing values, or certain people violated societal rules, or rules did not exist for certain situations, or rules conflicted. But some sociologists began to puzzle over why certain social phenomena achieved the status of social problems while others did not. Most often quoted (though often unheeded) in this regard is Herbert Blumer, who contended that to attribute social problems to "presumed structural strains, upsets in the equilibrium of the social system, dysfunctions, breakdown of social norms, clash of social values, or deviations from social conformity" is unwittingly to transfer to a "suppositious social structure" what belongs to the process of *collective definition*.[7] Blumer suggested that students of social problems should study the process by which a society *recognizes* its social problems: 1) the emergence of a social problem; 2) the legitimation of the problem; 3) the mobilization of action with regard to the problem; 4) the formation of an official plan of action; and 5) the transformation of the plan in its empirical implementation. Similarly, Fuller and Myers offered a "natural history approach," suggesting that a social problem is always in a state of "becoming," passing through the natural history stages of awareness, policy determination and reform.[8]

Kitsuse and Spector further developed Blumer's admonition regarding the false picture presented by singular attention to structural conditions, when they proposed that the central interest of sociologists of social problems should be the interaction of claims-making groups and others about the definition of social conditions and what should be done about them. "What is in contention throughout the social problems producing process . . . are the definitions of reality that groups and organizations assert, sponsor, impose, reject or subvert." [9] Special note was taken by Kitsuse and Spector of a significant prerequisite for a sociology of social problems—the importance of taking the members' perspective as the starting point, focusing in particular on definitional and claims-making activities as the primary subject matter. From this perspective, the sociologist would arrive at "macro-sociological" concerns from a direction that differs from the traditional route:

> Rather than investigating how institutional arrangements produce certain social conditions, we examine how individuals and groups become engaged in collective activities organized and directed toward establishing institutional arrangements, recognizing putative conditions as problems, and attempting to relieve, ameliorate, and eliminate them.[10]

This I have seen as the task of my work: if the social problem of alcohol use has grown from an invisible social problem to one of heightened visibility, how, to use Kitsuse's and Spector's terminology, has its definition been "socially processed"? What are the collective activities that have become organized around the assertion that alcohol use is a problem? What has been the career of this definition?

The waxing and waning of political responsibility for social problems has been characterized by Gusfield as "the ownership of social problems," [11] signifying in regard to alcohol use, the shifting roles played by religious institutions, the alcoholic beverage industries, and the government in the assumption of leadership. However, as Gusfield specifies, ownership and responsibility *may* coincide, but this is not necessarily the case. Quite often those who own a problem are trying to place obligations on others to take responsibility and behave in a "proper" manner. Owners of the problem must transmit their mission in the form of "public facts," which Gusfield sees as resembling Durkheim's "social facts"—products of collective entity.[12] The "discovery" of public facts requires that someone has monitored, recorded, aggregated, analyzed and transmitted separate and individual events into public reality. In making his point, Gusfield does a nice turn on Christie and Bruun's simile for the abundance of words used in relation to alcohol and drugs, which they say are "as many as pebbles on the beach." [13] To quote Gusfield:

> At every stage in this process human choices of selection and interpretation operate. Events are given meaning, and assumptions and values guide the selection. Public "facts" are not like pebbles on the beach, lying in the sun and waiting to be seen. They must instead be picked, polished, shaped and packaged. Finally ready for display, they bear the marks of their shapers.[14]

In another context, Gusfield has underscored his point: "There is, then, a crucial interaction between that which interests the public and that which is available to their interest." [15] Thus, a related task of my work has been to trace the shaping of public facts regarding the social problem of alcohol use.

In tracing the heightened visibility of the social problem of alcohol use and the shaping of public facts surrounding this problem, I have found that *collective definition* does not pass through stages sequentially as Blumer proposed, but that all the stages he identified intertwine. For example, after a plan of action is implemented, legitimation of the social problem may be continually threatened. Nor is "the formation of an official plan of action" as purposeful as that phrase would suggest. The plan is constantly emerging and being refashioned by the actors who have been "mobilized." Following Blumer's shift of emphasis away from "a suppositious social structure," I have identified the integrants of the collective definition of the social problem of alcohol use as: *animating* the problem (establishing turf rights, developing constituencies, funneling advice and imparting skills and information); *legitimizing* the problem (borrowing expertise and prestige, redefining its scope, building respectability, maintaining a separate identity); and *demonstrating* the problem (competing for attention, combining for strength, selecting supportive data, convincing opposing ideologists, enlarging the bounds of responsibility). It is important to stress, however, that while I present these sub-processes sequentially, to ease the understanding of their various facets, this should not be interpreted as implying steps or stages, but rather, as a *continually ricocheting* interaction.[16]

More social problems are recognized by more people today than ever before in American history. Alcoholism and alcohol abuse must share the stage with child abuse, wife abuse, drug abuse, mental patient abuse, *ad infinitum.* An obvious contributing factor is government intervention. Perhaps less obvious is the additional explanation offered by Ross and Staines, who contend that the degree of divergence between ideal and reality which people will tolerate before recognizing a social problem has diminished:

> The expansion of material resources and productivity in the United States has meant that much more can be done to change reality in the direction of the ideal. . . . [and] the elaboration of the division of labor has created new occupational categories whose interest and concern have been to alert people to the discrepancies between ideal and reality. Whether called intellectuals, technocrats, conservatives, radicals, etc., this scatter of social roles, together with the interests they defend and attack, creates a steady percolation of potential social problems.[17]

Poorer societies allow much wider range for what constitutes acceptable health, tolerated illness, endurable existence. McCarthy and Zald have graphically captured the net effect of this composite of government intervention and a cadre of interveners: "If large amounts of funds are available, then, problem definition becomes a strategy for competing for them." [18]

The social worlds that interveners represent are themselves constantly in a state of flux, constantly splitting off and reshaping. This is reflected in the continual transformation occurring within the arena under examination. "Alcoholism," "alcohol abuse," "problems with alcohol"—these are very different problems to a lot of different people, who can still form marriages of convenience. Christie and Bruun, in their paper on the conceptual framework of alcohol problems,[19] talk about the function of vagueness, and how apparent agreements can be reached, for instance, on the disease concept of alcoholism, while the parties who reach that apparent agreement really have very different notions of what is going on. Coalitions are impermanent, and there is a great deal of sliding that goes on between various interests. People have come into the arena as volunteers, and ended up with careers. Others have come in for a summer job, and ended up with a commitment. Some serve on an advisory board out of genuine concern; others for one more prestigious notch on their belts; and some out of a combination of these and still other motives. All of the worlds represented by these actors are attentive to their own public relations, and all have stakes—not just economic, but ideological. All of the actors are exchanging time, advice, information, and have concerns for their individual self-respect, prestige and status.

In describing the influence of these actors on the arena, what may come across is more a "confected" than a "natural" history. I cannot stress enough that analysis of the processes of collective definition should not be interpreted to mean that the problem is entirely manufactured, and the actors all self-serving. Quite the contrary, people form beliefs, construct and fight for a reality from which they can act. Some assert a leadership role and help form that reality; others feel themselves prisoners of the constraints of their organizational and/or social worlds. That differing perceptions within an arena cause conflict in certain circumstances, and foster alliances in still others, should come as no surprise. My concern is to trace the way a collective definition emerges out of that interplay. I must emphasize that there is a real difficulty in studying a problem without reducing or demeaning it. In dealing with the politics of the social problem of alcohol use, and focusing on the growth of this arena, I am not denying the existence of people who are suffering because of their experience with alcohol, nor questioning the need to provide services for them. That is simply not what I have chosen to explore. It is important to state that it was neither possible nor desirable to cover all the highways and byways of the entirety of this arena—to provide detailed examination of all its facets. In order to maintain my focus on how the arena has grown, how its visibility has been enhanced, I have had to sacrifice detail and concentrate on the movement of events. In short, what follows is *not* a history (Gusfield has observed that sociologists rush in where historians fear to tread.[20]) It is, rather, an exploration of the collective definition of the social problem of alcohol use. My thesis is that building an arena around a social problem, in this case alcohol use, entails increasing its visibility by *animating* the problem, *legitimizing* it, and *demonstrating* it. While my theory has emerged from my data, I, too, have had to select and interpret. It would be naive not to acknowledge that I, too, have "picked, polished, shaped and packaged" these pebbles, in the hopes of transforming them into diamonds.

Notes

1. Dan Edward Beauchamp, *Precarious Politics: Alcoholism and Public Policy* (Ph.D dissertation, Johns Hopkins University, 1973).
2. Address before the North American Congress on Alcohol and Drug Problems, San Francisco, California, December 13, 1974.
3. *The Alcoholism Report,* Vol. 7 (January 26, 1979), p. 1.
4. Beauchamp, *Precarious Politics,* p. 53.

5. Ibid., p. 86.
6. Ibid., p. 85.
7. Herbert Blumer, "Social Problems as Collective Behavior," *Social Problems,* Vol. 18 (1971), p. 306.
8. Richard C. Fuller and Richard R. Myers, "The Natural History of a Social Problem," *American Sociological Review,* Vol. 6 (1941), pp. 320-28.
9. John I. Kitsuse and Malcolm Spector, "Social Problems and Deviance: Some Parellel Issues," *Social Problems,* Vol. 22 (1975), p. 593. An undergraduate textbook that has taken this approach is Armand Mauss, *Social Problems As Social Movements* (Philadelphia: J.B. Lippincott Co., 1975).
10. Ibid.
11. Joseph Gusfield, "Categories of Ownership and Responsibility in Social Issues: Alcohol Abuse and Automobile Use," *Journal of Drug Issues,* Vol. 5 (1975), p. 290.
12. Emile Durkheim, *The Rules of Sociological Method* (New York: The Free Press, 1962).
13. Nils Christie and Kettil Bruun, "Alcohol Problems: The Conceptual Framework," in M. Keller and T.G. Coffey (eds.), *Proceedings of the 28th International Congress on Alcohol and Alcoholism,* Vol. 2 (Highland Park, N.J.: Hillhouse Press, 1969), pp. 65-73.
14. Gusfield, "Categories of Ownership," p. 290.
15. Joseph Gusfield, "The (F)Utility of Knowledge?: The Relation of Social Science to Public Policy Toward Drugs," *The Annals of the American Academy of Social Science and Drug Policy,* Vol. 417 (1975), p. 5.
16. Fuller and Myers explained that the stages they outlined were not mutually exclusive and tended to overlap, but they still insisted on a temporal course of development of analysis of social problems. I have attempted to portray the overlap by avoiding a framework of temporal stages, focusing instead on the interrelationship between the processes and subprocesses I have identified.
17. Robert Ross and Graham L. Staines, "The Politics of Analyzing Social Problems," *Social Problems,* Vol. 20 (1972), p. 19.
18. John D. McCarthy and Mayer N. Zald, *The Trend of Social Movements in America: Professionalization and Resource Mobilization* (Morristown, N.J.: General Learning Press, 1965).
19. Christie and Bruun, "Alcohol Problems."
20. Seminar; Berkeley, California, January 12, 1977.

2.

Theoretical Stance

As described more fully in Appendix A, I have utilized an inductive method for collection and analysis of my data. That is, the purpose of my research is neither to test a hypothesis nor to impose an existent sociological theory (deviance, stratification, formal organizations) upon the data; rather it is to discover a theory "grounded" in that data. This is sometimes misunderstood to suggest that the researcher is professing a *tabula rasa* innocence, which, of course, is not the case. All sociological research is guided by a larger theoretical perspective regarding what makes society tick. Mine is a dual perspective: on the one hand I have followed the symbolic interactionist/phenomenological traditions, and on the other a less explicated, still emerging, concept of "social worlds in a social arena."

The Action Frame of Reference

According to the tradition of symbolic interactionism, based on the perspective of George Herbert Mead and developed by the Chicago school of sociology,[1] man in some sense selects and interprets the environment toward which he responds, forming many "definitions of the situation." The individual acquires a commonality of perspective with others by learning and developing together the symbols by which aspects of the world are designated. Phenomenologists call this "the social construction of reality." The commonly accepted way of doing things is transmitted from generation to generation, resulting in a totality that Berger and Luckmann call the "symbolic universe," which "hardens" and "thickens" to gradually assume the appearance of objective reality.[2] This is not to say that the world is not real, but rather to indicate *the manner in which it is real.*

I have taken some liberty in combining symbolic interactionism and phenomenology, which strict adherents of either orientation would not do. However, for precedence I can point to Talcott Parsons, who, while not in sympathy with this sociological stance, has aptly called it "the action frame of reference."[3] In describing its basic tenets, I borrow from Silverman:

> Sociology is concerned with understanding action rather than observing behavior. Action arises out of meanings which define social reality.
>
> Meanings are given to men by their society. Shared orientations become institutionalized and are experienced by generations as social facts.
>
> It follows that explanations of human actions must take account of meanings which those concerned assign to their acts; the manner in which the everyday world is socially constructed yet perceived as real and routine becomes a crucial concern of sociological analysis.[4]

It is not difficult to see that research stemming from this view of man and society would rely on hearing the subjects' own stories—hence the prevalent use of unstructured interviews. Not that the story is "the truth," or that the analyst always agrees with the subject's definition of the situation; rather it is the analyst's aim to comprehend and illuminate the subject's view. In symbolic interactionist parlance, the analyst is "taking the role of the other."

Explanations which assert that action is *determined* by external and constraining social or non-social forces are in contradiction to this stance. Thus research stemming from this perspective has been criticized as too often focusing on man's actions to the exclusion of the structural conditions affecting him.[5] However, those research endeavors which justify this criticism stem from a narrow reading of symbolic interactionism. Mead's notion of interaction was one of constant interplay between man and the environment, each affecting the other. The second "leg" of my theoretical stance, the concept of "social worlds in a social arena," provides a scheme to deal with this reciprocity between the individual and society.

Social Worlds in a Social Arena

The concept of *social worlds* floats throughout the sociological literature (and indeed, as "worlds," throughout the common language). But it
has received renewed interest following a paper delivered by Strauss
before the Society for the Study of Symbolic Interaction, June, 1975.[6]
Strauss noted the roots of this concept in Mead's "universes of dis-
course," by which Mead signified that the basic social processes of
communication occur within an enormous, unlimited and ceaseless proliferation of functioning groups—groups which are not necessarily clearly
boundaried or tightly organized. The formulation of "reference groups,"
as presented by Shibutani, caught the fluidity of this concept. Again
stressing that society exists in and through communication, Shibutani
described each social world as a culture area, the boundaries of which
are set neither by territory nor formal group membership, but by "the
limits of effective communication." [7] To underscore his observation that
for any individual there is a simultaneous participation in a variety of
communication networks, Shibutani drew upon the earlier image of Simmel, depicting each individual as standing at that point at which a
unique combination of his social circles intersect.[8] Our language reflects
this understanding: expressions such as "we come from different
worlds," "we are worlds apart," "he bridges different worlds" are commonly used. It is readily apparent that "society" breaks itself down into
worlds by virtue of people's own definitions of who they are and what
they do. Strauss lists as examples the worlds of opera, baseball, surfing,
stamp collecting, country music, homosexuality, medicine, law, mathe-
matics. He emphasizes that all these worlds vary—some small, some
large; some international, some local; some inseparable from given
spaces, others less spatially identifiable; some highly public and pub-
licized, others barely visible; some barely emergent, others well established and organized; some very hierarchial, some less so or scarcely at
all.

The origin of the term *arena* as a sociological concept can be found in
Psychiatric Ideologies and Institutions,[9] where Strauss et al. used an
arena-negotiation model to convey the processes of bargaining, tacit understandings, and shared agreements that characterize organizational
life. The imagery of an arena as a place of action and contest is apt, for
one of the challenges of this perspective is to identify and analyze the
domain in which issues are being fought out among social worlds. Where
is the competition, organizational building, extending, defending, invad-
ing, taking over, converting? Observing the range of discrepant positions
held by psychiatrists and allied professionals, the authors of *Psychiatric*

Ideologies and Institutions took as their subject matter "this battle of positions." Subsequently, Schatzman and Strauss [10] underscored this observation in a separate monograph, drawing upon Blumer's concept of "publics"—groups or aggregates who engage in controversy about issues. But as these authors point out, controversy is not a necessary condition. In their example, psychiatry is the arena, and there are publics whose identification can be determined by their patterned understandings and actions vis-à-vis psychiatry (police, the clergy, teachers, vocational guidance personnel, etc.). Farther out, in the sphere orbiting the psychiatric arena, are other universes, for example, the various news media which represent psychiatry to their audiences. Thus, a social worlds/social arena perspective carries forward the Blumerian/interactionist concept of society consisting of the fitting together of acts to form joint action.[11] Analysis of the interaction among the social worlds of a designated arena will reveal whether and when these joint actions are made on the basis of compromise, out of duress, because the actors are using each other to achieve their respective ends, because it is the sensible thing to do, or out of sheer necessity. These are Blumer's possibilities—research may unearth other causes for joint actions, and their consequences. Implicit in the general frame of reference of social worlds/social arena, is the expectation of *problems* of consensus, communication, and coordination.

Crucial to this perspective is the understanding that continual segmenting occurs within these worlds. As Strauss and other seekers have discovered, most social worlds seem to dissolve, when scrutinized, into a congeries of sub-worlds. To illustrate: a look at the homosexual social world reveals that "cruising" is anathema to one segment, while another finds "gay liberation" repugnant, and still another is scornful of "closet-protection." So that intersecting occurs usually between *segments of worlds.* Strauss indicates, and I can confirm, that this intersecting and segmentation creates difficulties for analysis by implying a universe marked by tremendous fluidity; it will not and it cannot stand still. But it is this very difficulty of looking at phenomena with a sense that constant change is occurring that enhances the sociological endeavor by insuring a focus on *process.*

This perspective picks up a Weberian strand in sociology, in its concern with the coordination of human activities through groups and organizations. "What we call a society is nothing more than a shifting network of groups and organizations, held together by . . . coalitions of interests, or dominance and submission." [12] This Weberian approach is in contradistinction to the "structural-functionalist" approach in sociology, whose very terminology assumes that common values hold all of society together and that a state of perfect value-integration is logically possible, the basic model against which all deviations are measured. The perspective of social worlds in a social arena affirms Weber's truism that individual interests diverge; hence a situation in which individuals are so socialized that no one would want to change things is impossible. The next logical step is to investigate the shifting of alliances which contribute towards change—the process Weber called *elective affinity* by which perceptions and interests of groups converge in an unintended way, possibly even in a way that contradicts the ideologies held by the groups involved.[13] (As I shall demonstrate later, an instructive illustration is to be found in the temporary alliance around a specific issue of the alcoholic beverage industries, and the volunteer action and recovery service worlds.)

Perhaps of greater significance for sociologists, a social worlds/social arena approach tackles the microscopic problem of the orientations and behavior of particular actors, without sacrificing the macroscopic problem of the structural conditions that impinge upon them. As mentioned earlier, this criticism has frequently been directed toward the action frame of reference, particularly as expressed by so-called "conflict" theorists. Conflict theory conceives of social structure as held together by latent force and constraint—coercion of some by others is the basis for society. A perceptive analysis is offered by Peter Hall, who has caught the significance of the interactionist concept Strauss et al. called "negotiated order." Hall finds this a useful political model for competing groups in society, a model which would address itself to the questions raised by conflict theory. Hereby, Hall says, joint action can be seen as involving all the manifestations of bargaining and negotiating—strategy, tact, maneuvering, persuading, constraining, exchanging. While retaining the basic symbolic interactionist precepts of man as actor, rather than reactor, and of man as interpreter, of meanings which evolve and change, he has not lost sight of the significance of power relationships.[14] A social worlds/social arena perspective provides the means to synthesize the action frame of reference and conflict theory, hopefully transcending both models with a more comprehensive one.

Distinguishing Between Physical and Social Science Concepts

The question that arises most frequently regarding this perspective, particularly from those who would find stability and equilibrium in society, is: how does one mark the boundaries of segments, or of entire social worlds? That boundaries are not the "problem" signifies the advantage of this perspective, for to concentrate on boundaries is to miss the relationship and the intersecting of segments. Boundaries are not fixed; they are constantly breaking apart and reforming. The major analytic task is to discover such relationships and intersections, and to trace the associated processes, strategies and consequences. What is more, the boundaries of most categories are fixed only insofar as the fixing is arbitrarily done by sociologists—Bennett Berger made this clear in reference to chronological age.[15] Is being "middle-class" a category with fixed boundaries when one considers the proliferation and variation of worlds which the "middle-class" person touches? By whose "definition of the situation" does a specific number of drinks separate a social drinker from a problem drinker? What is a family: may it be a mother and a child, or must it include a father?

Weber designed his ideal types to come to grips with the great complexities of social reality: "to use such concepts (merely) to classify descriptive materials is to waste them." [16] While sacrificing the pristine quality of clearly demarcated boundaries, a social worlds/social arena approach allows the researcher to move beyond classification in an attempt to capture the fluidity of human behavior.

Blumer, differentiating between physical science and social science, proposed that the aim of theory in the former is to develop schemes in terms of classes of objects and of relations between such classes. The concepts of physical science, then, are *definitive* concepts, referring precisely to what is common to a class of objects, by the aid of a clear definition in terms of attributes or fixed benchmarks. Social theories, such as the underlying framework of my research described above, Blumer calls *sensitizing* concepts, positing that they give the user a general sense of reference and guidance in approaching empirical instances: ". . . sensitizing concepts merely suggest directions along which to look." [17]

Application of the Theoretical Perspective

My research started after I reflected on issues raised at the North American Congress on Alcohol and Drug Problems held in December 1974, in San Francisco. I had just been awarded a fellowship from the National Institute on Alcohol Abuse and Alcoholism that required that my dissertation be concerned with some aspect of this problem, and I was attempting to comprehend its scope. What I found was that not only had this conclave attracted 64 sponsoring organizations, but attendance was so large as to require concurrent sessions in multiple rooms of two hotels. Forced to make choices between subject areas (criminal justice or research? training or client care?), I could not help but note how compartmentalized one's attention could be, or as in my case, how schizoid one could become. In retrospect, I realized what I had witnessed: a group of people brought together because of their common concern about alcohol and drugs, but representing different aspirations, perspectives, languages—in short, *a network of ideology bearers*. (I use the term "ideology" as it is employed by social scientists to denote a shared or collective set of ideas or beliefs.) Bacon highlights another distinction between physical and social science, which demonstrates the relevance of ideologies for social scientists:

> A major difference between the social sciences and the natural or laboratory sciences is that the latter . . . can dispense with non-real findings or thrusts or concepts as "trash"—perhaps dangerous and debilitating to science but in fact little more than garbage or moonbeams. But to the social scientist, mythologies and prejudices and fallacious descriptions and beliefs are themselves phenomena—highly significant factors in instigating, reinforcing or changing behavior and attitude.[18]

There is a relationship between ideologies and social movements which Hall has caught:

> The use of the term ideology often obscures the analysis of the situation since observers assume its existence in complete and static form over time. In fact, ideologies are most often incomplete or in process and as such always involve definition, ambiguity and interpretation. They parallel the social movement form of social organization and collective behavior. Social movements are themselves in flux and emergent; they represent coalitions of groups, quasi-groups, and individuals at different levels of commitment; they respond to internal dynamics as well as external pressures. Each leader and each group therefore puts forth their own variant of truth and seeks to have their interpretation of the scripture accepted as prophecy. Ideologies cannot be divorced from but should serve as rhetorical indicators of the conditions in which they are created, the intentions of the people who fashion and use them, and the consequences on the audiences for whom they are intended as well as those who respond against them.[19]

When I reflected on the network of ideology bearers whom I had observed at the San Francisco meetings, the implications of Hall's comments became heightened. Who were these people and why were they there? How long had they been around? Where did they come from? What kind of claims were they making? What kind of places were they building? In a curious marriage of need and happenstance, Anselm Strauss, chairman of my doctoral committee, was at that time developing his concept of social worlds. As we conferred over my dissertation possibilities, he pointed out that there are "little social movements" going on within the worlds whose ideology bearers I had observed. People get together, fight issues out; groups splinter, coalesce. Prior to the "public" formation of "public opinion," there is debate going on within each world, public opinion being formed within each world, and, most interesting, each world affects the others.

I decided that my research problem would be the building of this arena. Following the introduction provided by the North American Congress, I designated the major worlds to be examined as: bureaucratic (in which I include all government representatives), treatment, volunteer action, research, and law enforcement. In my ignorance, I specified the arena as alcoholism, not yet understanding the distinction between alcoholism and alcohol abuse. I have subsequently altered my language to "the arena of alcohol use," after the discovery that two additional worlds play large roles: the alcoholic beverage industries world and, less so, the temperance world. Learning that the word "treatment" creates anxiety among some people in this arena, I changed this to recovery service world. Furthermore, as my research progressed I discovered many peripheral worlds, and I proceeded with the following image: I see some segments of these worlds as many circles intersecting like Olympic rings, while others spoke outward to form orbiting circles. What is more, some people have allegiance to multiple worlds (for example, one can be a counselor in the recovery service world and a participant in the volunteer action world) and others are confined within one segment. Most important: It should be stressed that the worlds of any arena are open systems that are periodically intruded upon by *other* worlds which because of their own history intersect the arena.

In short, the combination of an action frame of reference and a social worlds/social arena perspective provided the *sensitizing concept* which led me to the *people* who are defining alcohol use as a social problem, and the *processes* whereby it is being defined for the larger society.

Primary data was drawn from interviews with arena participants. It is important to emphasize that these interviews were rich in *in vivo* categories, and that most of my codes (for instance, establishing turf rights, building respectability, maintaining a separate identity) employ the language of the respondents. If there appears to be an overconcentration on California sources, it is because these respondents were most accessible. On the one hand, this allowed me to go into some depth in relating California's history to the national scene; on the other, it is unfortunate that I was hampered by economic restrictions from gathering data that would be more reflective on the other 49 states. To compensate, I have relied heavily on the literature—not only the alcohol literature but related publications, such as journals of nursing, occupational counseling and social work. I have drawn liberally from the writings of arena elder

statesmen like Selden Bacon, Mark Keller, and Robert Straus, whose publications (fortunately) quite forcefully portray their view of the "story"; similarly helpful have been the publications of younger "alcoholologists" like Robin Room and Ron Roizen. *The Alcoholism Report,* through its succinct and reliable reportage on the national scene, was an invaluable means of keeping in touch with current activities in the arena; the *Journal of Studies on Alcohol* provided this service in regard to scholarly developments. I also made use of additional newsletters which proliferate within the arena. For the most part, I have quoted from the published data in order to indicate an argument or a position on a specific issue. Rather infrequently, I have used the literature for my own purposes—to point out factual deficiencies in reviewing other's arguments.

A third and abundant source of data was observation at public meetings, congressional hearings, sessions of summer schools, advisory board meetings, conferences. (A classification of sources of data is presented in Appendix B.) Although research was concluded in December 1977, I have updated major information, such as budget figures and legislative changes, wherever possible.

The Discovered Theory

As coding of all the above data proceeded, the incessant analytical questions were being asked: under what conditions does this happen, and with what mechanisms, strategies, rhetoric, and with what consequences? Since I had taken as my problem how this arena gets larger and larger, what has emerged in my theory is detailed analysis on that problem—not on, for example, what makes Alcoholics Anonymous "tick," or the specifics of an occupational alcoholism program. In other words, a good deal of the fine points are sacrificed, and problem focus allows the "telling" of only "some of what's happening." Also, it may be disturbing to some readers to find there is a shifting back and forth between microscopic and macroscopic elements. However, the value of a social worlds/ social arena approach is just that: it allows the analyst to cover a wider scope. I have been able, within this framework, to deal with organizational interrelationships, the formation of "public facts," the collective definition of a social problem, as well as *time* on a larger scale than would be possible in unit analysis—that is, time in a historical sense. In that regard, I have tried to be faithful to C. Wright Mills' instruction:

> No social study that does not come back to the problems of biography, of history and of their intersections within a society has completed its intellectual journey.[20]

I must emphasize that it is the framework *combined* with the method I would prefer to call "process analysis" rather than "grounded theory" that allowed me to do this. Hall has correctly observed that, "Sociology of all kinds typically answers the 'what' question by indicating relationships between variables but infrequently demonstrates the processes which, in fact, connect those variables, the answers to the 'how' question." [21] Human activity is too complex and diversified to be reduced to the "what" questions. Wilson, in an account of her own study, underscores the purpose of this approach as opposed to, for example, one that seeks to test hypotheses, or measure the magnitude of relationships, or yield frequency distributions:

> I sought to discover multiple and varied relationships between and among concepts rather than attempting to prove a linear causal hypothesis between two. Such an approach is designed to yield "molecular" rather than linear theoretical models.[22]

Philosophers have said that the question of whether the chicken or egg came first cannot be answered, since they are both part of the circle of life. So too, sociologists should be concerned with bending the straight lines—making some sense out of a labyrinth such as this arena, and then drawing the twisted and curving lines back in again—hopefully, with enhanced clarity.

The following theory emerged from my data: building an arena around the social problem of alcohol use entails increasing its visibility by *animating* the problem, *legitimizing* it, and *demonstrating* it. While these are the key processes, each of these in turn is broken down into component sub-processes, which I shall summarize.

Animating the problem includes:

• Establishing turf rights	The growth of associations, the burgeoning of the research world and the relationship to the macrosociological conditions of the history of the arena and federal, state and county programming.
• Developing constituencies	The growth of "citizen participation" through advisory boards, special minority boards and commissions, and the awarding of grants and contracts. The consequences in terms of interorganizational relationships and the building of a dependency within organizations.
• Funneling advice and imparting skills and information	The relationship of the National Center on Alcohol Education to the growth of area education and training, summer schools, and state

prevention programs; the increase in training courses; the role played by the National Clearinghouse for Alcohol Information and its effect on the Rutgers Center of Alcohol Studies. Consequence for the arena: the growth of a training constituency, and the assertion, re-establishment and enlargement of turf rights.

Legitimizing the problem includes:

- Borrowing prestige and expertise

The history of the arena's eclecticism. Roots of that eclecticism in closely protected turf rights; the intellectual isolation of the early "alcohologists"; and the disinterest and inability of other professional worlds to take on the problem of alcohol use. Consequence for the arena: a variety of treatment approaches which, also influenced by movements outside the arena, engage in mutual borrowing.

- Redefining the scope

The shift from a moral to a legal to a medical/psychological model of alcoholism; the conditions leading to a disease concept; the conditions undermining a disease concept. The next stage in the redefining process: social setting detoxification and the social model of recovery.

- Building respectability

Strategy for attaining respectability: the enhanced status lent to the problem of alcohol use by prominent recovered alcoholics; by interested legislators; by the existence of a national institute; by softening the labeling to "alcoholic persons." Consequences of the drive for respectability: the establishing of a clearinghouse for information, an epidemiology division and research centers. Further tactics: buying into the health insurance institution. The continuation of the redefining process: the search for a "disability" definition.

- Maintaining a separate identity

The rationale behind maintaining a separation from mental health and drug problems. Two consequences: the divisiveness over the issue of "straight alcoholism" versus "broad brush" occupational programs, and the thwarting of the California plan to combine the Office of Alcoholism with the Department of Alcoholic Beverage Control.

Demonstrating the problem includes:

• Competing for attention; combining for strength	Competing for jurisdiction, funding, eminence and the attention of the public eye. A consequence of the competing process: intersecting of worlds around the issue of the public inebriate; the relationship of this issue to the macrosociological condition of urban redevelopment and to the redefining process. Stratagem for alliances and cooperation; relationship of the combining process to the California tax bill.
• Selecting supportive data	Problems avoided and encountered by the need for accountability. Relationship to the macrosociological condition of cost-benefit thrust in government. Intersection of the bureaucratic world and the alcoholic beverage industries world over the issue of "responsible drinking." Strategy for developing sophisticated statistics: the search for causal relationships to explain alcohol problems.
• Convincing opposing ideologists	The contra-ideologies behind the "controlled drinking" issues. Relationship to organizational turf carving and to turf rights of the research world.
• Enlarging the bounds of respectability	The expanded "ownership of the problem" in terms of careers, prevention approaches and pressure on the alcoholic beverage industries world. New turf broken by the co-alcoholic. Relationship of career growth and prevention stance to the "professional reform" movement. Contrast in turf strength of the alcoholic beverage industries world and the temperance world. Relationship of prevention activities to insurance and legal worlds.

A point stressed in the Introduction bears repeating: although I shall present each of these components of my theory in a separate chapter, they are overlapping, not sequential, processes. To demonstrate the manner in which they overlap has been the challenge of the analysis.

An additional word of caution: it will be evident throughout the narrative that in some instances tactics are consciously being employed; in other instances some people will suspect a conscious strategy, which may or may not be the case. I have moved gingerly in such labeling of action, since it is the process (the continuous change in time) that interests me. Focus remains on the overall movement of events—tactics, conditions, consequences are of interest as they contribute to the larger flow.

As explained in Appendix A, I have sought to render a less awesome connotation to the word "theory" and the method called "grounded theory." The interconnections I shall demonstrate have been, after all, filtered through *my* perception. As Martindale has expressed it, ". . . theory has one function: to illuminate. The difference between one theory and another is in comparative candlepower." [23] The theory offered in this book—that building an arena around the social problem of alcohol use entails increasing its visibility by animating the problem, legitimizing it and demonstrating it—is presented in the Martindale spirit: with the hope that there is sufficient strength in its candlepower to enlighten the sociological pursuit.

Notes

1. Anselm L. Strauss (ed.), *The Social Psychology of George Herbert Mead* (Chicago: University of Chicago Press, 1956). *See also:* Berenice Fisher and Anselm Strauss, "The Chicago Tradition: Thomas Park and Their Successors," *Symbolic Interaction,* Vol. 1 (1978), pp. 5-23.
2. Peter Berger and Thomas Luckmann, *The Social Construction of Reality* (Garden City, New York: Doubleday Anchor, 1968).
3. Talcott Parsons, *The Structure of Social Action* (Glencoe, Ill.: The Free Press, 1949).
4. David Silverman, *The Theory of Organisations* (New York: Basic Books Inc., 1971), p. 126.
5. *See:* Alvin Gouldner, "Taking Sides: The Sociologist as Partisan and Non-Partisan," in Jack D. Douglas, (ed.), *The Relevance of Sociology* (New York: Appleton-Century-Crofts, 1970), pp. 112-48; and Richard Ropers, "Mead, Marx and Social Psychology," *Catalyst,* Vol. 7 (1973), pp. 42-61.
6. *See:* Anselm L. Strauss, "Social Worlds," in Norman Denzin (ed.), *Studies In Symbolic Interaction* (New York: J.A.I. Press, 1978). *See also:* Benita Luckmann, "The Small Life-Worlds of Modern Man," *Social Research,* Vol. 37 (1970), pp. 580-96.
7. Tamotsu Shibutani, *Society and Personality* (Englewood Cliffs, N.J.: Prentice-Hall Inc., 1961), p. 130.
8. Georg Simmel, *Conflict and the Web of Group Affiliations,* tr. by Kurt H. Wolff and Reinhard Bendix, (Glencoe, Ill.: The Free Press, 1955).
9. Anselm Strauss, Leonard Schatzman, Rue Bucher, Danuta Ehrlich, and Melvin Sabshin, *Psychiatric Ideologies and Institutions* (Glencoe, Ill.: The Free Press, 1964; Transaction Books, 1980).
10. Leonard Schatzman and Anselm Strauss, "A Sociology of Psychiatry: A Perspective and Some Organizing Foci," *Social Problems,* Vol. 14 (1966), pp. 3-17.
11. Herbert Blumer, "Sociological Implications of the Thought of George Herbert Mead," *The American Journal of Sociology,* Vol. 71 (1966), pp. 535-44.
12. Randall Collins, "A Comparative Approach to Political Sociology," in R. Bendix (ed.), *State and Society* (Boston: Little, Brown and Co., 1968), p. 51.
13. Max Weber, *The Methodology of the Social Sciences,* Glencoe, Ill.: (The Free Press, 1941).

14. Peter Hall, "A Symbolic Interactionist Analysis of Politics," in Andrew Effrat (ed.), *Perspectives in Political Sociology* (New York: Bobbs Merrill, 1976), pp. 35-75.
15. Bennett Berger, "How Long Is A Generation?" *British Journal of Sociology,* Vol. 11 (1960), pp. 10-23.
16. Collins, "A Comparative Approach," p. 63.
17. Herbert Blumer, "What Is Wrong With Social Theory?" *American Sociological Review,* Vol. 19 (1954), p. 7.
18. Selden D. Bacon, "Concepts," in W.J. Filstead, J.J. Rossi, and M. Keller (eds.), *Alcohol, New Thinking and New Directions* (Cambridge, Mass.: Ballinger, 1976), p. 99.
19. Hall, "A Symbolic Interactionist," p. 60. Since 1969, increased attention has been paid to the dynamics of collective behavior. However, for the most part, the study of social movements by sociologists and political scientists has dealt with the details of particular political, reform or religious movements. Most of these studies have stemmed from the researcher's interest in a specific social issue and/or philosophy and have followed the career of an association from an incipient aggregate to a formally organized group. For a review of the literature on collective behavior and social movements see Gary T. Marx and James L. Wood, "Strands of Theory and Research in Collective Behavior," in Alex Inkeles, James Coleman and Neil Smelser (eds.), *Annual Review of Sociology* (Palo Alto, California; Annual Reviews Inc., 1975), pp. 363-428.
20. C. Wright Mills, *The Sociological Imagination* (London: Oxford University Press, 1959), p. 6.
21. Hall, "A Symbolic Interactionist," p. 72. *See also:* Herbert Blumer, "Sociological Analysis and the Variable," *Symbolic Interactionism: Perspective and Method* (Englewood Cliffs, N.J.: Prentice-Hall, 1969), pp. 127-39.
22. Holly S. Wilson, *Infra-Controlling: Social Order Under Conditions of Freedom in an Anti-Psychiatric Community.* (Ph.D. dissertation, University of California, Berkeley, 1974), p. 45.
23. Don Martindale, *The Nature of Sociological Theory* (Boston: Houghton Mifflin, 1960) p. vii.

Part II

Animating the Problem

As explained in the introduction, when I propose to examine the process of animating the problem, it should not be inferred that this means the social problem of alcohol use has been artificially manufactured. Rather, it is my intention to show how this problem is infused with life: how the dimensions are carved out, how the number of people drawn into concern about these dimensions is increased, how a common pool of knowledge begins to develop for the arena participants, and how all these sub-processes increase the visibility of the problem. There is an organizational structure (only partially examined in this chapter) through which participants establish turf rights; a "citizen participation" ideology and a distribution of funds by which constituencies are developed; and a burgeoning of training grants, programs, schools and courses funneling advice and imparting information and skills. Since the underlying assumption of this book is that the way people and resources are committed contributes toward the collective definition of a social problem, this is where we shall first place our attention.

3.

Establishing Turf Rights

"Arena," while implying contest, also implies territorial space, which is useful as a metaphor. For within a problem arena, people—sometimes singly, sometimes through groups—are *establishing turf rights,* claiming title to the resources. They are part of the animation process in the sense of entrenching the problem, making a place for it, and for themselves in relation to it. For some of the worlds of this arena, one means of establishing turf rights is through association. For segments of the research world, research centers provide the means to this goal.

These groupings of arena-participants have careers just as individuals do. These careers are influenced by external forces, the most salient being the concept of "programming" as it emerged in the New Deal, and the increased funding of recent years. Since all of the associations and research centers were at different stages of development when the alcohol arena began to burgeon, the effect of growth is different for each. Some have been helped; some have been jarred from a previous, less competitive, position; some have come into existence *as a result* of the growth. In this chapter I shall present the major examples of this aspect of the process of establishing turf rights (other examples will emerge in later discussions). First we shall briefly look at the historical background of alcohol programming as seen from the perspective of California, in order to understand better the placement of associations. Examination of this process as it is reflected in the research world is presented at the conclusion of this chapter.

Dovetailing of Federal and State Programs

Recommendations for a "total alcohol program" were spelled out by the Cooperative Commission on the Study of Alcoholism, which, in its 1966 published report, called for a national coordination of policy regarding alcohol use. To rectify what is described as a patchwork approach, the commission recommended that a Center on Alcoholism be established within the National Institute of Mental Health.[1] Prior to 1966, no federal health, welfare, or rehabilitation statutes specifically referred to alcoholism. The 1963 Community Mental Health Centers Act included alcoholism among the authorized treatment services, but the first federal statute to deal with the problem was the 1966 Highway Safety Act, which called for reports to the Congress on the effects of alcohol on traffic accidents. This is the same year that the National Institute of Mental Health followed the recommendation of the Cooperative Commission and set up a National Center for the Prevention and Control of Alcoholism under the direction of Jack Mendelson.

In December 1970, the small core of volunteers in this arena, and their leader Senator Harold Hughes, were rewarded when Congress passed, and President Nixon signed, the "Comprehensive Alcohol Abuse and Alcoholism Prevention, Treatment, and Rehabilitation Act." Under this legislation, the new National Institute on Alcohol Abuse and Alcoholism (henceforth referred to as NIAAA) entered the bureaucratic world of acronyms. (A glossary of acronyms referred to in this book appears as Appendix C.) NIAAA was authorized to confer *formula grants* (i.e. based on a population formula) to the states in order to establish programs for treatment and prevention; *project grants* to public and private non-profit agencies to conduct demonstration projects, and provide education and training and services for the treatment of alcoholism; and *contracts* with public and private agencies for the above services.

The bestowal of formula grants meant that some states could begin programs; for others, these funds facilitated an *enlargement* of programs already developing. Reynolds places California in the early history:

> . . . the first modern attack on alcoholism at the state level was the formal establishment of a program by Connecticut in 1945. By 1952, thirty-eight states and Washington, D.C. had passed legislation recognizing alcoholism as a public health problem, and had created board or other official agencies to establish programs of treatment. The State of California was not among them.[2]

The California State Alcoholic Rehabilitation Commission was established in 1954, as a result of the work of several special committees and commissions which had examined alcoholism from the perspectives of mental health, public health, crime, and medicine. Reynolds remarks on the "political neutralization" of this commission:

> . . . it was an independent body which drew most of its membership from the laity; had no officially prescribed program, links with operating state agencies or other organization; lacked any responsibility, authority, or accountability to or for any other operating agency; and exercised no line responsibility or authority to control existing arrangements for the use, or control of use, of alcoholic beverages or existing procedures for dealing with situations arising from such use.[3]

For this arena, the governing rationale was augural:

> . . . the Legislature, in establishing an alcohol commission and by implication a program to accompany it, carefully refrained from defining its understanding of the term "alcoholism." This was done not because of oversight, ignorance, or carelessness, but because of insight. If the founding body had adopted a particular interpretation of the term, it would have aligned the Legislature solidly with one interest group or another.[4]

As to the consequences of the commission's political neutralization, Reynolds clearly establishes the line from its lack of status, power, and resources to its demise in 1957, when the Legislature failed to appropriate the necessary funds and transferred responsibility for this problem to the California State Department of Public Health. Former staff members of the Alcoholic Rehabilitation Commission were transferred to the newly created Division of Alcoholic Rehabilitation (DAR) in the Department of Public Health. DAR's approach was to contract with local agencies in various kinds of programs to provide rehabilitation of problem drinkers within their purview. The department did not have the authority to impinge on programs of these agencies. Neither did it know how much state money was being spent on the rehabilitation of alcoholics in the care of departments under the general supervision of the state Health Department which housed the money, personnel, authority, and responsibility for management of the problem of problem drinking.[5]

The July 1969 passage of the McAteer Act transferred responsibility for California alcoholism programs from Public Health to the Department of Rehabilitation; on the same date, the Lanterman-Petris-Short Act became effective, making alcoholism also the responsibility of the Department of Mental Hygiene. This same year, the state Human Relations Agency appointed a Task Force on Alcoholism. Composed of executives of related agencies and citizens prominent for their interest in the problem, this group pointed out that two agencies were now in effect competing for the same clientele and recommended coordination of all identifiable resources into a state-wide total delivery system under one office.[6]

The Office of Alcohol Program Management (OAPM) was created by the California legislature in 1970. With community mental health funding for alcoholism programs omitted from OAPM's responsibility, "comprehensiveness" was still only a promise. Coordination was improved in 1973, when local mental health funds for alcoholism became subject to review and approval by OAPM, and was reinforced with the passage in 1975 of legislation establishing an Office of Alcoholism, designated as "the single state agency to review all state federally funded plans relating to alcoholism and to approve and oversee administration of county alcoholism program budgets for state and federal funds for counties electing to apply for funds under such provisions." [7]

California funding for alcohol problems (not including government funding for control and distribution of the product) grew from approximately $1 million in 1965 to a budget of $38 million in 1977 (including $5 million which comes from the National Institute on Alcohol Abuse and Alcoholism), but was reduced to $36 million in 1978. During the McAteer era, a great deal of energy went toward defending the continuation of the program. To quote one respondent:

> The McAteer Act was on a year to year basis and the last six months of every year was spent justifying our existence. I remember the fight put on by people from Alcoholics Anonymous and the National Council on Alcoholism to retain the program each year, and the chairman of the Senate Finance Committee telling them, "you show us how many drunks you can salvage next year."

By the 1970s, state efforts had dovetailed with federal legislation. The Hughes Bill stipulated that any state desiring to participate in this new source of funds must submit a state plan. It did not stipulate that planning occur on the county level, but this choice stemmed from the role the counties had played in the development of alcohol programs in California. The result has been a mushrooming of the bureaucratic world.

Who Professes?

Tocqueville's amusement at the Americans' tendency toward affiliation appears in most of the literature on interest groups and voluntary associations. But it has been little noted that his example dealt specifically with association around drinking:

> As soon as several of the inhabitants of the United States have taken up an opinion or a feeling which they wish to promote in the world, they look out for mutual assistance and as soon as they have found one another out, they combine. From that moment they are no longer isolated men, but a power seen from afar, whose actions serve for an example whose language is listened to. The first time I heard in the United States that a hundred thousand men had bound themselves publicly to abstain from spiritous liquors, it appeared to me more like a joke than a serious engagement, and I did not at once perceive why these temperate citizens could not content themselves with drinking water by their own firesides.[8]

Temperance associations are now only a small part of the proliferation of groups that have grown up around the problem of alcohol use.

Since "every profession considers itself the proper body to set the terms in which some aspect of society, life or nature is to be thought of, and to define the general lines or even the details, of public policy concerning it,"[9] the professional associations of this arena are of growing importance. Prominent among these is the County Alcohol Administrators Association of California (CAAAC). During the McAteer era, directors of programs (primarily out-patient clinics) would get together, sometimes informally, most of the time at the behest of the state, for the sharing of information. When the OAPM was formed, many of these people became responsible for the extended operation of the county alcoholism programs, and they continued to discuss mutual concerns. At this time, the state bureaucracy was still feeling its way regarding its role and its support. Most of the programs were still under the Mental Health Department; the official authority as "alcoholism coordinator" was the Mental Health Director in most counties. The structural form varied from county to county, but in most counties, according to respondents, there was one administrator who "did all the work." The state began to call these individuals together to work out the programming of county services. With strong county Mental Health departments already existing, and their representatives taking a leading part in the development of programs, a state philosophy developed whereby funds were allocated to the counties which provided the services either directly, or by contract with private agencies. This was consistent with the McAteer days when the Department of Rehabilitation contracted with the counties for services; OAPM was staffed principally at that time by people who had been in the Department of Rehabilitation. The result has been organizational growth at the county level and an elevated status for the county administrators, who joined together to form their association in 1973.

From the county administrators' perspective, the bulk of their struggle has been to get the state to implement the philosophy of county-state partnership and county-run programs. Respondents referred to "lip-service" from the state, unsupported by action. As one leader of the county administrators association expressed it, "we have been engaged in a process of attaining political viability and visibility to be in a position of relative strength." When the drive was on to establish an Office of Alcoholism, the administrators' association was instrumental in neutralizing the negative reaction on the part of the mental health people to the prospect of an autonomous office for alcoholism problems. Thus the trade-off: built into the enabling legislation were specific articles delegating power to the counties, thereby establishing the legality of a state-overseen, county-run program. The administrators felt they had to have this strength behind them, to deal with their own mental health systems, which in some counties still constitute a significant obstacle. In these counties, the accounting of funds is made to OA, but the handling of funds still goes through County Mental Health. Buttressed by the role played in this fight, the CAAAC is bent on establishing a respected and authoritative position in the state arena.

Another organization, older and national in scope, the Alcohol and Drug Problems Association of North America (ADPA), has tried to widen its base—as the arena has burst forth around it—by offering membership to both government and private professionals and by combining alcohol and drug representation. Formerly the North American Association of Alcoholism Programs (NAAAP), this association was founded by a group of state Alcoholism Program Directors in 1949. In the 1960s, it increased its membership categories to include agency members, public or private; individuals who are engaged in activities related to alcohol and drug abuse, and students. In 1963, this organization established a full-time office in Washington, D.C., which remains the center of its activity. Hoping to become a gathering place for a splintered constituency, the organization also established special interest sections (for example, alcohol and traffic safety, occupations, church involvement). Each section was to develop its own bylaws and dues, and set up its own program as part of the ADPA annual meeting. Obviously, there are geographic barriers to this type of participation.

ADPA has joined with other organizations in lobbying efforts on behalf of alcohol and drug problems, and has organized conferences and seminars. It also provides information services such as an annual listing of alcohol/drug problems summer schools, a clearinghouse for employment, directory of treatment facilities, etc. The former director of California's Office of Alcoholism, Loran Archer, served for a year as vice-president of ADPA, but for the most part this organization has not made an impact among my West Coast respondents. ADPA has been visible around certain *national* issues, such as certification of personnel, and in a curious way has recently become revitalized with the demise of another organization, CSTAA, discussed in the next chapter.

Still another, and newer, professional organization is the Association of Labor-Management Administrators and Consultants on Alcoholism (ALMACA). Starting in Los Angeles in 1971 with forty people, AL-MACA, six years later, could boast 1,000 members, calling itself "the fastest growing professional organization in America." This association was formed out of the specialized need of people engaged as occupational counselors. The growing attention to ferreting out people with alcohol problems by identifying them at work is dealt with in a later chapter—suffice it to say here that California's Office of Alcoholism, with its vocational rehabilitation history, has encouraged this direction. ALMACA follows the usual format of professional organizations—providing a newsletter, resource materials, notice of occupational alcoholism conferences, workshops, and an employment referral service. It has opened up its membership to "associate" members, i.e. "those who wish to be kept informed of activities in the occupational field," explained as "researchers, medical directors, treatment people, job seekers." ALMACA maintains its distinction from ADPA by eschewing all lobbying activity. Asked why the need for a professional organization apart from ADPA, one founder replied:

> I was in ALMACA for a long time before I wondered why we weren't the occcupational branch of ADPA, and I'm not sure I have a good answer to that except that at the ADPA convention you'd go to their occupational meeting and there'd be five people there.

In San Francisco, the association holds a monthly no-host luncheon, which is open to non-members. The meetings serve at least three functions: 1) they are educational, always featuring a guest speaker representing one of the worlds of the arena; 2) they are convivial—many of the counselors are recovered alcoholics, and as the above founder explained, "we have to fight the stigma and loneliness of alcoholism and this is a nice way to overcome that"; and 3) they offer an opportunity for providers of services for alcoholics to increase *their own* visibility—a number of those who are regular recipients of referrals from occupational counselors are also in regular attendance at these luncheons.

Organizing the Volunteer-Action World

The prime forum for the volunteer-action world is the National Council on Alcoholism (NCA). Formed in 1944 as the National Committee for Education on Alcoholism, NCA follows the pattern of other voluntary fund-raising agencies like the American Cancer Society and the American Heart Association, but NCA maintains a director in Washington, who often joins forces with the ADPA director in lobbying efforts.

This arena is unique in having such a large mutual-help group, Alcoholics Anonymous (AA), in addition to the voluntary national and local organization of NCA. AA prohibits political participation under its aegis, but has been in existence since 1935, and so has had many years to build an army of volunteers—not only the recovered alcoholics, but potentially three or four people who have suffered with each one. Although grateful for the workers who come out of the ranks of AA, NCA is continually faced with distinguishing its separation from the self-help group. To illustrate: NCA prides itself on its counseling-for-referral service, but it has a constant battle getting volunteers to accept the fact that AA is not right for everyone, that alternative modes are available.

NCA has a much harder time raising money than comparable health associations. To quote one respondent, "The Heart Association does very well with memorials, but people don't want to say Joe died of alcoholism." Thus, the government funding explosion was looked upon as a boon. Some NCA veterans worry about the mixed blessing of government dollars: "Two-thirds of the budget for the six NCA councils in the San Francisco Bay Area comes from county funds—what will happen if a controversy should arise with the county and those funds should be withdrawn?" (A painful national NCA experience with government funding is discussed in Chapter 4.) Nevertheless, grants from the National Institute on Alcohol Abuse and Alcoholism, plus the publicity NCA gets when a NIAAA television message appears on the screen, have greatly increased NCA's visibility. In addition to referral, the money has allowed NCA to expand its services, such as public information, educational programs for professionals in allied health care, and schools for people convicted of drunken driving.

A Half-Way House Is Not a Home

The major association of the recovery service world in California is the California Association of Alcoholic Recovery Homes (CAARH). Like the county administrators, and perhaps in reaction to their growing strength, this association is intent upon both upgrading the standards of its member-homes and presenting itself as a bloc when making demands on the bureaucratic world. A national association, the Association of Halfway House Alcoholism Programs, was already in existence when this group began to coalesce; a number of founders of CAARH had been members of that organization, served on its board, etc. But the AHHAP had not mirrored the expansion of this arena in terms of its own growth and power. There was dissatisfaction over "the narrow AA orientation" of the AHHAP; despite many California leaders having either come out of AA or having respect for this approach, they had moved beyond it to what was evolving as a "social model," discussed in detail later. Thus, the use of the name "recovery homes," to pick up the sense of the continuum of recovery:

> The Eastern models are still tied to the medical approach. Half-way house is correct for them—it is a facility-oriented term, implying connection to the institutional system. Here we're trying to do away with institutionalization.

Martin Dodd further explains the distinction between an institution, "a hierarchical system of formally structured relationships" as against the model CAARH is promoting, which places the emphasis upon "peer-group orientation, a calm, accepting understanding atmosphere, and physical surroundings which are conducive to those factors." [10]

It is not surprising to find California in the vanguard of this movement, since until recently a disproportionate number of the recovery homes in the United States were in this state. When the emerging northern and southern groups joined forces to become CAARH in 1972, they brought together "homes" as diverse as the Salvation Army facilities, three or four large hotel-type establishments, and small residences. AHHAP had proposed that under no circumstances should there be more than twenty people in an alcoholic recovery home, an issue which has been fought out within CAARH among those who would stress "the dynamics of environment" rather than the size of the physical structure. CAARH leaders were determined to make these homes "accountable" and "professional," and have given considerable time to working out a detailed exposition for what has now been accepted as state standards; these leaders serve as consultants for the state in accrediting homes. CAARH documents are unique in an arena given to "fat words" [11] (loose, inconsistent words which carry several, sometimes opposing, meanings) in that they usually commence with specific definitions.

A number of the founders of this association are recovered alcoholics, and bring great zeal to their work (examined in Chapter 13). Beauchamp, in his discussion of the barriers to a public policy for alcohol problems, has said:

> It is probably the possession of a highly developed skill and technique that interests the public and public officials the most. Unfortunately, the work of treating alcoholism does not lend itself to being communicated as a highly skilled and dramatic routine. The task of rehabilitating the alcoholic is often prosaic in nature, consisting largely of talk and consultation.[12]

Accurate as Beauchamp's description is, the leaders of CAARH, a group of people both articulate at public gatherings and prolific in their production of position papers, have faced up to this public policy impediment and made a considerable impact on the state Office of Alcoholism, facilitated to some extent by the rehabilitation orientation of that department. During the 1950s, there had been acknowledged exploitation of alcoholics in the state hospitals; after they sobered up, they constituted the hospitals' major work force. At the same time, the early recovery homes were developing:

> Traditionally, such facilities were offered by men and women who had achieved sobriety themselves and as recovering alcoholics they reached out to help those who were still suffering. In some cases, this meant providing accomodations by opening their own homes—the early Recovery Homes were not identified as such in the community—they simply emerged in a natural, consistent pattern. Usually a fairly large house was leased by enterprising and concerned people who opened the doors to those who needed help . . . all who lived there were expected to behave somewhat as if in a "family" situation; that is—by undertaking the chores of the house and the provision of food, and sharing a common table.[13]

Gradually, as California closed down the state hospitals, the State Office of Alcoholism encouraged the counties to fund recovery homes, both out of its openness to a non-medical mode and out of awareness that costs for residential facilities are smaller than hospital costs. CAARH, armed with this support, and its own membership growth, is enjoying an enhanced position in the state arena.

Emerging Rights in the Research World

The present position of the emerging alcohol research world can only be appreciated when viewed against the obstacles encountered in the past. Faith in new knowledge, the development of techniques for scientific investigation, and the veneration of "experts" which mark the 1930s and 1940s, made their impact on this arena. In 1935, Norman Jolliffe, chief of medical services of the Psychiatric Division of Bellevue Hospital, conceived a multidisciplinary approach to the study of alcoholism, and when the Rockefeller Foundation backed out of supporting his research project, Jolliffe's advisory committee became the Research Council on the Problems of Alcohol. Its goal was to seek funds to support research on alcohol problems. The efforts of this group led to the first Center of Alcohol Studies at Yale University.[14] From Yale, came the early work of the apostles of "the new scientific approach"—Howard Haggard, E.M. Jellinek, Mark Keller, Selden Bacon. No one would deny the contribution made by the Yale Center in its publishing, abstracting and bibliographic activities (non-research activities are discussed later), which became organized around the *Quarterly Journal of Studies on Alcohol* and the Classified Abstract Archive of the Alcohol Literature (CAAAL). Therefore, it is not in any way to detract from the work of the center's academicians that Straus has pointed out the incompatability of their twin goals of attracting scientists of recognition and advancement and of pursuing a multidisciplinary perspective. One impediment to these goals, as identified by Straus, is the stigma of alcohol research:

> As with physicians and the other helping professions, with scientists, there is evidence that the shadow of derived stigma has been a deterrent to alcohol research.
>
> In the 1940s when the Yale program was emerging, the wide publicity it received was most distasteful and embarrassing to a majority of the Yale faculty. It was as though the Professor of English felt personally stigmatized because his colleague, the Professor of Applied Physiology, was an authority on alcoholism. Of more serious consequence was the reluctance of distinguished scientists or of young scientists who aspired toward distinction to risk their reputations or ambitions by showing an interest in alcohol-related research.[15]

Another obstacle was inherent in the internal organization of universities and the role played by departments as bases of power. Straus asserts that as departments are political units (competing in the university for funds, space, curriculum prominence, and faculty lines) so they have felt obliged to assume clearcut identities around which to stake their claims and to demand the allegiance of their members. On the one hand, the study of alcohol problems required a multidisciplinary approach—this Haggard and Jellinek recognized when they brought together scholars from the biological, social and psychological sciences, history, education, law and theology, and clinicians from diverse medical specialities. On the other hand:

> There was an inherent weakness in the laboratory's place within the political framework of the university. Scientists who joined the program from an academic base in other departments risked loss of reward and status

within their basic departments. Those who published their research in the interdisciplinary Quarterly Journal of Studies on Alcohol found that these publications were not recognized by or even known to their departmental colleagues because they did not appear in the principal journals of their own disciplines. Despite—and perhaps also because of—the great amount of favorable publicity which Yale's Center of Alcohol Studies received, and the plaudits it brought to the university from the outside world, the program was never appreciated or given stability within the University.[16]

In 1962, the center moved to Rutgers University, after Yale's president stripped his University of virtually all activities which did not fit the formal departmental structure. Rutgers has been somewhat more hospitable, but even here the center has remained a university stepchild. It has been aided by private foundations, the federal government in the form of specific projects and the alcoholic beverage industries. The only funds it has received from the State of New Jersey have been for a few small research projects. Partly because of the competition of a NIAAA sponsored information and education bank (the Clearinghouse for Alcohol Information, discussed later) and because NIAAA has been sparing in its support, the Rutgers people feel they been neglected as this arena has experienced its growth.

Other institutes for specific alcohol research are still rare, but they are a developing aspect of this world. State support has led to the establishment of a Research Institute on Alcoholism in Buffalo, New York (biochemical and animal laboratory research) and the Center for Alcohol Studies, in Chapel Hill, North Carolina (clinical and biological research and faculty grants for special projects in biochemical and psychological laboratory research). In September 1977, the University of California, Los Angeles was awarded a much coveted $2.3 million grant from the California Office of Alcoholism to establish the first state Alcohol Research Center.

Three centers have experienced growth as a result of the increased largess of recent years. The Oklahoma Center for Alcohol and Drug Related Studies in Oklahoma City, which has concentrated on animal and human laboratory studies and clinical research under the direction of Alfonso Paredes, has enlarged in terms of staff and publications since its establishment in 1971. In Seattle, the Alcoholism and Drug Abuse Institute was given a substantial start through a state initiative which earmarks taxes from liquor licenses for alcohol research and training. This institute enjoys the support of the volunteer-action world—the Washington State Council of NCA is a powerful body in that state, counting in its ranks a number of recovered alcoholics who are also legislators. Unlike the Rutgers Center, this institute, while multidisciplinary, also appears to have the support of the University community. University attitudes toward a multidisciplinary approach altered drastically during the 1960s in response to student agitation for "relevance"; the deans of the various disciplines involved in the institute serve on its advisory board. Under its research grant program, this center has supported faculty research on the UW campus, conducted workshops, seminars and special courses and holds an annual summer conference. In 1975, Marc Schuckit, a psychiatrist with experience in clinical and genetic research, took over the directorship. The institute is now carrying on its own research projects as well as offering a program in which health workers can spend time working with the institute staff in both health care planning and research.

Also, reflecting the expansion of this world in the Social Research Group of the School of Public Health, University of California, Berkeley, directly descended from a research project which was organized in 1959 by the Division of Alcoholic Rehabilitation of the State Department of Public Health. The founding investigators of this center, Wendell R. Lipscomb, Ira Cisin and Geneviere Knupfer, conducted the first national surveys of drinking practices based on a non-treatment population. This focus on general population drinking practices and drinking problems (and later on prevention alternatives) has continued under the supervision of SRG's director, Don Cahalan, and his successor, Robin Room.

Despite the increased visibility of these centers, it is important to understand that most of the work of the research world remains invisible, in that it is scattered all over the country, funded through individual grants and contracts. Federal support has gone toward the research of individuals who had already established a reputation prior to the establishment of NIAAA (people like Richard Jessor at the University of Colorado who directs sociological/psychological studies, and Donald Goodwin at Washington University, St. Louis, whose concern has been with the genetic factor in alcoholism, and to others associated with these institutions or, for example, with the University of California, Irvine, where they are engaged in brain studies). NIAAA also supports isolated studies which cover a wide range: for instance, alcohol-induced liver injury; alcohol influences on perceptual-cognitive behavior, cell membranes of nerves, motor control, the heart; alcoholic behavior in special populations, such as youth, ethnic groups, women; and an occasional "flier," such as the grant to develop a program for identification and referral using bartenders as "gatekeepers." That this world has benefited from the expansion of recent years is clear when one views the Congressional alcohol research budget—$15,474,000 in 1978, plus a 1979 estimated budget of

$21,976,000 and a 1980 estimated budget of $25,078,000 [17]—against the struggle of the pioneers of this arena to establish a place for alcohol research.

Summary

It has been my intent in this chapter to examine the relationship between the history of this arena and its present growth—to set the stage, so to speak—and to make the point that through whatever means the worlds described so far have found expression, they have, in the process of establishing turf rights and of increasing their own positions of strength, contributed toward increasing the public visibility of the social problem of alcohol use. There has been some displacement: Rutgers nee Yale no longer is *the* academic center; ADPA is not *the* professional organization. But each of these establishments continue to exist in altered form. This chapter is further meant as an *introduction* to the myriad groups and associations to be found in the arena.

One word about social worlds before proceeding: it is an underlying assumption of this perspective that within each world there are issues being fought out. (I have alluded to some instances, such as the debate within NCA over how dominant the AA orientation should be and the ironing out of differences between members of CAARH over standards.) Further, it can be assumed that what one judges from observing the leadership of associations is quite likely at variance with *some* members. If this study had been confined to organizational interaction, it would have been possible to pick up many more of the confrontations, compromises, strategies than I shall be able to do. Having chosen to look at an entire arena, I have had to be content with discovering only the most glaring examples, hoping that what has been sacrificed in detailed examination is compensated for by increased scope.

There is great variation in the extent to which the actors described so far represent a political constituency, as the term is usually employed. A number of them could undoubtedly be mobilized if the dollars were threatened; some perhaps could not. Many have little interest in any but their own domain; others have a heightened sense of the interrelationship at least with *some* of the other worlds. *All* have an interest in the continuance of national, state and county programming. Even in California, where only 14 percent of the total state budget for alcohol problems comes from NIAAA, no respondents denied that the NIAAA, by its very existence, has increased the visibility of the problem of alcohol use and contributed toward a favorable climate for state/county funding. In both county and private facilities, the impact is observable in the improvement of physical plants alone. And even in the midst of nostalgic reveries about the loss of volunteerism, the "good old days" when people could not buy resources and creatively developed their own, these people do not deny that they have an interest in the perpetuation of public funding.

Notes

1. Thomas F.A. Plaut, *Alcohol Problems: A Report to the Nation* (London: Oxford University Press, 1967).
2. Lynn M. Reynolds, *The California Office of Alcohol Program Management: A Development in the Formal Control of a Social Problem* (Ph.D. dissertation, University of California, Berkeley, 1974), p. 42.
3. Ibid., p. 51.
4. Ibid., p. 52.
5. Ibid., p. 98.
6. "Alcoholism Programs: A Need For Reform," report prepared by the Assembly Office of Research, California Legislature, March, 1970.
7. Senate Bill No. 744, State of California.
8. Alexis de Tocqueville, *Democracy in America,* Phillips Bradley (ed.), (New York: Vintage Books, Vol. II 1945), p. 117.
9. Everett C. Hughes, "Professions," *Daedalus,* Vol. 92 (1963), p. 657.
10. Martin Dodd, "How Big is a Recovery Home?" *The Hearth* (January, 1976).
11. Nils Christie and Kettil Bruun, "The Conceptual Framework," Proceedings of the 28th International Congress on Alcohol and Alcoholism, 1969.
12. D.E. Beauchamp, *Precarious Politics* (Ph.D. dissertation, Johns Hopkins University, 1973), p. 343.
13. Dodd, *"How Big."*
14. *See* Mark Keller, "Multidisciplinary Perspectives on Alcoholism and the Need for Integration," *Journal of Studies on Alcohol,* Vol. 36 (1975), pp. 136-38.
15. Robert Straus, "Problem Drinking in the Perspective of Social Change 1940-1973," in W. J. Filstead, J.J. Rossi and M. Keller (eds.), *Alcohol, New Thinking and New Directions* (Cambridge, Mass.: Ballinger, 1976), p. 37.
16. Ibid., p. 40.
17. *The Alcoholism Report,* Vol. 7, January 26, 1979, p. 1.

4.

Developing Constituencies

Life is infused into an arena in direct proportion to the growth of its constituency. In this chapter, we shall examine three means of *developing constituencies:* through establishing advisory boards, through enlisting representatives of special populations on commissions, and through awarding contracts and grants. Also examined are the consequences of this growth as it pertains to contracts/grants. To what extent does building a constituency also entail building a dependency?

More Generals for the Civilian Army

The Jeffersonian ideal of fullest participation of the citizen in government has enjoyed only wavering attention throughout American history. A useful analysis of its most recent adaptation by the bureaucratic world is offered by Elliott Krause:

> In those bureaucracies where the activity is of an "action" sort, involving direct community intervention for change, the need for the bureaucracy to justify its actions reaches a maximum. It is these sociopolitical factors which lead the "action bureaucracy" to develop ideologies to increase the acceptability of their actions to the influenced public. One of the most important of these new bureaucratic ideologies is "citizen participation." [1]

In the establishment of legislative boundaries, the "action bureaucracy" of this arena fell heir to the rebirth of this ideology as manifested in the programming of the 1960s. Model Cities Program, Office of Economic Opportunity projects, Mobilization for Youth undertakings all mark the discovery of community and of participatory democracy used (and misused) during those years.[2] Even more closely allied is the structure of Community Mental Health programming, which provided a close-at-hand model in drafting the 1970 Comprehensive Alcohol Abuse & Alcoholism Prevention Treatment and Rehabilitation Act. Not only did this act designate the establishment of a National Advisory Council, but it specified that any state wishing to participate (i.e. receive funding) must designate a state advisory council. In addition, California's enabling legislation specifies that each county shall have its own alcoholism advisory board.

The disparity between an ideology of citizen participation and its application in practice is a worthwhile subject of study. However, it would require a much closer examination of the workings of these advisory councils than was within my purview. Since the problem under attention here is the building and making visible of an arena, the more relevant question is how the adoption of the ideology of citizen participation has affected that growth. The important consideration is the extent to which the mandating of citizen advisory boards has provided a means for reinforcing an already existing constituency and for building upon it.

On a national level, the National Advisory Council has been comprised of people with a professional connection to the arena (such as a dean of a college of pharmacy, chairman of a department of psychiatry, a mental health commissioner), people with some program connection, and recovered alcoholics with seniority and prestige in the arena. These can be said to be political appointments, with all that this implies in terms of status; names are submitted to a special office in Health, Education and Welfare devoted entirely to such appointments. The potential power of this council can be judged by its mandate to approve grants after recommendations have been made by review committees; it has, in the past, varied in respect to an active/passive role based on the nature of its rotating membership and on the stance of the director of the National Institute of Alcohol Abuse and Alcoholism. Liaison members of the advisory council (i.e. representatives of the American Medical Association, the American Hospital Association, the American Nurses Association, the National Association of Social Workers) further enlarge the professional base of support, by serving as information conduits between NIAAA and the respective organizations for their reciprocal benefit. Additionally, efforts have been made to recruit people for grant review committees from professional worlds (e.g. architecture, law) beyond the recovery service world—people with no previous involvement in the arena, in order, as one respondent explained, "to get them sensitized and hooked in to the problem of alcoholism."

State advisory boards further enlarge the constituency. For example, under the legislation which replaced the California Office of Alcohol Program Management with an Office of Alcoholism in 1976, the composition of the state advisory board is as follows: five members to be appointed by the governor, five by the Senate Rules Committee, and five by the speaker of assembly. At least one appointee of *each* of these legislative bodies (thus three members) must be a person who has received treatment or rehabilitation services for alcoholism problems. Other members are to have "professional, research, or personal interest in the field of alcoholism" and to be "representatives from various economic, social and occupational groups"; membership must also "allow for geographic distribution throughout the state." Since there are only fifteen members, care must be taken to combine some of these criteria within a single person. Most of the members come from the recovery service and volunteer-action worlds.

The first year of operation under the new system in California consisted of a contest over power, i.e., clarifying the fine line between providing assistance and advice to the Office of Alcoholism and running the program. The intent of the law was to create checks and balances *vis-à-vis* the bureaucratic world, and this was subsequently spelled out by Senator Gregorio, author of the legislation. Since the present political climate of constituency politics is reflected in the political mode of selection, the end result is that the new board members represent a wider constituency than before. For example, they represent, and are accountable to, not only the recovery service and volunteer-action worlds but a specific sub-world such as an ethnic minority. The advisory/policy-making struggle is far from resolved; in an atmosphere of heightened political awareness, these constituencies will continue to pressure their board representatives to enlarge their advocacy role.

California county advisory boards are mandated to follow the same pattern, to include recipients of services for alcohol problems and to base the remaining representation on the criteria listed, excluding geographic distribution. Thus the constituency widens by exponential progression: specialized interests may include, to take San Francisco County as an example, a civil liberties lawyer concerned with public inebriates, a representative of the board of education, doctors, a policeman, a probation officer—this is only a partial list. All of the boards have a share of what one respondent called "professional board sitters," but for the most part members are connected to, or advocates for, some aspect of programming.

Obviously, the county boards are presented with the same advisory/policy-making issue vis-à-vis the bureaucratic world as that described on the state level. (I draw upon the San Francisco experience because it was the most accessible to my examination but it can be taken as illustrative of other counties.) That the people on the community level who had the expertise were working in agencies and services created a dilemma, since the board has the final say in the distribution of funds. It was the private agencies which fought to have more programs, and forced the issue in the community. Veterans look back on years when money was available but not spent, when development of county programs was impeded by the civil service system. A breakthrough came with the national and state developments described on the preceding pages, spurring the private agencies to convince the counties to try private contracting. When the first advisory board was to be recommended by the Mental Health advisory board, this body drew upon people already at work in the arena, some of whom turned out to be connected to recipient agencies. Senator Gregorio's subsequent legislation attempted to circumvent this "conflict of interest," still difficult to define. No member of a county advisory board may be an employee of an agency receiving funds, but the law says nothing about being a board member or volunteer in a recipient agency. And those who *are* excluded from advisory board membership serve as consultants, or on task forces or attend providers meetings. In addition, the interlocking of a growing constituency is given impetus when there are two active and adjacent counties. To illustrate, Marin County has had two board members who were providers in San Francisco County but residents of Marin. Thus, remaining active at this level, even when denied official board membership, becomes important for those who would protect their interests.

Those who are denied membership on an advisory board by virtue of their paid positions as providers feel some frustration over the exclusion, particularly "after I worked in this field for nothing." They view citizen participation from the volunteer-action world as offering up people less knowledgeable than they, and, in some cases, making a rubber stamp of the board. As with all boards, the balance between members and administrators depends on the relative strength of the personalities involved. Moreover, member participation varies greatly, depending on time, money, other demands. The interplay is seen by one board member as follows:

> Bureaucracy always resents citizens coming in and telling them what to do. The issue is to what extent the community is seen to have a mandated role

in determining the nature and distribution of the services it pays for and receives, and very often the bureaucracy thinks it is their money they are playing with. In _____County it took two years to work out the balance; in ours six months. A lot of times the board is kept off balance, they don't get the information they need, or it's given to them in bureaucratese, or they don't understand the funding channels, so they're ineffectual, and people get bored and drop off.

A Flurry of Dissent

One expression of the tug of war between the county administrators and their boards was the attempted formation of an Association of County Alcoholism Advisory Boards. At first blush, the title of this group suggests the American propensity for association carried to an ineluctable absurdity. In fact, this endeavor represents a logical outgrowth of the division of power. The conflict was neatly summed up by two respondents. From a board member: "advisory boards realized they didn't have much in the way of authority—in some cases they have to report to a Mental Health Advisory Board, and then there's this paid person sitting there and really doing what he wants to do." From a county administrator: "it was made up of the anti-anti people, the people most in need of recognition, strictly to put the administrators in their place." Ostensibly meeting to "upgrade our knowledge and discuss common problems," this group for now seems moribund. Originally organized with one representative from each of the counties, some of these people found it hard to travel to a central meeting point The organization received a further blow when the county administrators convinced the Office of Alcoholism to restrict compensation, for county board members, to travel expense within their respective counties. Denied this outlet, the county bureaucracies and their boards are forced to look for other vehicles to express their power struggle.

Providing the Basis for Mobilization

It would be difficult to assess the extent of practical application that exists in regard to this ideology called "citizen participation," and, as explained above, such an assessment is unnecessary for the purposes of this study. What is important is that the county board structure (and its related consultants, task forces, and provider meetings) provide an army at the ready. When the Gregorio Bill became effective in January 1976, *The Hearth* (newsletter of the California Association of Alcoholic Recovery Homes) was quick to mobilize its readers:

> . . . unpaid members of Boards of Directors or Advisory Boards of private facilities are eligible to be appointed to any County Alcoholism Board . . . it is vitally incumbent upon every interested, concerned person in the county, to call, write, or go see their Board of Supervisors and make known to them the names of persons who ought to be considered for appointment to the County Alcoholism Advisory Board.[3]

Pointing out that part of the law which states each county shall utilize available *private* alcoholism programs and services in the county *prior to developing new county-operated* programs and services, *The Hearth* instructed, "the County Alcoholism Advisory Boards must play a very definite role in insuring that this provision of the law is properly and fully implemented." By August, 1976, after the state significantly augmented each county's alcoholism budget, *The Hearth* told its readers that most counties were now in the process of negotiating proposals, and "It behooves every Alcoholism Advisory Board Member and provider to be fully aware of this activity." [4] Also during 1976, when there was a statewide lobbying effort in behalf of another Gregorio Bill (Senate Bill 204, which would have increased the tax on beverage alcohol, the proceeds to go toward more treatment and prevention efforts) board members and their constituencies in attendance at board meetings were repeatedly encouraged to make their views known to their elected representatives.

A concurrent development of a constituency has been occurring in the volunteer-action world, principally through the National Council on Alcoholism. There are now some 150 councils throughout the country, each one separately incorporated, with its own board of directors. Active councils, like that in the San Francisco Bay Area, have not only a board of directors but committees (public education, labor/management, fund raising). A concerted effort is made to attract to these boards and committees people who had no previous involvement with the arena—clergymen, lawyers, labor leaders, ethnic minority representatives. Since it was estimated by an NCA leader that at least one-third of these participants were new to the arena, I asked how many fall into the category of "professional board sitters." His response was, "There tends to be a conscientious commitment—there's not that much status involved in sitting on an alcoholism council board or committee." Elsewhere, the ratio of new participation varies; some councils still are totally composed of recovered alcoholics.

Drafting Constituents

Critics of urban renewal and anti-poverty programs have directed attention to the bureaucracy's role in energizing groups toward acting in their own behalf—"grievance manufacture," to use the phrase coined by McCarthy and Zald.[5] In this arena, the organization of constituency groups was instigated by John Wolfe, the former director of treatment and rehabilitation for NIAAA, who came out of the activist anti-poverty era, by way of Community Mental Health. Wolfe prompted the formation of a National Indian Board on Alcohol and Drug Abuse, a Commission on Alcoholism for Spanish Speaking Persons, a National Black Council on Alcoholism, a National Assocation of Anti-Poverty Alcohol Programs. Although initial formation was bogged down in a conflict between Wolfe and NIAAA's director, Morris Chafetz, the concept of attracting special population groups persisted, since it was in keeping with the national thrust on the part of ethnic minorities. (Indeed, one NIAAA national conference had been interrupted by a "mau-mauing" session, symptomatic of those years.)

As with all such groups, questions have arisen as to whether they are representative of their respective populations or of the leaders' self-interest, but in regard to enlarging the constituency of the larger arena, there would be no question. The result was an Indian desk in the Treatment division of NIAAA; an Indian review board for grants; there are specific programs for black people; and, by order of Congress, programs directed at two more population groups, women and youth. The rationale is that all of these groups have different needs based on who and what they are; [6] the end result is an ever-widening base of support.

The California minority commissions predate the national ones by a year, and came about in that curious combination of interests characteristic of any political interplay. Under the imperative imagery of a proposed "Strike Force," the state Secretary of Health and Welfare under then Governor Reagan called together people involved in alcoholism, venereal disease and dental programs to engage in a public information campaign designed to influence "major changes in behavior affecting major health problems." Bureaucratic representatives of these arenas fanned out throughout the state, encouraging service groups and schools to conduct forums and workshops, drawing in people who had never been involved with these problems before. Brochures were disseminated at these sessions, but the entire campaign was to culminate in Strike Force Sunday, when the brochure would be distributed door-to-door by a volunteer force which had grown from the early ground work. Since every brochure contained a picture of the Secretary of Health and Welfare, and since he often arrived at these sessions with great fanfare, and was coincidentally interested in running for United States Senator in the Republican primary, there were those who felt that the motivation of increasing the visibility of these health problems was secondary to in-

creasing the visibility of the secretary. Critics felt the costs far outweighed the possible benefits (the campaign also included television
advertising): some regions refused to cooperate. Nevertheless, the California Office of Alcoholism Programs (OAPM) looked upon this drive
as a good way to get information out to the public, and consequently
provided staff support. As the OAPM staff representative moved around
the state, she became impressed with the need for "grass roots organization," so that special populations could define and express their particular needs, monitor programs, and make an impact on programming. As
on the national level, the timing of the state's interest coordinated with
the power needs of ethnic minorities and women that were emerging at
the time. Also at the same time, another thrust within the volunteer-
action world coincided to give the grass roots movement added impetus.

The larger councils of the National Council on Alcoholism within
California had been meeting informally to try to develop opinions in
concert, mainly regarding legislation. When it was learned that OAPM
might be willing to let a contract to implement a state-wide organization
of volunteer groups, this informal group incorporated as the Alcoholism
Councils of California, hoping to stimulate the addition of new councils.
NIAAA became the funding source when California was chosen one of
six states for such a grant to the National Council. OAPM, worried lest
their vision of an organization representing *all* the private interests might
become subverted into NCA domination, drew upon the people who had
emerged through Strike Force, and provided funding to help special
population groups get started, so they could join the Council on an equal
basis. Armed with a rationale of "technical assistance," OAPM contracts
funded the establishment and the operating costs for a black, Spanish-
speaking, Native American and women's commission, circumventing all
the civil-service requirements that would have been entailed in bringing
these people into government employ. Of these, the women's commission has been the most active, and has included representatives of the
other minority commissions within its ranks.

After three years of operation, the state decided to discontinue its
policy of sole support; the commissions now must bid competitively with
other organizations to provide technical assistance. This is forcing the
commissions to work with county administrations for possible funding.
The commissions do not generate membership fees, as does for example
the California Association of Alcoholic Recovery Homes, and cynics
have asked if three years of "needs assessment" on behalf of ethnic
minorities does not suggest that a vacuum still exists. The strength of this
constituency is still to be demonstrated, with the real trial in the years

ahead. There is no question that through the vehicle of commissions, additional numbers have been added to the ranks of the alcohol problem arena; still to be answered is the extent to which these ranks represent local initiative and could be mobilized if needed.

Buying Constituents

Controversy has arisen over constituency building as it relates to NIAAA's funding mechanisms. Money comes to the states through *formula grants*, based on population (discussed in Chapter 11) and through *direct grants* for specific purposes (training, research, demonstration projects). Direct grants require review by a panel of experts, and final approval of the National Advisory Council. For a considerable period during the early years of NIAAA, this grant process was to some degree circumvented by awarding *contracts* to the private sector, as defended by then NIAAA Director Chafetz, for "expertise and quality endeavors." An added incentive:

> And when the contract had achieved its objectives, the personnel were not an entrenched part of the bureaucracy for whom new positions and activities (for which many were unsuited) had to be found.[7]

With this move, NIAAA stepped into the world of research marketing.

Initially, this resulted in a narrowing of the constituency to those who could bid competitively. Requests for Proposals (RFP's) appear in *Commerce Business Daily*, published by the Department of Commerce. Access to this publication, time limits on the preparation of proposals, and the tremendous cost of preparation, all created obstacles for the smaller contractor. Advantage fell upon large consulting firms, with people one respondent characterized as "good at being experts in anything—who have perfected the art of proposal writing and can include impressive credentials on their *vitae.*" Even from within this world, some have questioned the competitiveness of this system. To quote two employees of the Bureau of Social Science Research, Inc.:

> . . . success in the "RFP" game' depends heavily on an organization's ability to mobilize resources for making many proposals, for whatever work whatever agencies request whenever they request it and particularly during the end-of-the-fiscal-year contracting rush. Barring vast and conveniently idle resources for the purpose, it is difficult to see how such organizations can fail to subordinate study performance to study marketing. . . . Tossing together in one publication solicitations for bids for everything

from screws and bolts to the evaluation of large scale social experiments may by itself encourage the development of firms that are prepared to market anything whatsoever to the government, rather than appropriately specialized performance-oriented organizations.[8]

Gradually, some of the smaller would-be contractors emerging in the research and recovery service worlds have adapted to the "RFP Game," and picked up the "grantsmanship" that goes into tailoring proposals to meet the requirements of the granting agency.[9] Faced with a small staff, NIAAA found the contracting mechanisms the most reasonable way to extend services. With hindsight, one ex-bureaucrat summarized the problems:

The idea sounds good, free enterprise and all that. But you have to assume that the contracting agency knows what is best to do. The RFP is explicit, and it may leave out something that is important that the person filling the job maybe would think of if he did it himself. You don't appeal to people who are innovative and creative, you get entrepeneurs. Often the groups are hastily put together. Also, for it to work, you need careful supervision, and if the money is given to ethnic minorities, they'll have no part of outside supervision.

Seen from the perspective of the recipient, there are additional problems, as explained by one:

We have to modify our research aims to fit what the funding agency will approve, and to fit what we can do. It's hard to take on a long term project—you can't be certain of the kind of help you are going to sustain. So it's always a compromise between what is manageable, what can be funded, and what you're interested in.

And by another:

People on "soft money" tend to overgrow. You add more staff so as not to pass up this contract, for fear you may not be offered the next one.

Following press intimations of a sweetheart contract,[10] the institute shifted back to the grant process which requires peer review. Some of the same problems inhere, regardless of which process, but the important point, for our purposes, is that allocation of monies in smaller portions entrenches more recipients as interested parties in the continuation of the granting agency, NIAAA.

Building a Dependency

One thorny issue has arisen over such allocations with implications beyond this arena. That question is to what extent does building a constituency entail building a dependency?

NIAAA was established in spite of the opposition of the Nixon administration. During the first years, large amounts of the appropriation voted by Congress were regularly impounded. This situation was reversed after legal action instigated by the Alcohol and Drug Problems Association and the National Council on Alcoholism. Impounded funds amounted to approximately $800 million; the judge gave the institute one year from the day of his decision to spend this money. With staff size still restricted, the institute looked upon grants and contracts as the only way to distribute quickly the newly released funds.

To the National Council on Alcoholism went three multi-year grants totalling $6.9 million, to expand its information service, to develop new councils within the States and to establish occupational alcoholism programs in ten selected cities. The U.S. Conference of Mayors received $559,505 over two years to help demonstrate alcoholism programs for city employees and to draft city ordinances dealing with alcoholism. To Legis 50 (formerly the Citizens Conference on State Legislatures) went $1.9 million, which it added to $900 thousand from the National Institute on Drug Abuse and the Transportation Department, to provide the relevant state legislative committees with two staff members, one a generalist in the drafting of legislation and the other a specialist in alcoholism and drug abuse legislation. The National Association of Counties was granted $761,175 for three years, to inform county officials of their responsibilities regarding treatment for their own employees and the general public.

This is a partial list. Moving through and beyond the era of impounded funds, the institute has continued with grant awards to the Jaycees, the Educational Commission of the States, the PTA, the YMCA, the Girls' Clubs, the Boys' Clubs, all in a mass attempt to educate the public at large, to make these groups "change agents" in their communities. That there were uneven results can be partially attributed to the fact that these organizations had no clear concept of what the problem was or how to attack it. NIAAA could not render technical assistance in such a short time, and merely told the groups to "get involved." As quoted by one respondent, NIAAA Director Morris Chafetz often referred to these attempts as "rabble rousing programs." (Some grants/contracts were more specific: for instance, one to the Air Line Pilots

Association for an alcoholism occupational program, and one to the National Council on Aging to study the effects of retirement on drinking behavior.)

It will surprise no student of the bureaucratic world to learn that contracts were also awarded as outgrowths of these grants; for example $1.4 million to Arthur Young and Company to investigate the kinds of problems experienced by the institute's 450 grant recipients and to help recipients with accounting and programmatic difficulties arising from their grants, and $559,053 to Informatics Inc., to gather data on the kinds of clients who use the treatment centers supported by alcoholism grants and the kinds of treatment they receive. The latter is over and above contracts with the Stanford Research Institute for similar purposes, discussed in detail in Chapter 11.

The concept of building a constituency, which has thus far been interpreted as widening the base of support and increasing attention to alcohol problems, took on a negative tone when these large grants and contracts came under congressional scrutiny, in the spring of 1976. The House Interstate and Foreign Commerce Subcommittee on Health and the Environment "accused the institute of farming out work that could be performed more usefully by its own staff. It has asked whether the institute is trying to buy the political allegiance of organizations whose support would be helpful in getting more money from Congress for the fight against alcoholism." [11] In response, NIAAA set up a task force to review sixteen grantees whose continuation or renewal award times fell between July 1976 and the end of the year, including some of those listed above.

Caught in the crossfire was another organization, the Council of State and Territorial Alcoholism Authorities (CSTAA), whose entire support came from NIAAA. CSTAAA had come into existence in 1974 in a reverse lobbying effort. (The adjective "territorial" refers to U.S. Territories. This organization includes one director from each state and each territory.) It was NIAAA that urged a separate organization upon the state alcoholism authorities. Harsher critics at the time saw this move as an attempt to capture the state directors as a political force; a more moderate assessment was the expressed need on the part of NIAAA for a state organization which could deal with the institute as a united body, particularly in regard to regulations and policy direction. As explained in Chapter 3, the Alcohol and Drug Problems Association (ADPA) dated back to 1949, and was founded by a group of state alcoholism program directors. But this organization required a membership fee, and states are loathe to divert any part of their budgets in this way. The state directors would have been happy with a small grant to ADPA; NIAAA offered funding to get a new organization started. At the same time, the impounded funds were released with their expenditure deadline. The institute rushed its launching of CSTAA with a $3.3 million grant over a three-year period: $2.4 million was to enable the states to work out a uniform system of data collection; $255,000 to develop models for accreditation of facilities and certification of alcoholism counselors; the rest for a number of smaller tasks, and for staff administrators and travel.

Wariness was voiced at the time within the ranks of the directors, lest they lose their separate-but-equal status. Others felt the need for a strong state organization outweighed the risk, and preferred to see the funding as a vehicle by which there would be an eventual shifting of focus from direct project grants to state formula grants. A strengthening of the state authorities could make such a transition more orderly; armed with a uniform system of data collection and the visibility of a national organization they would be viewed as more capable of taking on the increased load of federal funding. Opposition also came from ADPA, whose main support was being diluted; this apparently subsided in the face of the inevitable. ADPA moved its offices in Washington, D.C. to larger quarters, subleasing part of the space to CSTAA, and thereby maintained a close relationship.

The question raised by Congress regarding total organizational reliance on the federal government is a legitimate one, even as viewed by CSTAA's director at the time:

> "The problem with a single source of funding is the control that goes along with it," Price said. The degree of the council's dependence on the institute is difficult to measure, but it was apparent recently when the institute persuaded the council to allocate $110,059 of the evaluation project money to an inventory of state alcoholism treatment resources. "I had to ask myself if I was doing it because it was useful to the states or because there was pressure from the institute," Price said. He said he concluded that the council's own membership would benefit from the inventory, but he said he could not be sure that the institute's position did not influence his recommendations to his board of directors to do the inventory.[12]

NIAAA's own task force report to Congress was frankly critical of procedures used in making these grants, and it is understandable that there was minimal effort to make the findings public. Released first by the Department of Health, Education and Welfare, it consisted almost entirely of blank pages, with all the panel's findings and recommendations deleted. Apologizing for its resemblance to "a piece of Swiss cheese," Harry Bell, information chief for NIAAA, said the deletions were simply following the letter of the Freedom of Information Act.[13]

Legal action led to publication of the full report, so the public no longer had to contend with sentences such as "in general the task force has determined (deleted)." In addition to references to past review procedures as "highly irregular and inconsistent," and a leadership and staff which "had little experience with traditional institutional constraints and safeguards regarding the review of grant applications," the most damning sentence contained in the report was: "some of the reviewers utilized also had potential conflicts of interest in that they were later employed by the grants which they recommended for approval." [14] The bulk of the report was much less severe, attempting to explain that the new federal agency "entered the public health arena committed to the rapid amelioration if not the resolution of a long neglected, serious, and poorly understood problem whose roots were deeply embedded in cultural habits" and took an active leadership role because it was encouraged "by an articulate constituency who projected an enthusiasm brought about by recognition that their cause was now given national visibility and credibility through Federal law and commitment." [15] Remedial action was offered in the promise of increased staff and improvement in program development, review, award, monitoring and evaluation functions for all grant and contract programs.

It should be stressed that there were no allegations of illegality. The task force criticism of the absence of rigorous review was based more on the tradition of the Public Health Service than on legal considerations. Moreover, to say, as the congressional subcommittee did, that it might have been more sound for the institute to perform some of the tasks itself, was to overlook the conditions at the time—the personnel freeze, the release of impounded funds, and the impact of such a large windfall on a fledgling agency.

CSTAA was the only organization *fully* funded by NIAAA, but Legis 50–The Center for Legislative Improvement—was most vocal about its sense of abuse under this investigation. Describing the history of its relationship with NIAAA, the National Institute on Drug Abuse (NIDA) and the National Highway Traffic Safety Administration (NHTSA) as "Kafkaesque," Larry Margolis, executive director of Legis 50 told the NIAAA Advisory Board:

> The project has been alternately ignored, delayed, disrupted, contorted, and then finally strangled by the funding agencies. Our organization has been maligned, mistreated, and frustrated in its efforts to conduct a reasonable program.[16]

CSTAA and Legis 50 were the only two organizations to feel the full brunt, the former because it appeared for a time to be out of business and the latter because it felt funds were cut off before it could complete its commitment. Ironically, CSTAA's denouement has redounded to the advantage of its parent organization, ADPA; CSTAA has become an affiliate of ADPA, now called the ADPA Council of Directors.

The National Council on Alcoholism, threatened with rejection of its request for renewal, demonstrated its strength. Responding to the accusation of "constituency building" as it was being interpreted by the advisory council, President Thomas J. Swafford described what NCA means by the term:

> A constituency that delivers direct services and influences delivery of services by others. A constituency composed of private citizens, lay and professional volunteers, over 4,000 volunteer board members at the national, state and local levels, 176 affiliate local councils, professional components for doctors, nurses and alcoholism researchers. A constituency that works with and through individuals, organizations, and groups such as labor, management, health professionals, civic and religious organizations and government at all levels to bring help to those affected by alcoholism, including women, youth, minorities and the aged. A constituency that provides public information, education, training, research and multiplies these effort through other groups.
>
> This is what we mean by building constituency—we mean an *alcoholism constituency, not an NCA constituency* (emphasis added).[17]

The result was that NCA received a six-month extension of its state voluntary association grant and third-year continuation awards for its labor-management and public information projects. When these terms expired, the state voluntary associations and public information projects were no longer funded.

Obviously NCA and the state directors (whether represented as CSTAA or the ADPA Council) have an abiding commitment to the arena. However, misgivings have been expressed regarding the long term effects of pulling national organizations, local governmental and voluntary community groups into the arena. To quote Room:

> . . . typically, the alcohol campaign fits in as one more in a jumbled succession of good works and interesting topics that the organization takes on as worthwhile content for its meetings, and the campaign may leave little legacy of organizational commitment, particularly in the absence of federal funding.[18]

Room's last phrase is key, for what *can* be expected is a commitment to continuation of federal funding. One cannot assess the larger commitment (as one respondent put it, "whether $23 million of rabble rousing was worth it"). However, many of the grantees formed steering committees (for example, the NCA grant counted representatives of labor and management among its ranks) and while some were surely figureheads, others were just as surely educated into a new interest.

Fall-out from this national experience can be observed in two illustrations. The first is that the State of California looked to the national experience in its decision to discontinue sole support for its minority and women's commissions, obliging them to demonstrate whether they do, in actuality, constitute a strong enough force to obtain county or private funding. Similarly, the Office of Alcoholism informed the County Alcohol Administrators Association of California that it would no longer pay travel and lodging expenses for county administrators attending meetings of CAAC, arguing that its role was not to fund the organizational entity but, rather, to contract for specific consultation services.

Summary

Having led the reader through a labyrinth of associations, advisory boards, constituency groups, minority commissions, contractees and grantees, it may be helpful to pause and reflect on what has been covered. This chapter underscores the point made in Chapter 2: although some actors may consciously employ stratagem, it is the overall flow of the process of developing a constituency that is of concern here. The tactics employed, for example, Wolfe's encouragement of minority involvement through special boards, are of interest only as they contribute to the larger current. Of equal concern is identifying the conditions in which the process flows, and the consequences that stem therefrom. For example, under the conditions of new-found wealth (release of impounded funds) and a newly-powered constituency of state alcoholism directors (required under the enabling legislation establishing NIAAA), another association, the Council of State and Territorial Alcoholism Administrators (CSTAA) was formed—only to find itself, two years later, the target of Congressional criticism. It is the consequences of this episode, fanning out through the arena, that are of import. CSTAA's unfortunate experience redounded to the benefit of the Alcohol and Drug Problems Association (ADPA), which has now solidified its base by taking the state directors in as affiliate members. But the national experience provoked a closer look at comparable state funding in California, and a pull-back decrease in the support previously extended to the commissions and the County Alcohol Administrators Association of California (CAAC).

Just as Chapter 3 was merely an *introduction* to the myriad associations in this arena, so it is with this chapter regarding the development of constituencies. We turn now to further processes by which the ranks increase, and to the attendant increase in the visibility of the social problem of alcohol use.

Notes

1. Elliott A. Krause, "Functions of a Bureaucratic Ideology: 'Citizen Participation,'" *Social Problems,* Vol. 16 (1968), p. 136.
2. *See:* Daniel P. Moynihan, *Maximum Feasible Misunderstanding* (New York: The Free Press, 1970); Joseph Helfgot, "Professional Reform Organizations and the Symbolic Representation of the Poor," *American Sociological Review,* Vol. 39, (1974), pp. 475-91; and Krause, "Functions," pp. 129-43.
3. "County Alcoholism Boards—Who Is Eligible?" *The Hearth* (January, 1976).
4. "News Notes From All Over," *The Hearth* (August, 1976).
5. John D. McCarthy and Mayer N. Zald, *Trend of Social Movements, in America,* p. 23.
6. *See:* interview with Ernest P. Noble, Director of National Institute on Alcohol Abuse and Alcoholism: Jay Lewis, "Washington Report," *Journal of Studies on Alcohol,* Vol. 37 (1976), p. 1390.
7. Testimony before the Subcommittee on Alcoholism and Narcotics of the Senate Labor and Public Welfare Committee, 1976, pp. 13-14.
8. Albert D. Biderman and Laure M. Sharp, "The Evaluation Research Community: RFP Readers, Bidders and Winners," *Evaluation,* Vol. 2 (1974), p. 40.
9. Keith Baker "A New Grantsmanship," *The American Sociologist.* Vol. 10 (1975), pp. 206-19, offers suggestions designed to reverse the "academic world's underrepresentation in receiving Federal applied social science research funds."
10. *The Washington Post* (May 19, 1975) p. C23.
11. Joel Havemann, "When Uncle Sam Pays the Way for State and Local Lobbyists," *National Journal* (August 7, 1976), p. 1116.
12. Ibid., p. 1117.
13. *The Christian Science Monitor* (January 18, 1977).
14. National Institute on Alcohol Abuse and Alcoholism. "Report on Grants and Contracts to National Organizations" (December 30, 1976), p. 20.
15. Ibid., p. 9.
16. *The Alcoholism Report,* Vol. 5 (February 11, 1977), p. 3.
17. Ibid.
18. Robin Room, "Draft Position Paper: Policy Initiatives in Alcohol Problems Prevention," Social Research Group Working F48, prepared for National Institute on Alcohol Abuse and Alcoholism Division of Prevention (1978), p. 46.

5.

Funneling Advice and Imparting Skills and Information

A third component of the process of animating the problem of alcohol use lies in the *funneling of advice and the imparting of skills and information.* What is more. these sub-processes tie into those described in the preceding chapters. Not only is the funneling and imparting dependent on NIAAA grants/contracts: but *because of* the funneling and imparting. a training constituency (a subworld of the recovery service world) is being built. And. a further consequence. in some instances these sub-processes have also entailed assertions. re-establishment. and enlargement of turf rights.

Contract for a Catalyst

The National Center for Alcohol Education (NCAE) was established by NIAAA under contract to the University Research Corporation. The intent was to: 1) produce training programs for practitioners and curriculum materials for public education; 2) develop models for state and community programs; 3) house a think tank for invited resident scholars; and 4) conduct seminars for training. Armed with $1.9 million to create "a center of excellence," NCAE ran into organizational problems, personnel and program conflicts with the institute, and the threat of a lost contract. After an eleven-month survival fight, in which staff time and energy was diverted to drawing up proposals and defensive briefs, University Research Corporation continued to be funded with annual contracts at $1 million.

Since 1975, NCAE has seen its function as playing "a catalyst role" regarding the development of three training constituencies: a regional training program that NIAAA was launching at the time, the summer school program, and a prevention program which NIAAA was supporting.

Again the release of funds that had been impounded during the Nixon administration played a part in the development of programs. A small group involved in the training world of this arena, expressing a need for coordination, proposed an experiment of regional training consortiums that could exchange information, share knowledge, and develop standards for certification of paraprofessionals. NIAAA, with its new-found wealth, converted this idea into a national project, developing the Area Alcohol Education and Training Program (AAETP). Four regional AAETP's were established, each with its own administrative staff and board of directors. As with the advisory boards discussed previously, these boards included people already involved in the recovery service world, but also enlarged the arena's constituency by conforming to the pressures of the times and seeking representation based on geographic distribution and special interests, e.g. minority groups and women. NCAE was given the role of consultant to the AAETPs.

The AAETPs were expected to "upgrade the qualifications of personnel in alcoholism education and treatment, promote alcohol education and training among service providers, increase the public's awareness of alcoholism in order to facilitate early identification of problem drinkers, and identify the special education needs of target populations such as high risk, low income, and minority groups." [1] This was a large order, and one that was not fully met. NCAE, which saw one of its roles as developing a cadre of "trainers of trainers," had designed material, and occasionally provided personnel to present this material in the regions, all with an eye toward testing the design in local situations. (A similar precedure had been followed in developing a training model for management skills in half-way houses.) In a classic confrontation, the rigorous standards of the educational research world with its "systems approach to modular development" (NCAE) intersected with the structural obstacles of the bureaucratic world, including review by NIAAA and postponements in the Government Printing Office. The result was a delay in getting the finished modules to the field. In isolated cases, area programs utilized developmental materials while they were being tested, but generally it can be said that this aspect of the program did not move with the speed desired by all concerned.

The AAETPs have mainly functioned as a conduit for fund dispersion. In the first eighteen months of operation, the four regions had made awards totaling over $2 million—115 training sub-grants had been awarded, and 229 stipend fellowship awards were made.[2] In California, for example, the sub-grants helped support eight regional training consortia, each with a small staff, and each holding short training sessions (often one day). A good deal of attention was given to "needs assessment," i.e. reviewing the states' plans and surveying the existing training and education resources. Predictably, board members were concerned with representing the interests of their respective states, and much time was spent "prioritizing"—with, on the one hand, the full range of differences emerging over what the area programs were and where they should be going, and, on the other, a sensitivity to the constraints inherent in NIAAA's power of approval. Of greater effect was the stipend component of the program. Originally conceived to make it possible for an individual to receive up to $6,000 for one year of full-time alcoholism training, the guidelines were changed and the amounts decreased when it was realized that the full-time requirement eliminated people already working in the arena. Consequently, this widened the number of recipients, further entrenching those who were already working in the field, but also encouraging the recruitment of new people.

A second task given to NCAE was as catalyst for the summer schools. Originating with the Yale Center of Alcohol Studies, these schools have been the water holes of the arena; their numbers and geographic locations have increased in recent years. Some are sponsored by state alcoholism authorities, others by universities or as adjuncts to regular training programs, (as in the case with the Berkeley Center for Alcohol Studies of the Pacific School of Religion). It was estimated by a respondent at NCAE that these schools attract about 11,000 people a year. NCAE brought key people from these schools together in 1973 for a conference, the first time they had ever met formally. Such meetings led ultimately to an application for an NIAAA grant in order that they might form a North American Association of Schools of Alcohol Studies. The grant was denied (which may have been a blessing, in light of the experience of CSTAA). NCAE, eschewing the role of advisor on organizational development, focused its attention on developing curricula, offering material plus a trainer to assist in their use in fifteen schools, again to test the design and revise if needed for wider distribution.

Grant denial was undoubtedly not the only impediment to forming an association; most of the schools operate in the black, or they would not be in existence. Tocqueville notwithstanding, it takes a large effort and a felt need to organize, and in this case at least the summer schools did not follow the conventional pattern. The Alcohol and Drug Problems Association has a summer school section, and publishes a list of the schools, which for now seems to serve their organizational purposes.

A third task given to NCAE was the training for another program undertaken by NIAAA in 1974 in order to implement community prevention. NIAAA's plan was to train one individual from each state to be its prevention coordinator. The coordinator's main task was to wean the bureaucratic world away from thinking in terms of secondary and tertiary prevention (early intervention and treatment) toward thinking in terms of primary prevention (public information and community organization work). The director of the NIAAA's Community Prevention Branch had in mind "changing attitudes by changing the environment" (personal communication). Each coordinator was to study the community (ascertain the sources of power); engage the community in a public education campaign; lead a public discussion on the community's attitude toward drinking; and get community groups (women's groups, task forces) to study drinking. NCAE brought the newly appointed state coordinators and their respective state directors together in Washington for the initial training session; brought them back mid-point and at the end of their two-year funding so they could share experiences and strategies.

The larger implications of the concept of prevention are discussed in Chapter 13. However, one aspect deserves cursory examination here, since it served as an obstacle to the State Prevention Coordinator Program, i.e., the relative emphasis placed on treatment and rehabilitation over prevention. Some states have not as yet implemented a treatment program; all states have some communities where no treatment program has been started. It is too much to expect a prevention program to take hold (especially one so ambitious as to expect changed attitudes toward drinking), in communities that have not gone through the process of establishing treatment. Room has drawn attention to the unsupportive environment in which the SPC's had to operate, observing: "The SPC's are typically not highly placed in the state administrative structure and a strong prevention program must often seem an irrelevant or diversionary proposal to those concerned with the provision of treatment and services."[3] Consequently, the SPC program suffered from this low priority:

> The hope of NIAAA was for the development of new approaches which would not be centered around treatment. To some extent this was the outcome. But the alternative usually adopted turned out to be very traditional: most strategies were centered around education of one sort or another. It can be assumed in the case of treatment tie-ins that a "treatable

disease" approach was utilized more often than not. The advantage to this approach was that a communication system probably already existed within a community and people were available for "prevention efforts" who had experience in the area (e.g. most communities have a speakers bureau traditionally made up of A.A. and treatment people).[4]

While it is not possible to assess the degree of environmental change (i.e., attitudes toward drinking), it *is* possible to assume there was a resultant increased visibility for the arena. In some cases, voluntary organizations held meetings, and there was considerable emphasis on school education and public information campaigns. NIAAA support was eventually phased out; some coordinators remained on their state payrolls, others left. But those who remained represent a change in the bureaucratic world. Regardless of whether the coordinator was newly recruited or simply reassigned, the concept of prevention has been legitimized in the bureaucracy. Furthermore, it can be assumed that *some* new people (bureaucrats and volunteers) were pulled in to the arena, and at the very least, the recovery service world was able to increase its own visibility.

A Little Training Here and a Little Training There

Over and above the training efforts mentioned above, other scattered attempts have been made—as described at the time by NIAAA Director, Ernest Noble,[5] "disparate efforts, a little training here and a little training there." [6] This would include NIAAA grants to individuals attached to universities, to train psychological specialists, community resources specialists, directors of services, rehabilitation counselors and masters and doctoral students in a variety of related fields (this is a partial list).

NIAAA and the state of California have supported a training program for clergy interested in alcohol and other drug problems at the Berkeley Center for Alcohol Studies at the Pacific School of Religion, which lays claim to giving the first masters degree in alcohol studies in the world. In some instances, this resulted in an increase in the constituency of the alcohol arena, but a loss to the clergy. Since this center had an early start in the burgeoning period of this arena (1968), its graduates were highly specialized and jobs became available to them as administrators of recovery homes or county coordinators of alcohol programs. This program now admits a limited number of professional and volunteer workers and holds one of the most popular annual summer schools.

University and college programs in alcohol studies, supported by the training branch of NIAAA, vary greatly in length and comprehensiveness. Some offer research training, others clinical/administrative training. Some are geared toward specific specialties, such as nursing, rehabilitation counseling, social work, or psychology. The Addiction Studies Program of the University of Arizona has a two year masters degree program with a major in addiction studies. The program at Washington State University offers a masters degree in sociology or psychology with a *specialty* in alcoholism. Similarly, Jackson State University has an Alcohol Drug Studies Center, whose masters degree program is designed as a specialty within the disciplines of sociology or health, physical education, and recreation. At the Johns Hopkins University, students who enroll in the School of Hygiene in alcohol may apply for any degree program for which they are qualified, most frequently a master of health science degree. The School of Public Health of the University of California Berkeley presents a three-quarter course in alcohol and other drugs; has designed a program to train Native Americans in the alcoholism field, culminating in a master of public health degree; and offers doctoral level training supported by NIAAA grants, as described above. Brandeis University has a program to prepare specialists at the doctoral level for positions as administrators, educators, and planners in the field of alcoholism.

For an arena filled with personnel who have lived through the years of rapid expansion, and with professionals who have transferred over from other fields (psychologists and social workers), re-training has become one of the greatest needs. Universities will continue to respond to that need as long as the classes fill up and remain profitable. Some courses hold forth a certificate as an inducement, such as that offered by the Alcohol Studies Program at Seattle University and by Counselors on Alcoholism and Related Disorders (CARD). (This name was subsequently changed to Counselors on Alcoholism, Addictions, and Related Disorders [CAARD]). CARD is a non-profit foundation which presents a one- to three-quarter course at the Los Angeles, San Diego and Irvine campuses of the University of California and at San Francisco State University. There is a brief field placement, but for the most part, the courses provide basic information as presented by a string of guest speakers—each course is different depending on the curriculum coordinator. CARD invites membership, and as West Coast affiliate of the National Association of Alcoholism Counselors and Trainers (NAACT), formed in 1974, is struggling to establish its little bit of turf along with the professional associations described in Chapter 3. Workshops and courses are also given by the University of California Extension and the Department of Independent Study, with such titles as "The Alcoholism Counselor as a Member of an Interdisciplinary Team," "Working with Depression and Self-Destructive Behavior" (also offering a certificate upon completion of fifteen units of study).

As can be expected, these efforts at training have their share of critics. When they consist of an array of guest lecturers, they are characterized as being simply "beginner courses"; if they are more intense (such as the one at U.C. Berkeley's School of Public Health, which compares different perceptions of alcohol abuse and alcoholism and highlights the ambiguities) they are accused of being "too theoretical"; if they include art therapy and biofeedback, as the extension courses have done, veterans in the arena ask, "what does that have to do with alcoholism?" As to CARD certification, the following was a typical response:

> They do no screening at all—a person has to be sober for a couple of months and he can get in, attend classes one night a week and end up with a little card that says he's a counselor. Where I came from the word counselor connoted a professional background.

Regarding one-day workshops: "They get people to say 'a-ha', and then go right back to what they were doing."

Support and interest tends to come from representatives of corporations and agencies interested in instigating alcohol programs, but an ample share of students are also people working in the arena who hope that a few years' experience coupled with the certificate will give them promotion preference. Again, one can defer judgment on the quality of the education and still acknowledge that these courses contribute toward the visibility of the arena, funnel *some* information into it, and increase the constituency of trainers and trainees.

Some providers prefer to handle their own training. Others start out training their own personnel and the enterprise is enlarged. A case in point is the Guerrero Street Program in San Francisco, which provides on-site training in its special mode of detoxification, attracting people from all over the world (and, it should be added, with some support from the State of California). In 1977, the California Association of Alcoholic Recovery Homes moved into training, and, in conjunction with the Office of Alcoholism and the State Department of Rehabilitation, offered a course in the fiscal and administrative management of recovery homes.[7] Thus does one's turf become enlarged.

Crosscurrents on the Information Front

One logical question arising from a "social worlds perspective" is: what happens when new sub-worlds rub up against old ones? We have seen that in the case of the state directors of alcoholism services, a new organization (CSTAA) diverted a large base of support from the older organization (ADPA), a situation that would have continued had Congress not made it incumbent upon CSTAA to return to the fold of its parent organization. Further illustration is to be found in regard to the establishment of the National Clearinghouse for Alcohol Information (NCALI), and its relationship to the Rutgers Center of Alcohol Studies.

Yet another beneficiary of NIAAA's funding mechanism was the General Electric Company, which created and operated the clearinghouse under contracts totalling $11 million over a four year period (1972-1976) and continued in succeeding years.[8] NCALI conducts a computerized system of information, housing a collection of contract reports, laws and decisions, semi-technical and popular journals, newspaper clippings, audio-visual materials, and pamphlets. It serves as an extension of NIAAA by handling information correspondence and reference inquiries and by providing the institute staff (which at times has been smaller than the clearinghouse staff) with specific information and literature searches. Of value to the larger arena has been the Current Awareness Service, whereby users may choose up to fifteen out of one hundred subject categories and receive notification of new publications (citation, abstract, document quality score, source of supply, and cost), and Grouped Interest Guides, containing annotated bibliographies of publications on various subjects (e.g., heredity, genetics and alcohol use; teenagers and alcohol; animal research on alcohol effects).

When the clearinghouse arrived on the scene, the Rutgers (formerly Yale) Center had been operating some thirty years. Howard Haggard, director of the Yale Laboratory of Applied Physiology, had been a member of the Research Council on Problems of Alcohol, formed to seek funds to support research on alcohol problems.[9] With a grant from the Carnegie Corporation, work commenced on a review of the biological literature on alcohol, eventually encompassing other disciplines as well. As the grant was exhausted, and no further funds for research were forthcoming, Haggard invited E.M. Jellinek, a biometrician from Worcester State Hospital in Massachusetts, to come to Yale and complete the writing of the review. Thus began the abstracting, indexing, content analysis and coding of several thousand articles on the effects of alcohol on the individual. In 1940-41, with Jellinek as its first director, the Yale Center of Alcohol Studies came into being, and for some time remained just that—the *center* of academic knowledge on this subject. Abstracts were typed on edge-notched cards denoting their topical code; the collection became the Classified Abstract Archive of the Alcohol Literature (CAAAL). In 1956, the Yale Center started an eight-year project of collecting the originals of all the abstracts contained in the CAAAL, successfully obtaining about 5,000 of the 10,000 abstracted articles. Grant support was given to the center starting in 1961, first from NIMH, later NIAAA, for its documentation and publication activities (a total of $6 million 1961-1977).[10]

Following questions raised by Congress in 1976 as to possible overlap and duplication of the clearinghouse and center efforts, NIAAA Director Noble requested an in-house evaluation. The resultant report contained background material explaining the basic differences between the two, and the consequent lack of coordination. One passage indicates just how inauspicious the initial climate was in terms of cooperation:

> Mark Keller, the Editor-in-Chief, of the *Journal of Studies on Alcohol* and a consultant to NIAAA at the time, said in an interview that he was not consulted about establishing a clearinghouse and only learned of the existence of the RFP [Request for Proposals] by accident while visiting NIAAA staff in his capacity as a consultant on other matters. According to Keller, he wrote a memo to NIAAA management suggesting that some of the function described for the clearinghouse in the RFP were being performed by the Documentation and Publications Division of the Rutgers Center of Alcohol Studies. He said that the NIAAA response to his memo was that Rutgers was free to bid "all or nothing" on the RFP. Keller did not think it was appropriate for a university library to attempt to become involved in such a large undertaking and did not pursue the matter further. Keller offered the opinion that NIAAA was indifferent to the potential impact on the Rutgers Center of the creation of the clearinghouse.[11]

The Report went on to contrast the resources of the General Electric Company "in information systems technology and a computer technology-oriented staff" to "the archaic CAAAL 'keysort' system"; it pointed out the differences in "user population size," stating that in 1975 the center answered 2,300 reference inquiries as against 96,500 answered by the clearinghouse. As to the *Journal of Studies on Alcohol,* a pioneer in the arena which dates back to 1940, the report stated it had a paid subscription circulation of 3,500, while the clearinghouse's *Alcohol Health and Research World* quarterly magazine had an unpaid subscription circulation of 22,500. Terms like "modern" and "dynamic" described the clearinghouse. Respectful credit was given to Rutgers with one hand and taken away with the other:

> The Center was a "venerable" institution with an established reputation and relatively small clientele, limited academic focus, leadership role in scholarly documentation of the alcohol literature, and very limited financial resources. On the other hand, the Clearinghouse was a new experiment whose scope of purpose and future were largely unknown, with a potential audience of hundreds of thousands, having a broad public/popular as well as technical information focus.[12]

The report was inadvertently passed on to Congress with none of the language softened, and the Rutgers Center personnel protested its prejudicial quality. Dr. Noble responded by setting up an *ad hoc* committee of scholars from the alcohol use arena and the library science world to study the two organizations, with an eye toward duplication. For the center, the closer scrutiny had produced mixed reactions. What at first looked like the last thrust in a suspected drive to push out the old for the new, had at least resulted in clear recommendations regarding the separate functions of both organizations. However, the center was informed it would henceforth be funded by contract rather than grant, which does not allow as much freedom of action. Told to modernize some of its procedures (such as the CAAAL indexing) the center had, for the first time since the establishment of NIAAA, been given some deserved attention only to have it tempered by the prospect of competitive bidding for future support.

The Rutgers/NCALI "story" is illustrative of the consequences that flow from the animating process. The *sentiment* behind this re-shuffling and establishment of turf rights is of course intense, and for some participants, painful—but the overall consequences are an enlarged constituency (the Rutgers Center *plus* a National Clearinghouse for Alcohol Information), and increased visibility for the arena.

Notes

1. *National Institute on Alcohol Abuse and Alcoholism Feature Service,* No. 10, April 1, 1975.
2. *The Alcoholism Report,* Vol. 5 (October 22, 1976) p. 7.
3. Robin Room, "Draft Position Paper: Policy Initiatives in Alcohol Problems Prevention," prepared for National Institute on Alcohol Abuse and Alcoholism Division of Prevention, 1978, p. 34.
4. Lawrence M. Wallach, "Analysis of State Prevention Coordinator Reports for the Period April through June, 1977," report prepared for the Division of Prevention, National Institute on Alcohol Abuse and Alcoholism, 1977.
5. Dr. Nobel served from 1976 to 1978, succeeding the institute's first director, Dr. Morris Chafetz. Loran Archer, former director of the California Office of Alcoholism, was acting director until April, 1979, when the post was assumed by John DeLuca.
6. Jay Lewis, "Washington Report," *Journal of Studies on Alcohol,* Vol. 37 (1976), p. 1386.
7. "Fiscal and Management Training for Recovery Homes," *The Hearth* (January, 1977).
8. Under the competitive procurement process, the contract was turned over to Informatics as of March 1, 1979.
9. See Chapter 3.

10. National Institute on Alcohol Abuse and Alcoholism, "Report of a Study of Overlap and Duplication Between Rutgers Center of Alcohol Studies and the National Clearinghouse for Alcohol Information" (April 30, 1976), Appendix D.
11. Ibid., p. 21.
12. Ibid., p. 24.

Part III

Legitimizing the Problem

It is not enough to animate a problem. Outside forces require that the problem be *legitimized* if the life that has been infused within the arena is to continue and grow. In this section, we examine the manner in which the legitimizing process occurs: through borrowing prestige and expertise from other arenas; through redefining the problem and thereby lessening the attached stigma; through building respectability in the eyes of those outside the arena; and through maintaining a separate identity for alcohol problems, as differentiated from other drug and mental health problems. Through the action that stems from all these sub-processes of legitimizing, new squares are added to the patchwork of collective definition already described, and visibility is further enhanced.

In this section, we turn attention to a crucial and divisive question: just what *is* alcoholism, and why the separate category, of "alcohol abuse"? At a public hearing in San Mateo, California, NIAAA Director Noble said he often deals with the blurring of these two categories by countering with another question: when does a cucumber become a pickle? As Part III will demonstrate, the cucumber/pickle dilemma strikes at the very core of this arena, creating problems *within* the legitimizing process.

6.

Borrowing Prestige and Expertise

A retrospective look at this arena—before the influx of programming, grants, contracts, and constituents—does not reveal a contested territory of clear goals and refined definitions. Rather, what one finds is an eclecticism (a *borrowing* process) born of closely protected turf rights and consequent intellectual isolation, as well as the disinterest and inability on the part of other worlds (universities, medicine, ministry, law enforcement) to take on the problems of alcohol misuse. This chapter deals with the interaction between the small group of pioneer "alcohologists" and the diverse professional worlds that crossed in and out of the arena in its early years. Also examined are the consequences of this history, a limitless variety of treatment approaches borrowed from other arenas. Next we shall look at the borrowing process as it has affected Alcoholics Anonymous and a new organization, Women For Sobriety; and at the manner in which all of the approaches are affected by conditions outside the arena: the self-help movement, the women's movement, humanistic medicine. The final consequence is a situation of mutual borrowing.

The Use of Other Worlds

Within the alcohol use arena, the process of carving territory and establishing turf rights has also entailed a modeling process—what Selden

Bacon has called "special purpose borrowing." [1] Bacon finds early evidence of this process in the actions of the Committee of Fifty, a group which addressed itself to the "liquor problem" in the United States from 1899 to 1905. These progressive reformers were mindful of the limitations of ideas and explanations provided by "alcohologists," i.e., persons whose claim to expertise rested solely on their knowledge (and feelings) about alcohol:

> Therefore, to prepare their reports, they used economists, physiologists, political scientists, ethicists, physicians, and, perhaps surprising in view of the pre-1910 date of this effort, they even mentioned sociologists.[2]

Right from the beginning, this special purpose borrowing created difficulties for the alcohol use arena, as these other worlds raised questions considered irrelevant or misleading by the "real" thinkers and planners in the "alcohol field." Bacon goes on to describe the manner in which what has come to be called the Classic Temperance Movement [3] in the United States (1830-1930) also utilized a wide variety of special disciplines. But, while the leaders of this movement recognized the worlds of physiology, theology, psychology, political science, medicine, and education as potentially contributing fields of knowledge, insight and experience:

> ... they did not, so to speak, trust them. They developed or nurtured their own varieties of such disciplines and organizations, set the limits and goals for each, bitterly attacked any independent variations, and maintained for the field both its problem-oriented stance and also its single and simple and specific solution.[4]

Of this problem-oriented stance and its single, simple and specific solution, much more will be said later. What is significant at this juncture is the consequence of this intersecting of worlds. For as Bacon points out, these disciplines were themselves growing in identity and confidence; as an occasional theologian or economist or historian questioned specific ways of using evidence or defining terms or testing assumptions, disagreements with the "alcohologists" resulted. The merit of their criticism aside, these specialists from other worlds lacked what Bacon calls "social power" in the alcohol use arena:

> And if they expressed their questions or doubts or criticisms, they were ridiculed and even labeled as immoral, tools of the "traffic" (the beverage industry), un-American, and very probably "drinkers" (meaning drunkards). And the movement found its own historians, economists, physiologists, theologians, etc., to stand up for "the real truth." [5]

Bacon notes two important consequences for the arena: 1) the other worlds increasingly avoided the "field of alcohol phenomena as it might relate to their concerns"; 2) the arena became "intellectually isolated and in many ways manifested what can only be termed an archaic image." [6]

True, attempts were made to instill a multidisciplinary approach, most notably by the Yale Center. Keller reports the deliberate effort to keep the documentation and publication division of the center as nearly multi- and interdisciplinary as possible, by gathering, processing and indexing into bibliographies and abstracts reports and information from *all* worlds. Keller, who had served for many years as the editor of the *Quarterly Journal of Studies on Alcohol* (now the *Journal of Studies on Alcohol*) wryly testifies to force-feeding this approach on Journal readers. Upon hearing that a neurophysiologist never read the table of contents beyond the first one-third of the journal (because he learned that all articles that might interest him would occur in that part), Keller promptly changed the order of the articles to a "systematic even if seemingly disordered cycle." [7] But Keller, too, admits that while the center had a multidisciplinary ideology:

> . . . it would be an exaggeration to claim anything like an interdisciplinary success. For the most part the psychologists studied psychological problems, the biochemists biochemical problems, the sociologists sociological problems, and so on.[8]

At the same time, there were a few triumphs. Keller cites these: the first outpatient alcoholism clinics with multidisciplinary teams; the first Summer School of Alcohol Studies; and the center's sponsorship of an inter-discipline-inspired organization for public education, which developed into the National Council on Alcoholism.

What Bacon calls social power, Gusfield treats as "ownership of the problem." [9] To return to the larger questions of how social problems come to be so designated, Gusfield has observed that often this involves not only a moral judgment, i.e., that a particular phenomenon is painful and should be eradicated, but a cognitive one as well. Many social issues involve disagreements about whether or not a given state of affairs *should* be altered (racial disputes, pornography, sexual equality); moreover, one generation may define situations as problematic which another has ignored. Gusfield identifies the Protestant churches as the owners of the problems of drinking in the United States during much of the nineteenth and part of the twentieth centuries. By publishing persuasional materials and developing their personnel as authoritative sources in regard to drinking, the churches became the legitimate source of public policies toward alcohol use. Gusfield explains:

Other possible sources of ownership were absent or weak. The medical profession was poorly organized in America and unequipped to present an alternative conceptualization until well into the twentieth century. The same was true of the universities, which were less autonomous from religious auspices than has been true in recent decades. Government was less the initiator than the recipient of alcohol policies. In general, the alcohol industry, both beer and spirits, "disowned" the issue, seeking neither to develop strategies toward drinking problems nor to counteract those developed by the churches.[10]

Ownership was dispersed after Repeal, but under the condition of avoidance described by Bacon. Regarding the worlds of medicine, teaching, ministry, and law enforcement, Bacon reports that studies of alcohol-related disease or crime by the practitioners, training of new members of the profession, or even minimally professional recordkeeping were almost unknown. Even as late as the 1940s and the 1950s textbooks and training schools for police would hardly mention alcohol problems in any way. And "in the 1950s the idea of requiring those hospitals which were used for training physicians even to admit alcoholics, so that medical students could see such cases, was considered such a radical notion that the AMA's own committee on alcoholism was rebuked for entertaining such an idea." [11]

Such ownership as obtained, then, was in the special-purpose-borrowing sense of being used. The manner in which this ownership was handled, and the conditions contributing toward the distribution, will be discussed in subsequent pages. What is important for now is the fact that ownership was frequently not sought, but inherited. For the recovery service world, this has resulted in a wide variety of treatment approaches, examined next.

Wearing Somebody Else's Clothes

Nowhere is the eclecticism of this arena more evident than in regard to treatment offered. A report on the trends in the treatment of alcoholics from 1940-1972 suggests that the treatment modalities may be more varied than for any other conditions, listing twenty-four drugs ranging from gold cures to barbiturates to bromides to vitamin therapy to emetics used in conjunction with aversive conditioning techniques. One quotation from this report suggests that not only was the alcohol arena borrowing from the pharmacological world, but alcoholic subjects were being borrowed as well:

> With regard to at least three types of drugs—tranquilizers, anti-depressants and emetics—it appears that at about the time when one drug or class of

drugs was found to have undesirable side-effects and/or to be of little value in treatment of either acute or chronic alcoholism another group of drugs with a seemingly greater promise would come upon the scene.[12]

In addition, Giesbrecht et al. found the full range of psychotherapeutic techniques—classical psychoanalysis for only a select minority, but for others, hypnosis, psychodrama, transactional analysis, encounter sessions, and the full scope of group modalities.[13] (Also used, but not listed by these authors are relaxation methods such as biofeedback and transcendental meditation.) As with the pharmacological approach, psychotherapeutic techniques have followed current American trends. Starting in the 1960s, renewed interest in behavior modification led to theories of alcoholism as learned behavior, reflected in aversive conditioning using not only emetics such as mentioned above but electric shock administered in a drinking situation. Here too the borrowing was two-fold: the psychologists who entered the arena just as it was mushrooming had come out of training in the new techniques of the 1960s; alcoholic patients provided a ready-made laboratory for them.

This diversity of treatment approaches is a relatively recent phenomenon. A few "homes" and "asylums" for inebriates could be found scattered throughout the states starting in the 1860s and 70s.[14] These institutions ranged from reliance on religious methods, to workhouse-hospital settings, to those based on a specific medical cure. An example is the Keeley Institute, which treated alcoholics with injections of double chloride of gold, based on the theory that alcohol poisons the nerve cells. Government-supported inebriate asylums also date from the late 1800s, although the growth of these institutions slowed considerably with the passage of the Volstead Act, establishing prohibition. After 1919, many of the larger institutions closed down, and even though "the fallacy of this attitude soon became apparent." [15] few were reopened. More frequently, alcoholics were to be found as part of the larger population of a state mental hospital. In California, in the 1950s, state hospital treatment consisted of thirty days to sober up and sixty to work, as described by one respondent:

> The major work force in the state hospitals were alcoholics. As a matter of fact, we just about devastated the state hospitals when we pulled the alcoholics out. Costs shot up, because there had been real exploitation—once they dried out, they really worked. There was no real treatment, just a few experimental programs, or AA people who came in.

An analysis by Wittman [16] of the settings and levels of care in the 1970s is indicative of the growth of the arena. This study divides alcoholism facilities into four major classifications, in a continuum from lesser to greater levels of support: casual, clinic, residential, and emergency [17] settings. Casual settings are those within the daily orbit of the client—for example, the living rooms of Alcoholics Anonymous members, neighborhood drop-in centers and skid-row storefronts. They provide immediate support through contacts with people who are familiar with the client's situation, who can often help just by talking. Clinic settings are more structured settings where the providers are expected to have special skills and techniques, the clients are expected to initiate contact and where there is scheduling of staff—for example, psychiatric, and medical services, both in-patient and out-patient. Residential settings provide basic functional living needs: food, clothing, shelter, access to jobs, access to social contacts, access to other needed services. Examples are recovery homes, Salvation Army live-in facilities, hospitals, and sanitoria. A director described the variety:

> I have never seen it done exactly the same in any one place. We had a meeting of medical directors of units like this recently in Southern California. Everyone brought their treatment schedule and we sort of compared things. Funny thing, the medical treatment schedules were all different.

Wittman found the array of settings and treatment bewildering: sexually segregated units in some, sexually integrated units in others; locked doors in some, open doors in others; highly structured use of time with an elaborate structure of rewards in some, a loose, unregimented approach in others; fixed lengths of stay in some, indefinite stays in others. (Wittman notes, as has Wiseman,[18] that clients have often "done the loop" in a dozen or more of these facilities.) Increasingly, private facilities pride themselves on offering a potpourri. To quote one director:

> We start with medical detoxification and medical survey. Then there are psychotherapy sessions two hours every day. There is what they call an alcoholism therapist who talks about alcohol the AA style—sincerity, anger, what your emotions are and how you react to them. There is a family therapist, a woman who is a social worker who counsels the family. The nurses are all trained to do psychotherapy. You can't sleep at night—you have a rap session with the nurse. The one at night for instance happens to be very good with yoga and relaxation exercises. I give a straight medical lecture with colored slides—anything you want to know, ask the doctor. You name it, it's there—you never know what's going to work.

In order to understand how such a wide variety of techniques has evolved, one must recognize the corresponding variety of theories concerning what makes an "alcoholic." Keller, in frustration, has treated this subject humorously after reviewing 30 years of studies:

> Compared with other populations, alcoholics are, for example, more allergic, less leptosomic, more pyknotic, less bald, more first-or-last-born, less introverted, more color blind, less socialized, more dependent, less responsible . . . less frustration tolerant . . . less religiously active, more accident prone . . . less mother-loved . . . more suicidal . . . less prosperous, more impulsive, less libidinous . . . more anxious . . . more compulsive . . . less treatable . . . more thirsty.[19]

(Keller qualifies his list as incomplete, explaining that the totality of examples would occupy more space than the subject can justify.) But Keller's Law—the investigation of any trait in alcoholics will show that they have either more or less of it—is not a laughing matter to some of the sub-worlds within the recovery service world. Argument is directed toward those who advocate flexibility and eclecticism.[20] As one respondent said:

> Among service providers there is an egalitarian notion that all philosophies of treatment should be given equal consideration. This is fair to the philosophers, but many of the techniques (TM, gestalt, psychodrama) are modalities that were not designed for alcoholism. Alcoholism is a step-child—you have to fit somebody else's clothes. Helping professionals are not trained in alcoholism but in psychosis and neurosis, and those are the tools they use. If the alcoholic goes away and stays sober, *we* succeeded; if he goes away and gets drunk, *he* failed.

Thus, no one denies that the increased visibility of the arena, and the attendant funding as set forth in Part II, have brought about a marked increase in facilities and their varied treatments. The source of consternation for some people is the manner in which the increased visibility and increased funding have also increased the borrowing process. Among respondents, and in the literature, there was wide agreement that the type of treatment is not the decisive factor in recovery; much more crucial is the length of time a client stays in *any form* of the recovery service continuum.[21] And there is agreement that the facilities invariably take on the philosophy of the director. One observation of Giesbrecht et al. emphasized the relationship of Keller's Law to the borrowing process:

> The disease concept has been widely accepted but the exact nature of the illness has not been determined, and thus the cure has easily been adapted to fit institutional requirments, the personal training of the therapist, and faddish influences from other treatment sectors.[22]

Criticism within the recovery service world comes from those who feel not enough attention is paid to techniques designed specifically for people with alcohol problems. (This ties in with criticism of training courses discussed in Chapter 5, for example one offered by U.C. California Extension that focused on "common alcoholic behaviors such as denial, self-pity, helplessness, hopelessness, lack of motivation, resistance to treatment, and rationalization.") One large sector of the arena objects vociferously to any attempts to treat alcoholism as a symptom of a neurosis. For this group, real treatment lies in educating the afflicted person as to the effects of alcohol upon him and in helping him to maintain his sobriety—in other words, drawing him into the fellowship of Alcoholics Anonymous, or into techniques that have borrowed from AA its "sobriety-first" stance.

Alcoholics Anonymous: Tailor-Made Clothes

Alcoholics Anonymous was omitted from the discussion of voluntary associations in Chapter 3, not because it has not gained from the enhanced visibility of the arena (through increased sources of referral), but because it is not a formal organization. It is considered by its members to be a "fellowship"; members are those who so define themselves and present themselves at meetings. There are no membership lists, no dues, merely local groups who "take responsibility for promoting their mutual progress in abstaining from alcoholic drinking." [23]

The impact of AA on a score of self-help groups, from Weight Watchers to Schizophrenics Anonymous to Gamblers Anonymous, is widely acknowledged.[24] However, AA too had prototypes from which to borrow. In the nineteenth century, groups called The Washingtonians grew from the impetus of six drinkers who pledged not only to abstain, but to bring a new convert to each meeting. Sagarin reports that faced with the problem of making meetings interesting enough so that members would not slip (or sip) away from the fold, groups began the practice of having each member relate his drinking experiences, defining the depths to which he had sunk, and praising his new freedom.[25] Yet another source of special purpose borrowing for AA was Moral Rearmament (or the Oxford Group) founded by a Lutheran minister, employing as did the Washingtonians the confessional, but looking upon the confession as a surrender to God.

AA originated in 1935, when a New York stockbroker named Bill Wilson, who had had some contact with the Oxford Group, and a doctor, Bob Smith, discovered that they could stop drinking through mutual support. They embarked on a search for others similarly in need, and, in 1939, the small movement published a book, *Alcoholics Anonymous,* which told the personal stories of its first one hundred members. A 1941 article in the *Saturday Evening Post* by Jack Alexander touched off the spread of the movement. AA's borrowing from the Oxford group is most clear in the Twelve Steps, designed to guide the alcoholic's personal inventory; intrinsic to the AA path is the belief in a power greater than the self for restoration to sobriety.

AA's growth is related not only to the increased visibility of the arena, but to conditions in the larger society. As noted above, AA is now one of a multitude of self-help groups reflecting what Taylor underscores: "a change in social climate as various forms of deviance have come to be understood as sociological and psychological rather than moral issues." [26] Sagarin underscores Ross and Staines' observation [27] about the discrepancies between the ideal and reality, as seen from the perspective of the "handicapped":

> The days of passive acceptance of one's fate are over, whether for welfare clients or for ex-convicts. In the secular society, no one is predestined to purgatory, neither symbolically in this world nor religiously in the other. If a man today cannot change the condition that constitutes a handicap, then he changes the situation in which it becomes a handicap. People have decided that they can decide their own fate now. In so doing, they will naturally commit excesses. . . . What matters, though, when their acts are viewed in a wide sweep as part of an outcry against injustice, rather than in a narrower range of whether a single scientific contention is correct? [28]

In the case of AA, "the single scientific contention" is salient, for this not only is the dividing line in treatment but has implications for other issues, as we shall see later. AA's premise is that there is a physiological component separating the "alcoholic" from the rest of the drinking universe—call it addiction, allergy, tissue tolerance—a metabolic confrontation of alcohol on susceptible individuals resulting in a "loss of control" and a specific withdrawal syndrome when alcohol is removed. Nevertheless, in spite of the controversy surrounding this belief, with the expansion of the arena, cross-pollination of treatment philosophies was bound to occur, and has.

Mutual Borrowing

The very same therapeutic techniques that are scorned by strict AA proponents are making inroads in the larger society. Many AA members are coming out of treatment programs where they have been exposed to other techniques (therapeutic communities, transactional analysis, assertiveness training) and continue to be involved with these ideas and to talk about them. The California Association of Alcoholic Recovery Homes provides a forum for exchange of treatment philosophies. Some homes have borrowed generously from the drug use arena, e.g., Delancey Street and Synanon. One director found a parallel for his stance ("everyone must take charge of what's happening in his life") in today's thrust toward "humanistic medicine," such as advocated by Carl and Stephanie S. Simonton, in cancer therapy.[29]

Yet another example of special purpose borrowing is provided by a new organization, Women for Sobriety. Its founder, sociologist Jean Kirkpatrick, readily acknowledges the derivation of her philosophy in Emersonian "self-reliance," Norman Vincent Peale-type "positive thinking," the current consciousness-raising thrust, and the philosophy of the women's movement, tailored for this purpose: "women alcoholics are different from men alcoholics because they have lower profiles in self esteem than do men." [30] Based on Kirkpatrick's own experience with recovery, the organization offers an "acceptance program" consisting of recording in a personal journal the innermost feelings that contribute toward one's destructive drinking and the positive ways of dealing with them. Thirteen "Statements of Acceptance" [31] provide the central core of the program; meetings are held for reinforcement, sharing, and mutual support. Some AA groups feel threatened by this new organization, but leaders insist that they are not in competition. To quote one member of both:

> For AA the primary objective is not to drink—to get sober, and stay sober. It doesn't say we're going to help your depression, or help you examine your life style, or establish your role identity. It is an implicit rule that certain subjects (e.g., sex) are taboo. You talk about how you use the AA program, the twelve steps. In Women for Sobriety the emphasis is on self esteem, can you make decisions, etc. You move beyond what you get out of AA.

Many women belong to both groups; for others, Women for Sobriety offers an organization toward which to move after AA; for still others who did not find AA helpful, it is a substitute program.

Some AA proponents continue to lament the use of "totally secular methods for what is essentially a condition of the soul"; [32] others feel that treating the soul is precisely the business of behavior psychology. Burt has traced the similarities between AA and psychology: 1) steps four through ten of AA, which ask alcoholics to assess themselves and their actions toward others and to make amends wherever possible, Burt likens to techniques which teach people to make new responses, such as behavioral contracting and assertiveness training; 2) the religious aspect of AA he sees as compatible with the psychological emphasis on offering alternatives for destructive behavior, as expressed by one respondent, "you know church can be behavioral modification too, so can work, so can hobbies"; 3) for the AA practice of "telling one's story," the "drunk-alogs" that constitute the format of AA meetings, Burt finds analogues in two practices of behavior therapy, modeling and covert sensitization (similar to aversive conditioning).[33]

Even the Salvation Army has partaken of the eclecticism of the arena. As one Salvation Army Captain explained:

> The alcoholics I met all spoke very strongly against alcohol—it had ruined them, it was killing them. And I had difficulties as to why such a bad thing is so attractive, until I began to ask different questions. I started to do psychological testing and things like that to ascertain what was the underlying problem. I found there's no such thing as an alcoholic, because every one is different. At one time, the whole focus was on the conversion experience. But now the Death of God movement hasn't helped the poor person who is struggling with feelings about where do I go with this problem. The program developed by AA allowed for all the defenses and attitudes the alcoholic had to adopt to defend his use of alcohol. And instead of suggesting as we did years ago that the first thing to do is to surrender to God and give up and convert, now we say there are several other steps that can be taken first. The spiritual awakening is the last step, instead of the first.

AA, too, has done a little borrowing from the current resurgent "constituency consciousness." In San Francisco, it has been estimated there are from 30 to 40 homosexual AA groups; in nearby Marin County special AA groups have been formed for the deaf and for Spanish-speaking people. As clarified by Patricia Tate, executive director of the California Black Commission on Alcoholism:

> The reasons for alcoholism vary. The rich drink for different reasons than the poor. Women drink for different reasons than men. No one solution works for everybody. Some blacks perceive Alcoholics Anonymous as a middle-class white group. When they become involved in white groups, they become more conscious of their racial identity than their alcoholism.[34]

In sum, there is a growing admission that people with problems of drinking have different needs—not only for different levels of care, as discussed above, but for different environments in which to deal with their problems. While, as one respondent put it, "not everyone wants to keep talking about drinking," some people want to do just that, and some, not surprisingly, find this easier to do among people with whom they share more than their drinking problem. It is over the issue of measuring the success of the varying formulas (specifically over the question of abstinence) that a sharp cleavage occurs. This will be discussed in Chapter 12, but first we shall turn attention to how alcoholism has come to be defined as a disease.

Notes

1. Selden D. Bacon, "Concepts," in W.J. Filstead, J.J. Rossi, and M. Keller (eds.), *Alcohol, New Thinking and New Directions* (Cambridge, Mass.: Ballinger, 1976), p. 66.
2. Ibid., p. 65.
3. *See:* Selden D. Bacon, "The Classic Temperance Movement of the U.S.A.; Impact Today on Attitudes, Action and Research," *British Journal of Addiction,* Vol. 62 (1967), pp. 5-18.
4. Bacon, "Concepts," p. 66.
5. Ibid.
6. Ibid.
7. Mark Keller, "Multidisciplinary Perspectives on Alcoholism," *Journal of Studies on Alcohol,* Vol. 36 (1975), p. 139.
8. Ibid.
9. Joseph Gusfield, "The Prevention of Drinking Problems," in W.J. Filstead, J.J. Rossi, and M. Keller (eds.), *Alcohol, New Thinking and New Directions* (Cambridge, Mass.: Ballinger, 1976), p. 270.
10. Ibid., p. 271.
11. Bacon, "Concepts," p. 67.
12. Giesbrecht et al., "Sociological Trends in the Treatment of Alcoholics," paper presented at the 21st International Institute on the Prevention and Treatment of Alcoholism (Helsinki, 1975), p. 8.
13. *See also:* Eva Maria Blum and H. Richard Blum, *Alcoholism: Modern Psychological Approaches to Treatment* (San Francisco: Jossey-Bass, Inc., 1967).
14. For the early history of these institutions, *see:* E.H.L. Corwin and E.V. Cunningham, "History of Special Institutions for the Treatment of Alcohol Addiction," in *Institutional Facilities for the Treatment of Alcoholism* (New York: Research Council on Problems of Alcohol, Research Report No. 7, 1944), pp. 12-19.
15. Ibid., p. 19.
16. Friedner D. Wittman, "Alcoholism and Architecture: The Myth of Specialized Treatment Facilities," paper presented at the American Institute of Architects meeting, Los Angeles, January, 1971.
17. Emergency settings—hospital emergency rooms, city jails, detoxification centers—are discussed in later chapters.
18. Jacqueline P. Wiseman, *Stations of the Lost* (Englewood Cliffs, N.J.: Prentice-Hall, 1970).
19. Mark Keller, "The Oddities of Alcoholics," *Quarterly Journal of Studies on Alcohol,* Vol. 33, (1972), pp. 1147-48.
20. *See, for example:* H.M. Tiebout, "The Role of Psychiatry in the Field of Alcoholism. With Comment on the Concept of Alcoholism as a Symptom and as a Disease," *Quarterly Journal of Studies on Alcohol,* Vol. 12 (1951), pp. 52-59; R. Fox, "Treatment of Chronic Alcoholism," in Jules H. Masserman

(ed.), *Current Psychiatric Therapies.* Vol. 5 (1965), pp. 107-11; A. Silber, "An Addendum to the Technique of Psychotherapy With Alcoholics," *Journal of Nervous and Mental Disease,* Vol. 150 (1970), pp. 423-37; J.H. Conn, "The Decline of Psychoanalysis—Commentary," *Journal of the American Medical Association,* Vol. 228 (1974), pp. 711-12.

21. *See, for review of studies:* C.D. Emrick, "A Review of Psychologically Oriented Treatment of Alcoholism. II. The Relative Effectiveness of Different Treatment Approaches and the Effectiveness of Treatment vs. No Treatment," *Journal of Studies on Alcohol,* Vol. 36 (1975) pp. 88-108. *See also:* Reginald Smart, "Do Some Alcoholics Do Better in Some Types of Treatment?," *Drug and Alcohol Dependence,* Vol. 3 (1978), pp. 65-75.

22. Giesbrecht et al., "Sociological Trends," p. 8.

23. Mary Catherine Taylor. *Alcoholics Anonymous,* p. 6. *See also: Twelve Steps and Twelve Traditions* (New York: Alcoholic Anonymous Publishing Company, 1952); Margaret B. Bailey and Barry Leach, *Alcoholics Anonymous: Pathway to Recovery* (New York: The National Council on Alcoholism, Inc., 1965); Robert F. Bales, "The Therapeutic Role of Alcoholics Anonymous as Seen by A Sociologist," *Quarterly Journal of Studies on Alcohol,* Vol. 5 (1944), pp. 267-78; Freed Bales, "Types of Social Structure as Factors in 'Cures for Alcohol Addiction,'" *Applied Anthropology,* Vol. 1 (1942), pp. 1-13; and Milton A. Maxwell, "Alcoholics Anonymous: An Interpretation," in David Pittman and Charles R. Snyder (eds.), *Society, Culture and Drinking Patterns* (New York: John Wiley & Sons, Inc., 1962), pp. 577-85.

24. *See, for example:* Edward Sagarin, *Odd Man In* (Chicago; Quadrangle Books, 1972), and Mary Catherine Taylor, *Alcoholics Anonymous.*

25. Sagarin, *Odd Man In,* p. 35.

26. Taylor, *Alcoholics Anonymous,* p. 179.

27. See, Chapter 1.

28. Sagarin, *Odd Man In,* p. 246.

29. *See:* O. Carl Simonton and Stephanie S. Simonton, "Belief Systems and Management of the Emotional Aspects of Malignancy," *Journal of Transpersonal Psychology,* Vol. 7 (1975), pp. 29-47.

30. Jean Kirkpatrick, as quoted by Doris B. Wiley in "Focus," *The Evening Bulletin,* Plymouth, Pennsylvania, (July 19, 1976).

31. Women For Sobriety, Thirteen Statements of Acceptance:
    1. I have a drinking problem that once had me.
    2. Negative emotions destroy only myself.
    3. Happiness is a habit I will develop.
    4. Problems bother me only to the degree I permit them to.
    5. I am what I think.
    6. Life can be ordinary or it can be great.
    7. Love can change the course of my world.
    8. The fundamental object of life is emotional and spiritual growth.
    9. The past is gone forever.
    10. All love given returns twofold.
    11. Enthusiasm is my daily exercise.
    12. I am a competent woman and have much to give others.
    13. I am responsible for myself and my sisters.

32. Wayne Goethe, "The Death of a Philosophy," paper presented to the

Association of Halfway House Alcoholism Programs of North America, 1975.

33. Daniel W. Burt, "A Behaviorist Looks at Alcoholics Anonymous," paper presented to the North American Congress on Alcohol and Drug Problems, San Francisco, December, 1974.

34. *San Francisco Chronicle* (June 16, 1977), p. 18.

7.

Redefining the Problem

Who are these alcoholics, these people with drinking problems? What is the nature of their affliction? How have others gone about defining and *redefining* this problem in order not only to give it legitimacy but to generate and increase the previously described animating process?

Early in the interviewing, it became evident that respondents, when pressed to explain what they meant when they spoke of alcoholism as a disease, had been influenced by the eclecticism of the arena. Alcoholics have a genetic pre-disposition, and/or a physiological dependence, and/or specific psychological traits, and/or are affected by sociological and cultural factors—these definitions of the disease appeared in varying combinations.

The Southern Chapter of the California Association of Alcoholic Recovery Homes has attempted to compile a glossary of alcoholism terms designed to draw distinctions between inappropriate and proposed usage for such words as treatment, counselor, client, detoxification, etc.[1] This is no fools' pastime since the terms, and their disparate uses, represent clear philosophical differences among those who use them. For example, as explained by one respondent, "We object to the term 'rehabilitation,' which means returning to a former state; 'recovery' means to grow beyond what you were before." As mentioned in Chapter 1, quests for clarity, such as CAARH's endeavor, were challenged some years back by

Christie and Bruun who asked what would happen if people actually understood each other, all the time, completely—pointing out that disguise is often needed when the conceptual framework is so diffuse.[2]

As with the fine differences contested by Chinese radicals and anti-radicals concerning Mao's last words, the weight of history lies behind these distinctions. A verbatim account of the dialogue with another respondent is illuminating:

> A. We just got the definition of alcoholism and the alcoholic written into our (CAARH) standards. We've been trying to do that for two years.
> Q. But you're still calling it an illness. Doesn't that get you into the whole treatment/cure trap?
> A. No, only if you use disease. Illness can be applied to dysfunction, whereas disease a person has no control. We've still got some old-line people. Moving from a disease to an illness is a step—not very much, but a step.

The road from a moral to a legal to a medical/psychological model of alcoholism has not been an easy one. That it has been a journey in search of increasing humanitarianism is undeniable, but this does not detract from the judgment offered by Seeley:

> . . . the bare statement that "alcoholism is a disease" is most misleading since . . . it conceals what is essential—that a step in public policy is being *recommended,* not a scientific discovery announced.[3]

Less than a scientific proposition, the statement "alcoholism is a disease" (or illness) represents a response, a social imperative that is expressed in different social institutions, and in bureaucratic actions. The redefining of the problem of alcohol use, as dealt with in the remainder of this chapter, reflects changes in social location, a redefining of the social rubric various interests have sought to have applied to this problem. Moreover, as one respondent characterized the naming of the national agency, based on his own experience at the time:

> Calling it the National Institute on Alcohol Abuse and Alcoholism represents the feeble struggle to demonstrate that we couldn't really define either term.

After six months as director of NIAAA, Ernest Noble found that the struggle persists:

> In some ways you can look at alcoholism as like a cancer, having many different kinds. We have to begin to define more clearly what is alcohol abuse, and what is alcoholism. It would be a mistake to put the abuse of alcohol under the big umbrella of alcoholism. There is a tendency by some to do that. That's because they haven't taken the burden of defining alco-

hol abuse. We, as an Institute, have to define that more clearly. Is a father who occasionally drinks and comes home and beats his children an alcoholic, or is he abusing alcohol? A child who perhaps drinks twice a year, and goes out and gets involved in an accident—is he an alcoholic child, or is he a child who happens to abuse himself by drinking alcohol? [4]

To understand this struggle of language, and to discover how the "drunk" became an "alcoholic," one must trace the origin of the disease concept of alcoholism, as it hopped from the temperance world to the worlds of law and of volunteer-action, to the worlds of medicine, psychiatry, psychology and related health services, to its current movement into a world which is attempting to replace the disease concept with a "social model" of alcoholism.

Early Warning Signs of the Disease

Nineteenth-century America, out of which grew the temperance world, was dominated by middle-class values—the maintenance of self-control, the formation of good habits, the pursuit of purposeful activities. Appeals to the drunkard's better nature were made both by the Church and by the temperance literature, which in its early years was a persuasionist movement.[5] It is generally assumed that this period stressed a moral model of alcoholism, but the seeds of a fuzzy disease model begin to emerge even here. For while the drunkard was seen as suffering from a failure of will, therapy for moral problems took the form of "moral treatment" in asylums, the newly discovered cure-all of Jacksonian America. Following the boom in almshouses, orphan asylums, and reformatories, whose purpose was to aid inmates "in forming virtuous habits, that they may finally go forth clothed as in invincible armour," [6] came the accompanying growth of inebriate asylums.

To this faith in moral reform, the temperance movement added a fateful concept—that of loss of self-control. The habitual drunkard was portrayed as a slave to the poison alcohol:

> The temperance movement's most important and enduring contribution to popular and scientific thought about alcohol and drug use and abuse was the concept of addiction—of an overpowering craving for a particular substance. Temperance's contribution was not, as is widely assumed, the notion that individuals who became drunkards had unusually weak or depraved characters. In general, the movement countered that idea, arguing that even those with relatively good and strong characters became drunkards as well.[7]

It was not until the 1890s that temperance became a totally prohibitionist movement, as it became part of the Progressive effort to achieve social reform through government regulation.[8] The attempt to substitute national law prohibiting the substance for moral treatment of the addicted has been exhaustively recorded; [9] the relevant point for this discussion is that the country emerged from that period with the addiction concept still intact.

The Emergence of the Clinical Perspective

The addiction concept, or disease concept of alcoholism as it shall be referred to henceforth, is part of a clinical perspective that has its roots in American pragmatism—"the philosophy of possibility" [10] that was the spirit of the Progressive Era. Rejecting the determinism and *laissez faire* philosophy of the Social Darwinists, Dewey preached social responsibility and the effectiveness of intelligence as an instrument in modifying the world. A rebel against systems which are impervious to chance or choice, James held forth the possibility of active human effort in bettering life. Such were the concepts of social engineering that fell on ground ripe for this philosophy; Tocqueville had earlier observed that the promise of equality brings a concomitant promise of the infinite perfectibility of man. Obviously, this phenomenon did not spring full-blown in the United States, but rather stems directly from the optimism of the Enlightenment. Furthermore, the economic and political gains of the middle-class in the nineteenth and twentieth centuries meant that the standards for assessing progress were constantly rising. Marshall has captured the net effect: as "ever deeper probing into the social situation kept revealing new horrors which had previously been concealed from view, the glorious achievements of the past became the squalid heritage of the present." [11]

The pragmatic impulse, which makes it un-American to identify a problem as intractable, gained momentum as America became increasingly urban, industrialized, and wealthy:

> Between the two world wars, America chose social welfare over social Darwinism which meant, in part, that it chose to engineer a social order marked by upgraded and equalized participation in political democracy, material consumption, and multiple styles of urbanity. . . . America pours its wealth into vast numbers of opportunity programs to achieve its goals and names almost any conceivable group, event, or thing a social problem if it can be seen as threatening the achievement of these goals. Hence, its concern for the "culturally deprived," the under-achievers, the school dropouts, the job displaced, the aged, the ill, the retarded, and mentally disturbed. . . . American pragmatism is in full bloom, having converted most person-social events into "problem solving" or clinical situations.[12]

What in the nineteenth century had been a division, with Darwinism pervading the human scene (in a fateful, self-healing perspective) and science the material scene (in an engineering perspective) was transformed into social intervention, leading eventually to government programs for the afflicted.

If the pragmatic strain in American thought provided the underpinnings, contributing conditions emerging in the twentieth century moved that impulse in the direction of a clinical perspective in regard to the problem of alcohol use. These contributors were the growth of the health professions, the veneration of scientific thought, and the economic resources provided by foundations.

In the previous chapter, allusion was made to the "benign neglect" that has characterized the attitude of the medical profession toward alcohol problems. Bacon avers that the "disease notion" was an alien view to the medical profession during the 1930s (and that even now, those who call alcoholism a disease refer patients to AA for treatment). According to Bacon, the disease concept was "inserted," "foisted upon" or "sold to" the medical profession chiefly by outsiders who were significantly helped by a handful of insiders:

> In some ways the movement to place "alcoholism" in the professional "disease" world might be likened to inventing "larcenism" or "kleptomism" as a label to describe the assertedly most significant aspect of abuse of property, to indicate its essential bio-psycho-behavioral nature among chronic thieves as a pathology and to insist it was both a treatable disease and a public health responsibility.[13]

The medical profession was fortuitously emerging as a legitimizing agent just as those concerned with alcoholism were looking for a new way to attack the problem. A reform movement had taken place within its ranks around 1900 as concerted efforts were made (especially by the elite, Eastern physicians) to eliminate private medical colleges, weed out the quacks, develop standards and strict licensing procedures, involve foundation money in the building of laboratories and medical schools, and consolidate universities with teaching hospitals.[14] This led to the enhanced image of medical science which reached its zenith in the period from 1930 to 1950.[15]

Simultaneously, there occurred the growth of the psychiatric profession and the Freudianization of society, adding to the pragmatic impulse the potential discovery of the psychological components of alcohol dependence and of personality types prone to alcohol problems. Sagarin notes a curious irony:

. . . the formation of AA and other groups—all essentially hostile to psychotherapy of every type but their own distinctive brand—was actually aided by the popularity of psychotherapy at this particular state of American history. What Freud and his followers—novelists and educators, journalists and scenarists—did for the deviant was to popularize two distinct concepts about behavioral disorders and peculiarities: first, that they are within the area of human control, and second, that they should be looked upon with the same blameless compassion and sympathy that is extended to most victims of physical disorders.[16]

In addition, a transference of the alcoholic to health professionals occurred when the quasi-psychiatrists (social workers, psychologists) needed careers. Social workers were following the psychiatric route and psychologists were establishing new techniques, as adaptable to alcoholic patients as to any other patient population. The clinical orientation took hold, as institutions developed and graduates of professional schools needed "patients" to "treat." Moreover, it is not difficult to see how such a problem-solving philosophy, an approach that said "at least do *something,*" provided a fertile ground for the susceptibility of treatment approaches to the sway of fashion, as discussed in Chapter 6. As to the public health profession, Bacon recalls:

Just as "outsiders" pressed the disease-treatment concept upon the medical institution, so did "outsiders," in fact, mostly the same people, press the "public health" concept upon the world of public health. . . . And just as "public health" was exhibiting great difficulty in establishing its identity as something rather different from the treatment of disease, so did these "outsiders" from the alcohol problems world confuse (or perhaps entirely ignore) this central difference. As the three slogans of the National Council on Alcoholism put it: (1) alcoholism is a disease; (2) alcoholism can be successfully treated; (3) this is a public health responsibility. One conclusion from this tripartite statement is that the "public health" responsibility consists of (1) reinforcing and extending the disease concept and (2) making treatment (a) more attractive, (b) more effective and (c) more available to wider and wider sectors of "the public." This, however, is a public treatment not a public health interpretation.[17]

Bacon rightly points out that these professions were *not* struggling to take responsibility for alcohol problems, nor taking the leadership to reduce stigma or increase services, and were not instigating relevant research or training. On the contrary, to this day health professionals continue to look upon the patient with alcohol problems as undesirable and a poor risk. For example, physician-respondents, while affirming that alcoholism is a disease, would then proceed to blame the victim, as summarized by the following dialogue:

A. They fail to keep their appointments, don't follow instructions, phone in the middle of the night.

Q. But you could also say of another population, the aged, that they don't listen to or follow instructions, don't remember what you tell them, etc.

A. I have compassion for the aged—they've worked hard, we'll all be old some day, they can't help it. But the alcoholic *does it to himself.* If you're treating someone for liver problems it's hard enough; if it's self-inflicted it's discouraging.

A review of the nursing literature reveals a self-conscious movement away from a judgmental, moralistic or punitive attitude in which the alcoholic is regarded as lacking in character or will power toward an attitude which is accepting, non-stereotypic and therapeutic. The repeated emphasis on these points suggests that for nurses, too, practical application has not caught up with current theory. In spite of proclamations by the World Health Organization, American Medical Association, and the American Hospital Asociation, two nurses expressed the dilemma:

> ... few of us would reject this concept at the intellectual level, but many of us still have real difficulty *feeling* it is an illness.[18]

Faith in the rewards of scientific investigation is a cornerstone of this period. To refer back to Bacon's allusion to a "small group of insiders" within the medical profession, credit must be given to the medical/psychiatric worlds for the instigating the "new scientific approach." The Research Council on Problems of Alcohol, formed in 1937,[19] quickly achieved stature and respect both in enlisting prominent personalities and in gaining status as an affiliated society of the American Association for the Advancement of Science. Nevertheless, obstacles still remained in raising money. One grant, however, for $25,000, was significant for the arena, for it enlisted the services of Norman Jolliffe, chief of medical services at Bellevue Hospital in New York, and Karl M. Bowman, director of the Psychiatric Division of Bellevue and chairman of the Department of Psychiatry at New York University Medical College, as principal investigators for a review of the biological literature on the effects of alcohol on humans. As previously explained, for the position of director of this project, Jolliffe conscripted E.M. Jellinek, whose voluminous reports moved way beyond the confines of biology:

> Meantime, Howard W. Haggard and his small staff of physiologists and biochemists at the Yale Laboratory of Applied Physiology had for several years been conducting researches on alcohol metabolism and its phys-

iological effects. The publication of their findings had attracted some popular interest, resulting in the address of many questions to them which could not be answered from the knowledge of physiology and biochemistry or medicine alone. Haggard solved several problems, first by founding the *Quarterly Journal* of *Studies on Alcohol* in 1940; next by inviting E.M. Jellinek to come to Yale to complete the writing of the review whose funds were exhausted; and then by encouraging Jellinek to start what was to become the Yale Center of Alcohol Studies, beginning with the recruitment of a multidisciplinary staff.[20]

Keller portrays the center as projecting to the nation and to the world an image of science in action, solving or getting ready to solve the problems of alcohol, calling attention to the problems of alcohol as well as alcoholism. The center also assisted the volunteer organization, the National Council on Alcoholism, to start toward its goal of popularizing "the new approach"—a small group of reformers attempting to merge the American pragmatic spirit with new-found knowledge.

Brief note must be made of the symbiosis between reformers and philanthropists which marks this period. The growth of the medical profession was greatly enhanced by its connection with the Rockefeller and Carnegie Foundations;[21] the initial funding for the Research Council on Problems of Alcohol came from Carnegie.[22] The Christopher Smithers Foundation over the years has been the single largest contributor to the National Council on Alcoholism and the Alcohol and Drug Problems Association, and to the Yale School, support which continued following its move to Rutgers in 1962. According to its own testimony, the Smithers Foundation had given nearly $3 million for alcohol education, research and treatment by 1968.[23]

To these conditions—an underlying American pragmatism, the growth of the health professions and institutions, the veneration of scientific thought, and the beneficence of foundations—must be added two historical developments, which intertwined to put the seal on the disease model of alcoholism: the branching off of a sub-world of the legal profession, civil rights law; and the mushrooming of a constituency of "recovered alcoholics." These legitimizing developments will be examined next.

Civil Libertarians and the Alcohol Movement: Two Worlds Intersect

Running counter to the temperance world's emphasis on addiction, was an equally important American stress on individual responsibility, exhibited in the retention of criminal law sanctioning incarceration for public inebriates. While Prohibition had placed the blame on the bottle, state legal statutes were based on the assumption that offenders act out of rational choice and should be held responsible.[24] However, as Room points out, the merchant may have wanted the drunk off his doorstep, but the justice people were faced with an overcrowded system, and through refusals to convict, provided "passive cooperation" in a growing effort to nullify the public drunkenness law.[25]

Room, in his careful analysis of the steps leading to the Uniform Alcoholism and Intoxication Treatment Act, places great emphasis on the contribution of the civil liberties lawyers:

> During the 1960s, the concept of civil liberties, and in particular the concerns of the American Civil Liberties Union, broadened beyond earlier narrower concerns with first and fifth amendment rights. Lawyers, law students and civil libertarians started to take a strong interest in and seek reform of what were seen as the effectively discriminatory or unjust effects of the existing legal system in a number of areas—juvenile court proceedings, mental illness commitment hearings, capital punishment determinations, etc. In line with these interests, a spate of articles about arrests for intoxication appeared in law school journals, starting in the mid-1960s.
>
> ACLU lawyers took a primary role in the test cases concerning public intoxication. In alliance with elements of the alcoholism movement, and as I have mentioned often with the cooperation of the municipal court judges, the test cases concentrated on the disease concept of alcoholism, seeking to apply to alcoholism the precedent set for opiates in Robinson vs. California (1962), that a person could not be punished for illness.[26]

The point made clear by Room is that the disease concept was not the only possible ground for attacking the drunk court system, but rather was a preferred strategy of defense, and reflected the alliance of the civil liberties lawyers with the "alcoholism movement."

Room describes the "alcoholism movement" of the 1940s and 1950s as a coalition of interest united around a disease concept of alcoholism but without agreement on what this meant. Furthermore, "to a considerable extent lay thought in the movement led professional thought, rather than the reverse." [27] Bacon concurs in citing in this regard Jellinek's classic disease concept papers [28] and their dependence on data from a questionnaire *designed by and administered to* members of Alcoholics Anonymous. According to Bacon, Jellinek received about 160 completed questionnaires out of 1,600 or more possibles: "he finally used ninety-eight of the forms and emerged with a description of something called alcoholism." [29] Bacon asserts that Jellinek's first analysis bore almost no resemblance to the brilliance and high standards of Jellinek's previous academic work and was originally known as "Jellinek's doodle." Of course, public disclosure of such disparagement was not made until many years had passed. On the contrary, Jellinek's scheme was interpreted as presenting an inevitable downhill course of four phases (from social drinking to relieve anxiety; to surreptitious drinking, onset of blackouts, increasing consumption; to physical dependence and loss of control; to the onset of "benders," prolonged daytime drunkenness, neglect of responsibilities, "hitting bottom," in AA parlance), and was considered *the* definitive work for many years. Later, Jellinek-directed interviews with 2,000 AA members made it evident that there were "alcoholisms" and he proposed a five-type classification. Jellinek's 1960 qualification,[30] that "alcoholism" should denote any use of alcoholic beverage which causes any damage to the individual or to society, and "disease alcoholism" should be confined to addiction, or loss of control over drinking behavior, has been bypassed in the history of this arena. Nevertheless, the Jellinek-confirmed credo of addiction was adopted by the "alcoholism movement" (AA/NCA/Yale Center) as it became allied with the civil liberties lawyers in the 1960s over the issue of involuntary commitment.

As Room documents, the movement had a historical predisposition toward voluntary treatment, expressed by AA as "motivation": "an unmotivated alcoholic, one who was not 'ready,' could not be helped; the objection was thus pragmatic rather than explicitly ethical." [31] But in the early 1960s a drift was occurring in the alcoholism literature toward involuntary treatment as an alternative to public drunkenness arrests, harkening back to the "moral treatment" of the nineteenth century. It is here that the intersecting of the alcoholism movement and the civil liberties lawyers takes place. The lawyers, fresh from legal attacks on involuntary commitment for mental illness, became interested in test cases because of their abiding concern with the civil liberties issue. The defense strategy employed, however, promoted a disease model of alcoholism.

The year 1966 marked two district court decisions (the *Easter* and *Driver* cases) based on the principle that an alcoholic drinks involuntarily, and therefore cannot be criminally punished for intoxication—that as a disease, public intoxication is properly handled as a public health, welfare, and rehabilitation problem. Two years later, a similar case *(Powell vs. Texas)* reached the Supreme Court, which failed to move in the direction of the *Easter* and *Driver* cases, as had been expected.

Most important for our tracing of the clinical perspective are the consequences of the Supreme Court opinion in the Powell case. In an opinion with which Justices Warren, Black and Harlan concurred, Justice Marshall observed that both the arena and the medical profession were divided on definitions of alcoholism (and indeed the two leading organizations at the time, the National Council on Alcoholism [NCA] and the North American Association of Alcoholism Programs [later ADPA], could not even agree enough to combine their efforts in a single *amicus curiae* brief). The judgment was read as a mandate by NCA,[32] leading eventually to the publication in 1972 of NCA's "Criteria for the Diagnosis of Alcoholism." [33] Although refuting the unilinear progress of the disease, as presented in Jellinek's earlier work, this pronouncement attempted to place different weights upon the symptoms, dividing them into three diagnostic levels, from "classical, definite, obligatory" to "probable, frequent, indicative" to "potential, possible, incidental." The result was a mixture of *physical* (cirrhosis, pancreatitis, tachycardia) and *behavioral* (preference for drinking companions, bars and taverns; anxiety-relieving mechanisms, such as telephone calls inappropriate in time, distance, person or motive, i.e., telephonitis) symptoms. The "alcoholism movement" had bought the clinical perspective as a way of moving from a penal approach to humane assistance through treatment, carrying forward the American pragmatic thrust. But in regarding alcoholism as a clear-cut condition "like pregnancy," [34] and in clinging to the label "disease," movement representatives did little to clarify the matter.

For all of its tortuous elaboration, the NCA Criteria, still used as a reference point by many people in this arena, do not deal with the critics of the disease concept, who assert that drinking may *cause* illness but in itself is not a disease. And the situation continues to be blurred by positions such as that of the AMA in their 1972 statement:

> The American Medical Association identifies alcoholism as a complex disease with biological, psychological and sociological components. . . . By early recognition of drinking problems prior to biological injury, nonmedical treatment of psychological and sociological components may obviate the need for medical care.[35]

Nor is the disease concept given greater credence by statements such as that of the former director of the National Institute on Alcohol Abuse and Alcoholism: "We . . . must conclude that alcoholic excesses, alcoholic problems, alcoholism, or any label you care to affix is produced by complex, multidimensional factors, and that, in fact, there is no such thing as an alcoholic." [36] The distinctions remain muddy, with Keller trying to separate the stages which mark vulnerability,[37] and Senator William Hathaway, former chairman of the Senate Alcoholism and Narcotics Subcommittee (now the Senate Subcommittee on Alcoholism and Drug Abuse), telling a conference of clinicians: "Let researchers try to determine whether alcoholism is a disease. Let *us* concentrate on the fact that alcoholism *is* one of America's most serious health problems." [38]

Marty Mann, founder of NCA, herself a recovered alcoholic, has said that the disease concept is "one of the most powerful therapeutic tools to help an alcoholic. [Those who reject the concept] don't know the problems of alcoholism first hand." [39] This division between clinicians and theoreticians centers around the still unanswered question of addiction. It is not difficult to see why those who are exposed daily to a treatment population, as well as those who have recovered from the depths of alcohol withdrawal (and indeed, many times they are one and the same), find a physiological addiction ideology a compatible definition of the situation. For them, the issue is one of separating the "alcoholic" from the remainder of the drinking universe, of seeing "alcoholism" as a separate entity from drinking. To which Shore and Luce answer:

> This is a static notion which tends to freeze drinkers at points along a spectrum of experience and does not encourage a dynamic view of alcoholism. Indeed, it fosters a bookkeeping approach in which one's status as an alcoholic depends on a tabulation of the symptoms one has or has not accumulated in the course of his or her disease.[40]

In spite of its value as legitimation for increased and humane services, a progression of conditions have undermined the disease concept. It is to these we turn now.

A Shift in the Theoretical Framework

While American pragmatism set the stage for the clinical perspective, this tradition, intertwined with other underlying conditions, also set the stage for pointing out the clinical perspective's weakness of fit. Previous reliance on moral-religious restraints to establish order and compliance began to fall apart in the twentieth century, when mobility and the rise of cities undermined the religious institutional structure. As America has become increasingly secularized, the threat of perdition from demon rum has had diminished significance; the middle-class values of discipline and sobriety are no longer paramount, and have been replaced by moral relativism.

American pragmatism's roots can be traced to German "historicism," a philosophical emphasis on development—that is, how things come to be as they are. Dewey and Veblen were part of a generation whose early work had been done in an atmosphere dominated by Hegel and Kant. But White reminds us that right-Hegelianism and conservative social Darwinism represent the conservative wing of historicism from which American pragmatists split: "None of them ever accepted the doctrine that whatever is, is right; indeed Veblen questioned it to the point of maintaining its perverse contrary: 'Whatever is, is wrong.' " [41]

Add to this consciousness of the relativity of all values the impact of the drug culture of the 1960s. While there still is only conjectural knowledge about addiction, the alcoholism arena has exploded with new questions. The antithesis of a classical addiction theory, and one which reflects both this moral relativism and the twentieth century drug-consciousness, has been expressed by Scott, summarized as follows: people seek an altered state of consciousness for a variety of reasons, and an individual becomes "addicted to" or "dependent on" the agent that produces the greatest benefit in attaining that altered state. People seek that state either by healthy or unhealthy means. For the alcoholic, drinking is an unhealthy method of securing that state, yet it is sought in spite of the problems on the way to the goal. To concentrate merely on the *price* of the goal is a tragic misunderstanding of alcoholism.[42]

Against the background described above, developments have occurred—one within the world of sociology, another within the world of psychiatry, and a third in that branch of the research world called survey research—which have had a sizable impact on perspectives on alcoholism.

Historicism's effect on sociology is expressed in the philosophy that social reality is socially constructed, as witness Durkheim's "collective consciousness"[43] and Sumner's demonstration that varieties of moral beliefs and practices are relative to the customs of the time.[44] As Collins and Makowsky point out, the implications of the profound relativism of Sumner's "the mores can make anything right" is a far more sophisticated perspective than the moral absolutes of the sociologist-reformers of the time, whose interest was in the elimination of what they saw clearly as problems.[45]

This tradition, which focused on the relativity of social reality, has been carried forward by certain branches of sociology (symbolic interactionism, phenomenology, ethnomethodology), and specifically by sociologists of the "value-conflict school" and by those sociologists who have themselves been labeled "labeling theorists." The former[46] stress the value-judgment implicit in the designation of social problems, as stated by Fuller and Myers, "Social problems are what people think they are."[47] The latter[48] base their work on the general view that "deviance is not a quality that lies in behavior itself, but in the interaction between the person who commits an act and those who respond to it."[49] In combination (and there is overlap between these two "schools") these sociologists have shifted attention away from the behavior of those who constitute the problem, and on to the symbolic process through which the meaning of such behavior is constructed.

Gusfield's writings provide examples of this perspective as it relates to alcoholism. Gusfield has demonstrated that it is not the frequency of deviant acts, but how they affect the status of the norm (the predominant set of values) which determines whether the deviant actor is perceived by society as repentant and accessible to moral suasion, or as an enemy and needful of police intervention.[50] In his oft-cited analysis of Prohibition, Gusfield argues that this movement represented a reaction of the dominant group (native American, middle-class, evangelical Protestant) to a changing, industralized city, overrun with immigrants in need of reformation.[51] In another context, Gusfield makes an illuminating distinction between the symbolic import of alcohol as compared to drug use: experimentation with alcohol on the part of young people has been interpreted as part of "growing-up," while drug use is seen as "growing-away":

> Public attention to drugs, as an object and as a problem, is not one of American Puritan concern about mood-alteration, per se. Rather it is about the form and character of mood-alteration which occurs outside the scope and control of adult agencies and models.[52]

Concurrent with this development in sociology, there has run a similar movement in psychiatry, dubbed anti-psychiatry, which poses the question previously left for literary minds to ponder: who is really mad—the labeled schizophrenic, or the "normal" who adapts to a dysfunctional society?[53] Positing that what traditional psychiatry has called "psychosis" may in fact be an explosive breakthrough toward sanity, this school attributes the designation of mental patients as "ill" to the mere fact that their behavior is unacceptable. It is Szasz who has applied psychiatry's labeling theory specifically to alcoholism, for to him "excessive drinking is a habit, and according to a person's values, he may consider it a good or bad habit."[54] A person who is sensitive to alcohol and nevertheless imbibes. is like the allergic man with ragweed on his lawn who spends his leisure time in late August working on his yard. Others may consider it unacceptable behavior, but it is a matter of individual choice, and not one to be labeled an illness.

It is important to re-emphasize that which was stated in the introduction: inherent in such sociological and psychological theorizing is the danger of imparting the feeling that there really is no problem. Thus, while such theories have had a notable impact on changing perspectives on *just what constitutes* the problem, an equally sizable impact has been the manner in which such theorizing has divided some people within the recovery service and volunteer-action worlds from their counterparts within the research world. Interviews revealed that for those with a clinical, i.e., action-oriented, perspective, such "egg-head ruminations" are far removed from the "real" problem of addiction. What is lost in such judgment is the sense that these major ideas were not meant to explain individual casualty, or to explain away individual suffering, but are rather at the level that Blumer calls "sensitizing concepts." [55] And such they have been for the group most involved with examining American drinking practices.

Another "New Scientific Approach"

A third development, equal in importance to those occurring within the worlds of sociology and psychiatry, and indeed related to them, was the follow-through on the suggestion first proposed by the Yale Center to study "drinking" instead of "drunking." For this critical departure from the previous Jellinek-based emphasis on the study of inebriety, Selden Bacon must be given full credit. It was his 1943 paper, buttressed by subsequent publications, which first called for the study of the sociological aspects of drinking behavior.[56] In 1960, with the support of the California Department of Public Health and the National Institute of Mental Health, interest in alcohol consumption moved beyond previous cultural interpretations [57] through the efforts of Ira Cisin, Wendell Lipscomb, and Genevieve Knupfer, who began the first national surveys of drinking practices based on a *non*-treatment population. The early work of this group (later to become the Social Research Group in Berkeley) and of their colleagues in Finland and England, pointed up sub-group differences in drinking practices, values and attitudes, and the variation in the extent to which a drinker's normal social network tolerates drinking behavior, raising questions about the variables by which a heavy drinker does nor does not become labeled an alcoholic. Illuminated as well by the writings of this group, was the public's confusion concerning what should be an appropriate stance *vis-à-vis* drinking and drunkenness.

It was not the intent of these researchers to dispute the disease concept of alcoholism as it was being presented by segments of the volunteer-action and recovery service worlds. But in their continued search for the social dimensions of alcohol use, they have undermined the pure clinical perspective.[58] For example, Room [59] has questioned the conservative interpretation of addiction by demonstrating that being glued to a particular set of behaviors does not imply that the glue resides in an addiction to a substance. Glues may be found at many different levels of analysis, i.e. socio-cultural, or psychological. Surveys have verified that having any particular drinking problem is only a modest predictor of having any other particular problem, and having a problem at one particular time is only a modest predictor of having the same problem at another time [60]—that in regard to heavy drinking, there is what Cahalan and Room have called a "maturing-out process," at least among American males. As Room has reviewed these findings:

> There is considerable turnover in a period of a few years in the persons who are in the relatively heavy-drinking fraction of the population. . . . Among those drinking relatively heavily at any particular time, the occurrence of particular problems with drinking may be a matter as much of situational and social factors and of chance as of relatively permanent characteristics of the individual's psychological state and lifestyle.[61]

Such findings have raised myriad questions: 1) about the reliability of looking only to treatment populations for characteristics of the "alcoholic"; 2) about the interactive nature of social problems that are connected with drinking—for example, the association of a greater level of drinking patterns with a greater probability of social consequences of drinking in dryer than in wetter parts of the U.S., and conversely, the greater social acceptability of heavy drinking among certain groups, such as business executives; 3) about the ambiguity of the connection between, for example, marital problems and drinking, driving and drinking, the tendency to assume alcohol is the primary cause if it is present in any problematic situation, and the equally suspect assumption that a break in a relationship is always a problem when in fact it may be a solution; and 4) about the extent to which many of the problems associated with drinking are carry-overs from situations where drinking was appropriate to where it is not, such as driving after a party. A finding with perhaps the greatest import is the existence of a considerable age gap between general population problem drinkers (early 20s) and the typical age-distribution in clinical populations (35-60), leading Room to suggest that perhaps drinking problems among young men should be interpreted as "normal" or tolerated deviance. He points out that young men have quite a wide margin of social credit concerning risky behavior:

> The labelling of middle-aged problem drinkers and their extrusion from the general milieu and incorporation into the clinical population thus derive not only from the fact that they are now old enough to have a considerable if often sporadic history of problems—which is in itself seen as implicative—but also from the fact that their behavior is not uncommon and considered inappropriate to their age group. The middle-aged heavy drinker may indeed have changed his drinking style as part of his gravitation into an enclaved subculture, but the more important fact is that those around him changed their drinking habits. The emphasis on surreptitious drinking in the classical Alcoholics Anonymous drinking history is an indication of this ecological problem for the middle-aged heavy drinker.[62]

By focusing over time on what it is people do with drinking that gets them into trouble with other people, the work of the Social Research Group has evolved into a "drinking problem perspective." The departure from a clinical perspective was enunciated early on by Knupfer:

> We wish to avoid getting into the question, "what is a real alcoholic?" or "does the person have the disease called alcoholism?" We take the point of view that a problem—any problem—connected fairly closely with drinking constitutes a drinking problem.[63]

In other words, for the clinician the term "problem drinker" excludes "alcoholics"; for the Social Research Group the term "problem drinker" includes "alcoholics." While granting that benefits have derived from the disease concept in the form of increased treatment facilities and expanded support of research, their perspective continues to lead them along a line of questioning antithetical to the concept of a clear-cut alcoholic syndrome. Cahalan and Cisin [64] have warned that by implying an all-or-nothing division point between alcoholics and non-alcoholics, the disease concept provides an out for the problem drinker, who continues to maintain "I'm not an alcoholic yet." Roizen, Cahalan, and Shanks have employed an ironic touch, using the language of the disease model to undermine its basic precept. They report that analysis of general population data suggests there is a substantial amount of "spontaneous remission" from alcohol-related problems, i.e., that a number of people "recover" without treatment.[65] And Room has drawn attention to the gap in our understanding of just how the problem drinker becomes an "alcoholic" by entering the clinic population, an area only partially examined in the work of Wiseman [66] and Bigus.[67] To quote Room:

> Presumably admission to a clinic often involves a lengthy process of wearing out the patience of everyone in the potential client's immediate environment; the clinic is a last resort when all social resources have been exhausted, often after the client has lost both spouse and job. Frequently the major potential function of the clinic for the client who wishes to re-establish himself is to serve as a vouching agency which may help to revive his credibility and social credit with those outside the clinic door.[68]

The Issue of Social Control

Eroding the disease concept has not been reflected only in the work of the Social Research Group. Comments such as that made at a public hearing, "maybe the time has come to un-disease alcoholism," have been made by people who had looked upon the concept as beneficial, and now see, ". . . our current unreflecting medicalization of almost all public problems is itself becoming a major health problem." [69] One segment of concern centers around the clash between the general ideology of voluntary treatment as against the clinical compulsion that "something has to be done." By increasing the number of treatment facilities and buying into the concept of alcoholism as a disease, NIAAA has institutionalized this concept—some feel replacing one stigma with another.

Sociologists and psychiatrists of the labeling school of thought had dealt with one aspect of medicalizing a social problem, suggesting that the designation of a "sick role" could in some cases make people worse not better, that a double bind results from the dual messages.[70] On the one hand, the assignment "sick" may legitimize deviant drinking as being caused by a pathology rather than inappropriate behavior; on the other, the labeling process may lead to a change in the individual's self-concept and in the way he is seen by others, with the result that the behavior which is assigned is carried out.[71]

There is yet a broader issue: criticism of the medicalization of a host of social problems, not just alcohol use, has centered around the fact that removal of penal sanctions does not mean removal of social control. As Zola argues, the medical model is not a neutral one, but merely an alternative strategy for securing desired social change—with implications, such as "what happens when a problem and its bearers become tainted with the label 'illness'?" [72] The crucial variable which Zola highlights ties in with labeling theory: the existence of a power imbalance. A social illness is by definition to be eliminated, regardless of the wish of the individual. The illness is only to be diagnosed and treated by certain specified and licensed and mandated officials, and the patient has little right of appeal to the label-diagnosis. Szasz, too, had raised the question of involuntary treatment, the issue which had excited the civil-liberties lawyers. Comparing the alcoholic to a Jehovah's Witness who refuses blood transfusion in spite of a bleeding ulcer, Szasz said some alcoholics simply do not wish to be "treated":

> The ordinary medical patient, let us remember, has the right to be sick and refuse treatment. When we proclaim the alcoholic as sick, are we prepared to accord him the same right? Or do we intend to view his illness as similar to mental disease—that is, as a condition for which the patient lacks understanding and one, moreover, that threatens the safety of others—and hence prescribe involuntary treatment for it? [73]

While most alcoholic treatment is voluntary, there is usually coercion from others, most often family, but as government increasingly funds industrial and community outreach programs in search of "the hidden alcoholic." from these sources as well. AA meetings are held in jails or in the county hospital ward. In some places, attendance at AA meetings is checked during parole; in others a sentence for drunken driving may be commuted if the driver agrees to take Antabuse (a drug that causes a violent physical reaction if combined with alcohol ingestion).

Clearly, questionable uses of authority should be individually judged, but terms like "social control" and "power imbalance" have strong imagery which do not pick up the degree of severity that must be addressed if one is going to consider the issue of coercion. It is a legal axiom that protective privilege ends where the public peril begins, so that programs addressed to convicted drunken drivers cannot be equated with community outreach (early case finding) programs. Although even here the lines are not so clear, for presumably the "early case" is a potential drunken driver. Obviously, the presence of *any* authority throws a moral-ethical blanket over the "deviant." Experience has shown that a social services model would not eliminate social control and power imbalance.

Regarding family pressure, some have argued that rather than coercion, family reaction is more frequently denial; that the label "alcoholic" is withheld long after evidence for the problem is clearly available. Robins suggests this is a consequence of the matter illuminated by the drinking-problem theorists, that because there is no sharp breaking point in the drinking continuum, "a decision that the limits of social drinking have been crossed tends to be deferred until the criteria have been met beyond any doubt." [74]

What seems to be ignored in discussions of social coercion, is the empirical reality of people who *feel afflicted* by their dependence on alcohol—those who are asking society for help. People who are experiencing a disorder that is difficult for themselves and/or others would quite likely consider the voluntary/involuntary issue an academic irrelevance. Wittman has drawn attention to the interweaving of treatment types with client circumstances—the homeless alcoholic goes to a center with beds and meals, while the one with a home seeks out a non-residential treatment center.[75] The important component of the centers seems to be that they provide an environment where a person can experiment with abstinence, a convivial setting where people can look at their lives, amid peer and counseling support, and get out of their drinking pattern *if they want to.* In many of the psychodynamic techniques discussed in the previous chapter, the counselor is not in a position of authority, but serves more as a group catalyst. If the growth of these techniques (and of the social model discussed next) results in the replacement of a disease ideology with a mutual-support model, some degree of coercion may be reduced. In any case, the foregoing debate illustrates the manner in which the redefining process is influenced by a complexity of opposing viewpoints. Both the disease proponents and the drinking-problem proponents are concerned with replacing a punitive with a humanitarian approach. Differences between them regarding the route to this goal (the issue of social control is one dimension) are developed in subsequent chapters.

Old Wine in New Bottles

Occurring amid the counter-positioning of the clinical and the drinking-problem perspectives has been another development of note. There may not be a clear-cut shift away from the disease concept of alcoholism in California, nor a marriage of the clinical and the drinking-problem perspectives, but the two concepts—or their advocates at least—may end up living together.

Detoxification is a term that came along in the wake of the disease concept, a term of unknown origin, suggesting, like "intoxication," roots in the temperance concept of the drunkard's addiction to the poison, alcohol. (One respondent suggested that "detoxification center" was chosen in preference to "sobering-up station," an Eastern European term, and consequently too left-wing for the time.) The first "detox centers" were in hospitals where many different things were (and still are) used or done under this rubric—pills, vitamins, blood tests, acute care for complications arising from alcohol use. These centers grew out of the initial move to get public inebriates out of jail and into treatment through the Uniform Alcoholism and Intoxication Treatment Act of 1971. But this did not mean that such units sprang up all over the country. In California, where the legislative policy has existed since 1969, only a few counties have initiated the civil option procedures provided for in the statute, and even in these counties, the detoxification alternative has not eliminated arrest and jail as a means of addressing the public inebriate problem.[76] In jail, the alcoholic "dries-out" without medication or personal contact. In the hospital, symptoms are treated with drugs, but often personal contact is hostile. In either case, alcoholics are dismissed to return to their previous environment, usually without referral.

In reaction to these perceived deficiencies, social setting detoxification has emerged. Two related conditions discussed earlier have contributed toward this development: the self-help movement and the disagreeable experience of many recovered alcoholics in relation to the health services. Taylor's observation concerning one facet of the self-help movement is relevant:

> On one level the growth of the self-help movement is part of a general process of the democratization and demystification of professional skills. Nurse-practitioners and Physician's Assistants take on increasing numbers of functions once zealously monopolized by physicians . . . The same movement is occurring today in dentistry; it occurred long ago in psychiatry as social workers began to share most psychiatric functions except for prescribing medication. The same development continues in psychiatry, with the development of the "human potential" movement and such mass forms of "treatment" as Transcendental Meditation, biofeedback, EST Seminars, Scientology, and the encounter group movement.[77]

One important component of the acceptability of social setting detoxification is its drug-free, doctor-free nature. Another is that it surmounts the disease/problem-drinker dichotomy. Operating on the premise that genetic, biochemical and metabolic factors *may* determine *who* becomes an alcoholic, the basic tenent is that alcoholism does not depend solely upon what happens inside the victim, but largely upon the personal and social surroundings within which he lives. "He must be extricated from contexts in which the message *drink* is present, and placed in a context in which another set of messages is dominant." [78] Medication is not used in social setting detoxification centers: "Recovery is facilitated instead by person-to-person contact. Individuals in a toxic state from the effects of acute alcoholism are assured that someone is going to stay with them until they feel better." [79] Proponents claim that an unusually low number of clients experience withdrawal symptoms in such a setting. This is partially explained by the high proportion of recovered alcoholics among the residential assistants: "a counselor's ability to reassure the hallucinating patient on the basis of his own experience appears to be a major reason for the rapid decrease of symptoms and the general well-being of the clients." [80] An expression of the inherent medical antipathy came from one respondent:

> The whole medical mystique will freak you out if you're lying in a bed with all these white coats standing around talking Latiny phrases at you. But if you're in a place where the environment is engineered so as to precipitate those kinds of reactions—five to eight percent of the alcoholic population actually need acute medical attention.

Another summarized the advantage as follows:

> In medical detox, except for complications, there's nothing you can do medically anyway. The body will metabolize alcohol at a set rate, but there's no way to speed that up. What happens is that physicians use drugs because they don't have time to do anything else. Social setting is what a physician would do if he had the time.

Opposition came initially from the medical profession. To quote another respondent, "They didn't want to treat alcoholics but they didn't want anybody else to treat them." This attitude is changing, particularly following a study which found that non-medical personnel could be trained to recognize conditions requiring referral to medical backup.[81] Most significant were the plaudits of Dr. Jack Gordon, who conducted all the medical evaluations for the study. Weighed against Dr. Gordon's expertise in (and support of) medical detoxification, his comment in the final report. "I think we're ready to get (alcoholism) out of the mainstream of medicine and get it into the behavioral side where it is much more appropriate." has heightened impact.

The pacesetter of this approach, the Guerrero Street Program in San Francisco, is patterned after a model developed and implemented in Canada by N. William Petersen. Petersen, who directs the San Francisco Program, and Dr. Robert O'Briant, the other early advocate of this model, have always stressed the continuum of recovery—that detoxification must be followed by suitable referral to an individually suited recovery home. In California, these units have set the tone for an ideology which is developing in many recovery homes, called a "social model." Simply stated, responsibility is squarely placed on the individual, but with an expressed understanding of the community reinforcement sobriety requires. Proponents speak of a "continuum of relationship building" of "social growth"; staff members are "guides," "role models," "relate as peers." There is "follow-through" not "follow-up"; there are "recovery services" not "facilities." [82] The word "treatment" is assiduously avoided, for the goal is much less ambitious than cure of disease would imply. Substituted is an "exit plan," whereby the person examines his needs (food, housing finances, leisure time) and assesses how he will attend to them.

Whether acknowledged or not, the social model is compatible with the self-help mutual support aspect of the psychological techniques discussed earlier, but bears a closer relationship to AA, shorn of the spiritual and disease components. AA's emphasis on social fellowship separates it from the psychological concept of behavioral modification. In many ways, AA is its own world; members have their own parties, get married, have children, all within that world. Similarly, the social model recovery homes have alumni groups, pot luck dinners and other planned social activities for those trying to adjust "outside."

As indicated earlier, the leadership of the California Association of Alcoholic Recovery Homes is heavily inclined toward this model, a position fortified by the admission to their organization of social setting detoxification centers. One gets the impression when talking to proponents that social setting "detox" is the universal panacea for which this arena has been waiting. It *is* appropriate for a large group of people, but as respondents pointed out, its success is directly related to the fact that it is a self-selected group. Residents have to be able to walk in unassisted, or with slight assistance; they have to want to stop drinking; they have to be willing to risk a drug-free withdrawal. Often forgotten is that for some the medical aura still exists:

> For some people if we say we're going to put you in a place where they are going to talk you down it will be a deterrent, but if I say you'll be put in clean sheets and taken care of as a medical case for whatever time you need. . . .

Also, it is important to remember that most people with alcohol problems do not present themselves while intoxicated, so detoxification centers are not the only entry point for recovery; conversely, many who need care, notably public inebriates, have little contact with such homes. A considerable problem, as explained by a county administrator, is the fact that the popularity of this approach has led to the abused notion that non-medical detox and social setting detox are synonymous:

> Some of the anti-medical/psychological people interpreted social setting to mean that now we have permission to practice our anti-program, and this aligns the county administrator against these programs. Because by its nature it's not well-defined, I can open an operation that does nothing else but have people attending AA meetings every hour of the day, and demand my share of the pot to run a social model program that everybody says is the way to go. Which puts the county administrator in a position of saying that's all well and good but you've got beds piled up three high, you're forcing people to respond to a particular approach that is too narrow for me to allocate limited funds. The lack of definition has left us in turmoil.

In spite of these impediments, this approach signifies an attempt to redefine the problem of alcohol use beyond the moral and/or disease concepts.

Summary

The complex interplay of worlds described in this chapter laid the groundwork for the burgeoning of the arena that has occurred in recent years. Hence this chapter and the one preceding it provide a larger picture against which the animating process discussed in Part II can now be assessed.

In this chapter we have examined the conditions that led to a disease concept of alcoholism:

- the philosophical stance of American pragmatism, and its relationship to the clinical perspective;
- the growth of the health professions and institutions;
- the veneration of scientific thought;
- the beneficence of foundations;
- the intertwining of civil rights law with a constituency of recovered alcoholics.

Also examined are the conditions that have undermined the disease concept:

- the philosophical stance dealing with the relativity of social reality;
- the growth of a labeling school in sociology and an anti-psychiatry perspective in psychiatry;
- the development of a drinking-problem perspective;
- the questioning of the humanitarian aspects of the disease concept as it relates to the issue of social control.

Finally, I have introduced the philosophy behind social setting detoxification and the social model of recovery, *and* the relationship of these movements to the self-help movement and to the historical antipathy many recovered alcoholics harbor toward the health professions.

Since the goal of the social model of recovery is to prepare the recovered alcoholic for adjustment "outside," it is important to look at the way the "outside" must also be prepared—in other words, at the attempts to reduce the stigma of alcoholism. It is to this we turn now.

Notes

1. "Thoughts on Definitions of Terms," *The Hearth*, (January, 1977).
2. Nils Christie and Kettil Bruun, "The Conceptual Framework," in Keller and Coffey (eds), *Proceedings of the 28th Int. Congress on Alcohol and Alcoholism*, Vol. 2 (Highland Park, N.J.: Hillhouse Press, 1969), p. 70.
3. John Seeley, "Alcoholism Is a Disease: Implications for Social Policy," in D. Pittman and C. Snyder (eds.), *Society, Culture and Drinking Patterns* (New York: John Wiley & Sons, 1962), p. 593.
4. Interview with Ernest Noble: Lewis, "Washington Report," *Journal of Studies on Alcohol*, Vol. 2 (1974), p. 1388.
5. *See:* Seldon D. Bacon, "The Classic Temperance Movement," *British Journal of Addiction*, Vol. 62 (1967); Joseph Gusfield, (1967) "Moral Passage: The Symbolic Process in Public Designations of Deviance," *Social Problems*, Vol. 15 (1967), pp. 175-88; and Harry Gene Levine, *Demon of the Middle-Class: Self-Control, Liquor and the Ideology of Temperance in 19th Century America.* (Ph.D. dissertation, University of California, Berkeley, 1978).
6. Asylum manager quoted by David Rothman, *The Discovery of the Asylum; Social Order and Disorder In The New Republic* (Boston: Little Brown, 1971), p. 212.

7. Harry G. Levine, "The Curse of the Middle Class: Social Problems and the Anti-Alcohol Movement" (Unpublished dissertation prospectus, University of California, Berkeley, 1975), p. 20.

8. *See:* Harry G. Levine, "The Discovery of Addiction: Changing Conceptions of Habitual Drunkenness in America," *Journal of Studies on Alcohol,* Vol. 39 (1978), pp. 143-174; James H. Timberlake, *Prohibition and the Progressive Movement* 1900-1920 (New York: Atheneum, 1970); Richard Hofstadter, *The Age of Reform* (New York; Alfred A. Knopf. 1955); and Ernest H. Cherrington, *The Evolution of Prohibition in the United States of America* (Montclair, N.J.: Patterson Smith, 1st ed. 1920, 2nd ed. 1969).

9. *See, for example:* Joseph Gusfield, *Symbolic Crusade: Status Politics and the American Temperance Movement* (Urbana: University of Illinois Press, 1963); Gusfield, "Moral Passage"; John Kobler, *Ardent Spirits: The Rise and Fall of Prohibition* (New York: G.P. Putnam, 1973); Peter H. Odegard, *Pressure Politics: The Story of the Anti-Saloon League* (New York: Columbia University Press, 1968), Andrew Sinclair, *Era of Excess: A Social History of the Prohibition Movement* (New York: Harper, 1964).

10. *See:* Richard Hofstadter, *Social Darwinism in American Thought* (New York: Alfred A. Knopf, 1955).

11. T.H. Marshall, "The Welfare State and the Affluent Society," in T.H. Marshall, *Class, Citizenship and Social Development* (Garden City, N.Y.: Doubleday and Co., Inc., 1964), pp. 257-58.

12. L. Schatzman and A. Strauss, "A Sociology of Psychiatry," *Social Problems,* Vol. 14 (1966), p. 12.

13. S.D. Bacon, "Concepts," in W.J. Filstead et al. (eds.), *Alcohol, New Thinking and New Directions* (Cambridge, Mass.: Ballinger, 1976), p. 94.

14. *See:* Gerald E. Markowitz and David Karl Rosner, "Doctors in Crisis: A Study of the Use of Medical Education Reform to Establish Modern Professional Elitism in Medicine," *American Quarterly,* Vol. 45, (1973), pp. 84-107.

15. For the history of this period, *see:* Elton Rayack, *Professional Power and American Medicine* (Cleveland: World, 1967); and Rosemary Stevens, *American Medicine and the Public Interest* (New Haven: Yale University Press, 1971).

16. Edward Sagarin, *Odd Man In* (Chicago: Quadrangle Books, 1972), p. 30.

17. Bacon, "Concepts," p. 104.

18. J.F. Mueller and Terrie Schwerdtfeger, "The Role of the Nurse in Counseling the Alcoholic," *Journal of Psychiatric Nursing and Mental Health Services,* Vol. 12 (1974), p. 26.

19. See Chapter 3 and Chapter 5.

20. Mark Keller, "Problems with Alcohol: An Historical Perspective," in W.J. Filstead, J.J. Rossi and M. Keller (eds.), *Alcohol, New Thinking and New Directions.* (Cambridge, Mass.: Ballinger, 1976), pp. 21-22.

21. Markowitz and Rosner, "Doctors in Crisis."

22. Mark Keller, "Multidisciplinary Perspectives," *Journal of Studies on Alcohol,* Vol. 36 (1975).

23. Smithers Foundation, *Understanding Alcoholism: For the Patient, The Family, and The Employer* (New York: Scribners, 1968).

24. *See:* Norman R. Kurtz, and Marilyn Regier, "The Uniform Alcoholism and Intoxication Treatment Act: The Compromising Process of Social Policy Formulation," *Journal of Studies on Alcohol,* Vol. 36 (1975), pp. 1421-41; and B.C. Hollister, "Alcoholics and Public Drunkenness: The Emerging

Retreat From Punishment," *Crime and Delinquency*, Vol. 16 (1970), pp. 238-54.

25. Robin Room, "Comment on 'The Uniform Alcoholism and Intoxication Treatment Act,'" *Journal of Studies on Alcohol*, Vol. 37 (1976), pp. 113-44.

26. *Ibid.*, p. 120.

27. *Ibid.*, p. 114.

28. E.M. Jellinek, "Phases in the Drinking History of Alcoholics," *Quarterly Journal of Studies on Alcohol*, Vol. 7 (1964), pp. 1-88; and E.M. Jellinek, "Phases of Alcohol Addiction," *Quarterly Journal of Studies on Alcohol*, Vol. 13 (1952), pp. 673-84.

29. Bacon, "Concepts," p. 96.

30. E.M. Jellinek, *The Disease Concept of Alcoholism* (New Haven: College and University Press, 1960).

31. Room, "Comment," p. 121.

32. *See:* remarks of Dr. Frank Seixas, Medical Director, National Council on Alcoholism, New York, in Neil Kessel, Ann Hawker and Herbert Chalk (eds.), *Alcoholism: A Medical Profile,* proceedings of the First International Medical Conference on Alcoholism, London, September 10-14, 1973 (London: B. Edsell & Co., Ltd., 1974), p. 20.

33. National Council on Alcoholism, "Criteria for the Diagnosis of Alcoholism," *American Journal of Psychiatry.* Vol. 129 (1972), pp. 127-216.

34. Genevieve Knupfer, "Ex-Problem Drinkers," in Merrill Roff, Lee Robins and Max Polack (eds.), *Life History Research in Psychopathology*, Vol. 2 (Minneapolis, Minn.: University of Minnesota Press, 1972), p. 258.

35. "AMA" Extends Alcoholism Policy," *The Journal*, Toronto, Vol. 1 (August, 1972), p. 11.

36. M.E. Chafetz, "Alcohol Excess," *Annals of the New York Academy of Sciences.* Vol. 133 (1966), p. 810.

37. Keller, "Multidisciplinary Perspectives," p. 145.

38. *The Alcoholism Report,* Vol. 4 (January 9, 1976), p. 2.

39. *The Alcoholism Report,* Vol. 3 (May 9, 1975), p. 3.

40. Richard S. Shore and John M. Luce, *To Your Health* (New York: The Seabury Press, 1976), p. 159.

41. Morton White, *Social Thought in America.* (Boston: Beacon Press, 1947), p. 65.

42. Edward M. Scott, "An Attempt at Reworking the Definition and Dynamics of Alcoholism," paper presented to the North American Congress on Alcohol and Drug Problems, San Francisco, December, 1974.

43. Emile Durkheim, *The Elementary Forms of the Religious Life* (New York: The Free Press, 1st ed. 1915, paperback 1965).

44. William Graham Summer, *Folkways* (New York: Mentor, 1961).

45. Randall Collins and Michael Makowsky, *The Discovery of Society* (New York: Random House, 1972), p. 71.

46. *See for example:* Willard Waller, "Social Problems and the Mores," *American Sociological Review,* Vol. 1 (1936), pp. 922-32; Richard C. Fuller, and Richard Myers, "Some Aspects of a Theory of Social Problems," *American Sociological Review,* Vol. 6 (1941), pp. 24-32.

47. Fuller and Myers, "Some Aspects." p. 25.

48. *See for example:* Edwin M. Lemert, *Social Pathology* (New York: McGraw-Hill; 1951); Howard S. Becker. *Outsiders: Studies in the Sociology of*

Deviance (New York: The Free Press. 1963); John I. Kitsuse. "Societal Reaction to Deviant Behavior," in Earl Rubington and Martin S. Weinberg (eds.), *Deviance/The Interactionist Perspective* New York: The MacMillan Co., 1970), pp. 19-29; and Kai T. Erikson. "Notes on the Sociology of Deviance" *Social Problems*, Vol. 9 (1962), pp. 307-14.

49. Becker, *Outsiders*, p. 14.
50. Gusfield, "Moral Passage."
51. Gusfield, *Symbolic Crusade.*
52. Gusfield, "The (F)Utility of Knowledge?" *Annals of the American Academy of Social Science and Drug Policy*, Vol. 417 (1975), p. 10.
53. *See for example:* Ronald D. Laing, *The Politics of Experience* (New York: Ballantine Books, (1969); Edwin Fuller Torrey, *The Death of Psychiatry* (Radnor, Pa.: Chilton Book Co.., 1974); Richard Korn, "The Autoplastic Self-Changing Solution and Its Treatment: Medical Models of Deviance and Therapy," in National Commission on Marihuana and Drug Abuse, *Drug Use in America: Problem in Perspective*, The Technical Papers of the 2nd Report, Vol. 4, Treatment and Rehabilitation, Washington, D.C., G.P.O., 1973; and David Cooper, *Psychiatry and Anti-Psychiatry* (New York; Ballantine Books, 1967).
54. Thomas Szasz, "Bad Habits Are Not Diseases: A Refutation of the Claim that Alcoholism is a Disease," *The Lancet*, Vol. 2 (1972), p. 84.
55. See Chapter 2.
56. Selden D. Bacon. "Sociology and the Problems of Alcohol: Foundations for a Sociologic Study of Drinking Behavior," *Quarterly Journal of Studies of Alcohol*, Vol. 4 (1943), pp. 402-45. For an analysis of the contrast between the Jellinek and Bacon approaches, *see:* Robin Room, "Priorities in Alcohol Social Science Research," paper prepared for presentation at the Symposium on Research Priorities, Rutgers Center of Alcohol Studies, New Brunswick, N.J., October 7-9, 1977.
57. *See for example:* Robert Bales, "Cultural Differences in Rates of Alcoholism," *Quarterly Journal of Studies on Alcohol*, Vol. 16 (1946), pp. 482-98; Robert Straus and Selden Bacon, *Drinking in College* (New Haven: Yale University Press, 1953); and Albert D. Ullman. "Sociocultural Backgrounds of Alcoholism," *Annals of the American Academy of Political and Social Science*, Vol. 315 (1958). pp. 48-54.
58. *See:* Ronald Roizen. "Drinking and Drinking Problems: Some Notes on the Ascription of Problems to Drinking," paper presented at the Epidemiology Section meeting, 21st International Institute on the Prevention and Treatment of Alcoholism, Helsinki, Finland, June, 1975.
59. Robin Room, "The Social Psychology of Drug Dependence," in *The Epidemiology of Drug Dependence*, report on a conference organized under the auspices of the Regional Office for Europe of the World Health Organization and the United Kingdom Department of Health and Social Security, Copenhagen, September, 1972, pp. 69-75.
60. *See:* W.B. Clark, "Operational Definitions of Drinking Problems and Associated Prevalence Rates," *Quarterly Journal of Studies on Alcohol*, Vol. 27 (1966), pp. 648-68; W.B. Clark and Don Cahalan, "Changes in Problem Drinking Over a Four-Year Span," paper presented at the annual meeting of the American Public Health Association, San Francisco, November, 1973; and Don Cahalan and Robin Room, *Problem Drinking Among*

American Men (New Brunswick, N.J.: Rutgers Center of Alcohol Studies, 1974).

61. Robin Room, "Measurement and Distribution of Drinking Patterns and Problems in General Populations," in G. Edwards, M.M. Gross, M. Keller, J. Moser and R. Room (eds.), *Alcohol-Related Disabilities* (Geneva: World Health Organization offset publication #32, 1977), p. 80.

62. *Ibid.,* p. 83.

63. Genevieve Knupfer, "The Epidemiology of Problem Drinking," *American Journal of Public Health,* Vol. 57 (1967), p. 974.

64. Don Cahalan and Ira Cisin, "Drinking Behavior and Drinking Problems in the United States," in Benjamin Kissin and Henri Begleiter (eds.), *The Biology of Alcoholism: Volume 4; Social Biology* (New York: Plenum Press, 1976), pp. 77-115.

65. Ronald Roizen, Don Cahalan and Patricia Shanks, " 'Spontaneous Remission' Among Untreated Problem Drinkers," in Denise Kandel (ed.), *Longitudinal Research on Drug Use: Empirical Findings and Methodological Issues* (Washington, D.C.: Hemisphere Press, 1978).

66. J.P. Wiseman, *Stations of the Lost* (Englewood Cliffs, N.J.: Prentice-Hall, 1970).

67. Bigus, *Becoming "Alcoholic"* (Ph.D. Dissertation, University of California, 1974).

68. Room, "Measurement and Distribution of Drinking Patterns and Problems," p. 82.

69. Dan Edward Beauchamp, "Comment on the Uniform Alcoholism and Intoxication Treatment Act," *Journal of Studies on Alcohol,* Vol. 37 (1976), p. 1112.

70. Paul M. Roman and H.M. Trice, "The Sick Role, Labelling Theory, and the Deviant Drinker," *International Journal of Social Psychology,* Vol. 14, (1968), pp. 245-51.

71. For a discussion of this process, *see:* E.M. Lemert, "The Concept of Secondary Deviation," *Human Deviance, Social Problems and Social Control* (Englewood Cliffs, N.J.: Prentice-Hall, 1967).

72. Irving Kenneth Zola, "In the Name of Health and Illness: On Some Socio-Political Consequences of Medical Influence," *Social Science and Medicine,* Vol. 2 (1975), p. 85.

73. Thomas Szasz, "Alcoholism: A Socio-Ethical Perspective," *Washburn Law Journal,* Vol. 6 (1966-67), p. 262.

74. Lee N. Robins, "Alcoholism and Labeling Theory," in Walter R. Gove (ed.), *The Labeling of Deviance* (New York: Sage Publications, 1075), p. 30.

75. Friedner Wittman, "Alcoholism and Architecture," paper presented at the American Institute of Architects meeting, Los Angeles, January, 1971. *See also:* Sidney Cahn, "Alcoholism Halfway Houses: Relationships to Other Programs and Facilities," *Social Work,* Vol. 14 (1969), pp. 50-60.

76. Steve Thompson and associates, "An Overview of State Alcoholism Services," report submitted to the Senate Health and Welfare Committee, State of California, 1975, p. 4.

77. Mary C. Taylor, *Alcoholics Anonymous,* Ph.D. dissertation (1977), pp. 178-179.

78. Robert G. O'Briant, Henry L. Lennard, Steven D. Allen, and Donald C. Ransom, "Recovery from Alcoholism: A Social Treatment Model," *Alcohol Health and Research World,* (Fall 1973), p. 27.

79. R.G. O'Briant, "Social Setting Detoxification," *Alcohol Health and Research World,* (Winter 1974/1975), p. 15. *See also:* R.G. O'Briant, L. Lennard, S. Allen, and D.C. Ransom, *Recovery From Alcoholism* (Springfield, Ill.: Charles C. Thomas, 1973).

80. R.G. O'Briant, "Social Setting Detoxification," p.15.

81. Guerrero Street Program, San Francisco, "A Medical Evaluation of the Safety of Non-Hospital Detoxification," report prepared for National Institute on Alcohol Abuse and Alcoholism, October, 1976. *For summary see:* Robert O'Briant, N. William Petersen, and Dana Heacock, "How Safe is Social Setting Detoxification?" *Alcohol Health and Research World,* (Winter 1976/1977), pp. 22-27.

82. See Chapter 3.

8.

Building Respectability

Legitimizing the problem of alcohol use by *building* its *respectability* is a concern that runs throughout the history of this arena.

As we have seen, behind the disease concept was an interest in improving the public image of the alcoholic, a goal of replacing punitive measures with humane services. This was a reciprocal interest among the worlds involved in the arena. Out of Yale came the development of a community outpatient clinic approach to the treatment of alcoholics, and the discovery (through a study of male patients seen in nine Yale Plan Clinics) [1] that their clientele came from "the more stable elements of society." [2] Equal credit is given to the fame AA received in the 1940s, which not only expanded its own capacity, but helped the Yale Center "by reinforcing the teaching that alcoholics were not all skid row bums, that they could be rehabilitated." [3] Keller adds that this, in turn, helped the center in reinforcing the teaching that there were other things to do about alcohol problems (e.g. help its victims) than just to fight alcohol. And, he reports, it also served as an inspiration for many church people and "less rigidly doctrinaire temperance people" to take a new look at *their* ideologies about alcohol.

Distinguishing the alcoholic from the prevailing stereotype of the skid row image became an important turning point. To quote Room:

> A major thrust of the disease concept was to find, save, and preserve the
> social status of the hidden "respectable" alcoholic; the Skid Row stereo-
> type was seen as a small and overpublicized part of the problem.[4]

Straus affirms that the prototype Yale Plan Clinics of 1944 and similar
programs which developed throughout the country in the late 1940's
often justified their original funding by promising to reduce the public
investment in jails and mental hospitals, but he presents the emergence
of this newly recognized, more stable, clientele as unexpected. Room
agrees, taking issue with Kurtz and Regier's portrayal of the alcoholism
movement's cynically *using* skid row as a "threatening image" to secure
public financing of alcoholism programs.[5] Furthermore, Room counters,
most of those involved in the alcoholism movement continued to regard
the public inebriate as a millstone, discussed as a "special problem" in
carefully segregated sections of comprehensive reports such as that of the
Cooperative Commission.[6]

In this chapter, we shall examine the course the respectability process
has taken: the publicity given prominent recovered alcoholics; the enhanced status provided by interested legislators and a national institute;
the softening of language; the improved image inherent in the establishment of a clearinghouse for information, an epidemiology division
within NIAAA and of research centers devoted solely to problems of
alcohol use. Also explained is the manner in which the disease concept is
related to the drive for respectability, specifically as a means of buying
into the health insurance institutions. Next, we shall look at more recent
developments in the process of building respectability which, in effect,
represent a continuation of the *redefining* process: the search for, and
implications of, a "disability" definition of alcoholism.

Respectable People, Respectable Language

As stated earlier, AA's anonymity made it difficult to call upon that
segment of the volunteer-action world to make respectability a visible
concern—a gap that was filled by the formation of the National Council
on Alcoholism. This group continues in its educational capacity to re-
mind the public that most alcoholics have a family, are paying off a
house, have a job, can go weeks without drinking. NCA's drive for a
respectable image has been assisted recently by what W.H. Auden characterized some years back as an increasing readiness on the part of many
to take their clothes off in front of total strangers. Whether it be President Carter sharing with Playboy Magazine his heartfelt lust, or Dave
Kopay the homosexuality he encountered in the world of football, the

need for self-revelation has made itself felt, and, as one popular colum-
nist has put it, "closet doors are banging open all around us." [7] This
trend has been advantageous to the arena, for just as movie stars and
politician's wives have turned their mastectomies into public service announcements for the American Cancer Society, celebrities have revealed
their problems with alcohol in order to reduce social disapproval and
encourage others to seek help. Much publicity was given a panel of fifty
prominent citizens (entertainers, sports and political figures, clergymen,
journalists, businessmen, even an astronaut) which highlighted the National Council's 1976 meeting.[8] Drawing upon the success of this endeavor, NCA launched the first national speakers bureau on alcoholism,
providing a stable of celebrity recovered alcoholics.[9] Local NCA councils
have an annual Alcohol Action Week, in which the media cooperate
with coverage. In 1976, this took the form of a Sobriety Safari—celebrities who flew all over California to meet scheduled appointments,
"focusing attention for the first time on the 'sober alcoholic,' living proof
that alcoholism can be treatable." [10]

In filling the need for respectable people to legitimate a concern, legislators are especially important. Such spokesmen become the symbolic
means by which an issue becomes personified. Senator Harold Hughes
performed this function for the alcohol use arena as Senator Lister Hill
had done previously when it was still part of NIMH; in California, Senator Arlen Gregorio carried the banner prior to his electoral defeat in
1978. Of course, the very establishment of a separate agency and proclamations of "a national health problem" give increased stature and dig-
nity to the arena, further enchanced by announcements of prestigious
appointments to the NIAAA National Advisory Council. As explained
earlier, in many states no programs had started until NIAAA came upon
the scene. But in some, like California, the funding, while helpful, was
almost secondary to the status that came in NIAAA's wake, as explained
by a respondent:

> NIAAA's money was reliant on there being a single state authority—that
> gave us some prestige, a special blessing from outside. Every time anything
> about alcohol comes up they can now say "that's the state authority."

Language, as well, can be employed as a device to enhance respectability. As we have seen, "alcoholic" as used to suggest disease, was prefera-
ble to "drunk" or "inebriate." Dr. Chafetz, the first director of NIAAA,
attempted a further upgrading, using "alcoholic people." (Using "alcoholic" as a modifier rather than as a noun is meant to emphasize that
alcoholism is an aspect of, rather than the totality of, the sufferer.[11])

The Bureaucratic Route to Respectability

In addition, it behooves any governmental agency to be constantly alert for ways to improve its own status, not only within its problem arena, but among other agencies. NIAAA has followed the route to respectability laid out by other health agencies by establishing a clearinghouse for information, an epidemiology division, and a number of research centers.

Clearinghouses, such as the National Clearinghouse for Alcohol Information (NCALI) discussed previously, [12] are not confined to health arenas. Already operating are National Clearinghouses for Drug Abuse Information, Smoking Information, Mental Health, Health Planning, Criminal Justice, Child Abuse and Neglect, Female Offenders, Disaster Relief, Revenue Sharing, Computer Programs, plus seventeen Educational Resources Information Centers—and this is a partial list. Some are run by the agency itself; others are contracted to a private company as is the National Clearinghouse for Alcohol Information to General Electric Company. It is not within my capabilities, nor would it be my intent, to make any judgment on the service these clearinghouses perform. It is pertinent to say, however, that the establishment of many of them probably caused distress to organizations which considered themselves to be perfectly capable of serving the same publics, if only they were given the money and other resources. Surely the NCALI/Rutgers experience is not unique. For whatever reasons, not the least of which is the impact of computer technology, setting up a clearinghouse seems to rank in the first order of business within the bureaucratic world. Styles for legitimating social problems change from one era to the next, but one could hazard that the rise of clearinghouses in recent years and the fact that they are stretched into smaller and smaller territories, is indicative of their importance in maintaining respectability.

One could also view the 1976 creation of an epidemiology branch within NIAAA as another illustration of prestige seeking, in that it represents the bureaucratic attempt to signal a scientific approach. As explained in a Senate subcommittee report, the objective of this branch is to discover "who is most likely to become an alcoholic, how the problem is distributed geographically and demographically, and patterns of drinking related to alcoholism." [13] One aspect of program for this division is to collect data on the involvement of alcohol in various kinds of casualties, e.g., drowning, suicide, fire and child abuse (the turn this quest has taken is discussed in Chapter 11). Another is to set up a surveillance system of nationally collected data, using as sources agencies like the National Center for Health Statistics, the National Highway Safety Administration, the Department of Justice, in order to measure for trends. The rationale behind the search for more sophisticated statistics will become clarified in later discussion. For now, suffice it to say that NIAAA, as did its predecessors, has engaged in "special purpose borrowing," finding in a subworld of public health, epidemiology, a legitimizing model.

The relationship of this drive for respectability to the research world was made explicit by NIAAA Director Noble:

> . . . we need to make this a more powerful force, bringing the alcoholism researchers into the main line of the research community. I'd like to see people working in the alcohol research area receive recognition for their work by the highest and most prestigious bodies. I'd like to see alcohol research in the same kind of prestigious light as cancer and heart research. We have to bring alcohol research into the mainstream of scientific thought and scientific efforts. It's a big challenge . . . rather than an opportunistic kind of thing where if you can't get funded one place, you go to another to get the funds. I'd like to see the best minds come into the alcohol research field.[14]

To the scattered nature of alcohol research, as noted in Chapter 3, must be added the issue raised by Noble's allusion to opportunism. Some research worlds are more vulnerable than others to the capriciousness of grants/contracts bestowal. The transiency of funds for alcohol research means, as one respondent told me, "it's always a compromise between what is manageable, what can be funded, and what you're interested in." An illustration is the experience of an ichthyologist at the University of California at San Francisco, whose interest in the biological basis of aggression led him to the study of fish as a model system, since fish are naturally aggressive and their environment can be controlled. Approached by a NIAAA representative in its early days, this researcher applied for and was given a grant to study the effect of alcohol on aggression in fish. After four years of funding, the project was singled out for Senator William Proxmire's Golden Fleece Award, by which the senator publicizes what he considers wasteful government expenditures:

> NIAAA seems to be interested in testing what it means to be "stewed to the gills." Or perhaps they want to understand what is really behind the expression, "drinks like a fish." In any case, the application of this "fishy" research to understanding the problems of alcoholism and aggression in humans will not be swallowed hook, line and sinker by the American taxpayer.[15]

The researcher felt badly used. After all, it was NIAAA which had sought him out initially and clued him into "the RFP Game." [16] His rationale, and NIAAA's, was that animal studies have value for certain phenomena—in this case, inducing aggressive behavior in human subjects would raise questions not only of artificiality, but of ethics. But obviously this kind of visibility is not what the arena is seeking.

An attempt to avoid this type of situation and, as Noble suggested, to bring alcohol research into the mainstream of scientific thought, is now underway. The NIAAA announced in October 1977, a series of grants totaling $2 million for the first year, to set up five alcoholism research centers throughout the United States. The Social Research Group of Berkeley's School of Public Health was designated to study "Social Epidemiology of Alcohol Problems" (the only center concentrating its studies in the behavioral sciences); The Salk Institute for Biological Studies in San Diego, "Central Nervous System Effects of Alcohol: Cellular Neurobiology"; University of Colorado, "Genetic Approaches to Neuropharmacology of Ethanol"; Washington University's School of Medicine in St. Louis, "Neurobiology, Genetics, Epidemiology and Alcoholism"; and Mt. Sinai School of Medicine of the City of New York, "Pathologic and Toxic Effects of Alcohol." The program is planned as a five-year effort, to be funded by annual appropriations (with centers receiving up to $1 million annually)—designed to provide scientists "with a stable research environment." [17] That such an endeavor is expected to lend the arena not only knowledge but prestige, is evident from Director Noble's respect for the British Medical Research Council as a model, and his comment that "the English system of support has given that nation's research a very strong base of stability and resulted in a number of Nobel prize winners." [18] This intersection of bureaucratic and research interests ties in with the process discussed in Chapter 3; for the research world this represents an enlargement of turf rights, and a consequence for the arena of an expanded constituency and increased visibility.

Buying into the Health Insurance Institution

It should not be inferred that these three endeavors (a clearinghouse, an epidemiology division and research centers) are solely self-serving for the institute, but rather that whatever consequences each has individually, they all share in the enhancement of respectability. In another area, however, the respectability thrust is more evident, and that is in the pursuit of insurance coverage, or "third-party payments" (e.g., a third party, other than the client or the provider, pays for services).

In light of the previously discussed deficiencies, a logical question is: what is the staying power of the disease concept? Again, Krause's observation [19] is relevant: in those bureaucracies where activity involves direct community intervention for change, "action bureaucracies" develop ideologies to increase the acceptability of their actions to the influenced public. Hence, while individual NIAAA bureaucrats acknowledge flaws in the disease concept, it has been seen as an effective symbol. By removing stigma, it is felt to have increased the client population, and to have made to easier to obtain, and retain, federal funding. Administratively, it was a successful device for getting coverage in Veterans Administration Hospitals. As expressed by former institute Director Chafetz:

> Why was the disease model attractive and acceptable? Because it was a symbolic mechanism of communication, familiar and unfrightening in its acceptability.[20]

It was undoubtedly clear to NIAAA, as to anyone who has lived through the 1960s in the United States, that problem-specific funds are available for a relatively short period of time until public attention gets redirected, and that that time must be used to buy legitimacy in the major social institutions. Poverty programs and the Community Mental Health Program had been started on the premise that eventually, having created demands, local constituencies would continue with services once the federal government stepped out. Experience proved otherwise, particularly since there were limited resources at the local level. In this arena, the incentive of third-party payments has been seen as a means of transcending local funding inadequacies, at least in part, by buying into the health insurance institution. In this endeavor, NIAAA's interests coincided nicely with the worlds of volunteer-action, recovery service and training.

The drive for national certification of personnel began under the opposing tensions of impounded funds and a growing constituency within the recovery service world. John Wolfe, director of the institute's Division of Special Treatment and Rehabilitation Programs, became interested in third-party payments when faced with the possible closure of some "four hundred projects for the poor, Indians, blacks, public inebriates, drinking drivers, troubled employees."[21] In the expectation that a national policy would impart an image of reputability to insurance carriers, a contract was let to Littlejohn Company, a private consulting firm, to establish criteria for certification of personnel. Wolfe envisioned a national certifying body, which he saw as dovetailing with his interest in developing constituencies from among previously ignored minorities.[22] It was Wolfe's notion that a certifying board would serve as a means of bringing these minorities into the mainstream of the arena. Director Chafetz initially supported the national concept and then withdrew support. Some respondents attribute Dr. Chafetz's change of heart to what they see as "the threat of Dr. Wolfe's growing fiefdom." Chafetz has explained this conflict in retrospect:

> Credentialing, historically, creates a sense of elitism and leads to a destruction of humanistic responses. I agreed to spend tax dollars to develop mechanisms whereby state credentialing could become a reality. My reason for going part-way was that this was the only mechanism available to the field of making certain that alcoholic people received their fair share of the third party pie of financing of health care. When the push for national certification became prominent, my position was that if the constituency wished to create a national certifying body that was their prerogative but that I could not rationalize spending tax dollars to support what, in my opinion, is a form of self-indulgency for those who are care providers in the field.[23]

Wolfe subsequently left the institute, and what started out of the motive of obtaining third-party payments continued in turmoil.

Following a motion by the board of directors of the Alcohol and Drug Problems Association (ADPA) in the fall of 1975 to initiate the convening of the major national organizations interested in certification, the NIAAA advisory council instead directed that the institute become the convening agency. After a period of shuffling turf rights (for example Matthew Rose of the National Association of Alcoholism Counselors and Trainers said he would participate but called the plan as conceived by NIAAA "disruptive of efforts underway by his affiliates to establish voluntary certification on a state level"[24]) a panel was convened and charged with identifying issues related to certification. Executive directors of five national associations were named to the panel: the Alcohol and Drug Problems Association (ADPA); the Council of State and Territorial Alcoholism Authorities (CSTAA); the Association of Half-way House Alcoholism Programs (AHHAP); the National Council on Alcoholism (NCA); and the National Association of Alcoholism Counselors and Trainers (NAACT). Rose's contention was that "identifying issues" after the Littlejohn report had already developed standards and procedures was like "reinventing the wheel,"[25] but the administrative considerations extended beyond the question of pinpointing issues. Administrator James Isbister of the Alcohol, Drug Abuse and Mental Health Administration (ADAMHA), NIAAA's parent body, was looking for proof of a *developed constituency* before he was ready to approve the convening and funding of a national certifying body. After additional skirmishing, in which NCA pushed for the formation of a new organization devoted to the certification effort and CSTAA argued against the formation of a new body (CSTAA figuring most prominently as the organization for the job, due to its NIAAA grant to assist the states in their efforts), the panel came up with plans for a national board, only to run into funding difficulties. The timing of the national certification effort, which had started in 1974, had unfortunately coincided with the 1976 Congressional concern over NIAAA grants to national voluntary organizations. After another delay, the panel convinced all concerned that federal funding would only be temporary. Member organizations proposed establishment of a transitional board to phase into permanent status over a three-year period. Although expecting seed money from NIAAA for operating costs, the board still promised eventual self-sufficiency.[26] Expectations were summarized by Jay Lewis:

> Rough estimates devised by a finance subcommittee reportedly pegged first-year costs for the organization at about $160,000, growing to $190,000 by 1981-82. Income from credentialing and testing fees was seen as sparse initially but building to meet most of the costs by the fifth year. Presumably federal as well as private foundation monies would make up the difference in the early years.[27]

A National Commission on Credentialing of Alcoholism Counselors (NCCAC) was established in 1978 (with selection of members based on the panel's recommendations for maximum representation of arena interests), but continued without funding for the first year. At this writing, another delay has been imposed. Following the necessary publication of the contract proposal by the institute, NCCAC found itself in competition with three other bidders: Professional Examination Service, American Personnel and Guidance Association and Kearney Associates. Worse still, the new NIAAA director, John R. DeLuca (installed in April, 1979), reviewed the credentialing contract procedure and decided that it did not meet the HEW-wide "standard of impeccability": the institute's "confidential cost estimate had been published in a newsletter to which all potential offerors may not have had access." [28] It was estimated that recomputing the contract could mean another delay of from three to six months.

It is important to pause at this juncture to draw attention to the thesis of this book. The issue of certification provides an illustration of the inter-connection between the processes discussed so far, and the manner in which these processes are concurrent, not sequential. That this issue bears on *establishing turf rights* and *developing constituencies* is evident from the above. A comment by NCA's director George Dimas spells out a further relationship:

The NCA official said the panel did not know when the counselors would be able to pay for the core costs of the credentialing mechanism themselves since this would depend on activities in a lot of other areas, including enhanced training resources and third-party payment potential.[29]

Legitimizing the problem of alcohol used by *redefining* it as a disease and then by *building respectability* was seen by the worlds of this arena as leading to third-party payments. Action toward this goal required increased *imparting of skills* and *information,* and should augment the development of a budding constituency, the training world. It seems a bit circular that third-party payments were the motivation for the original concept of a national credentialing body, and then were presented by Dimas as a necessary condition if such a body is to subsist. But the point is that around this issue, the sub-processes of *animating the problem* and *legitimizing the problem* became inexorably linked—ultimate end, increased visibility for the entire arena.

A second prong of NIAAA's drive to buy into the health insurance institution focused on upgrading facilities. A contract with the Joint Commission on Accreditation of Hospitals (JCAH) in 1973, led to the creation of standards for facilities, in the hope that accreditation of alcoholism programs by that body would enhance their reputability. Membership on the Accreditation Council for Psychiatric Facilities (AC/PF) of JCAH was held up initially in another turf fight among *four* organizations (NCA, ADPA, AHHAP, and CSTAA) over three seats. This was resolved when all four organizations agreed (after lengthy debate) to present themselves as a coalition, with three members seated and one a secretary, all on a rotating basis—only to run into opposition from some members of the AC/PF as to the seating of *any* alcoholism representatives. In February 1976, the American Psychiatric Association reversed its position and voted to seat the alcoholism group, but eight months later there was another setback when the AC/PF was reorganized and the separate Alcoholism Division was abolished. It was announced that specialist surveyors for alcoholism (and children-adolescents, drug abuse, community mental health centers) would be replaced by generalists, and that the separate accreditation manual for alcoholism and the other specialities would be replaced by uniform standards for all programs.[30] This was followed by assurances from the alcoholism coalition that alcoholism programs will not suffer from the change.[31]

Although a number of facilities have sought accreditation, requests did not flood in. Various explanations were given by respondents: the essential parochialism of the arena, i.e. programs often operate in isolation from the rest of the health care delivery system, and providers are traditionally leery of anything new; a much more sophisticated system of bookkeeping is required than is presently employed by most facilities; there is no immediate pay-off, insurance coverage is still way down the road; costs of accreditation surveys must be borne by providers and range from $500 to over $1000.

The main objection is, however, ideological, as exemplified by the position of the California Association of Alcoholic Recovery Home (CAARH). Obviously, in light of its history,[32] the prospect of accreditation by a hospital, let alone a psychiatric board, is worrisome to this group and exacerbates unresolved issues:

> The confusion and concern surrounding this issue of accreditation, as I see it, is not the accreditation process. I feel that there is a disagreement about some of the standards, especially in the area of treatment. The problem is that alcoholism is an illness of unknown etiology and therefore subject to treatment from a variety of disciplines. I believe that we need to develop standards concerning the use or non-use of psychoactive drugs in the treatment of alcoholism and whether or not some of the questionable modalities, such as aversion therapy, are appropriate treatment for alcoholic people.[33]

This segment of the recovery service world has seen a way around the issue of certification of personnel and of accreditation of facilities, by calling first for certification of *program*. Since 1974, the CAARH leadership has devoted much of its attention to developing standards with an emphasis on "environment," "staff attitude," "what makes it possible for recovery to take place." A working relationship has been established with the California Office of Alcoholism: OA not only accepted CAARH's guidelines as state standards for recovery homes, but got them approved by the scientific committee of the California Medical Association so there would be a medical stamp of approval on non-medical homes; CAARH members serve as consultants in the state's certification program. Nevertheless, CAARH's philosophy is continually threatened by the medical mode which still prevails in the arena. Typical is the indignation of an editorial in CAARH's newsletter addressed to county administrators and insurance brokers who would have homes take out malpractice or professional liability insurance, *and* to homes which are "tempted or coerced" into accepting this directive. *The Hearth* editorial retorts:

> Homes do not engage in "practice" or make professional decisions for residents. . . . If one refers to the State Guidelines for Alcoholic Recovery Homes, it will be seen that "counseling" appears only twice—and then it is in the context of describing what Recovery Homes do not do. . . . Homes

> do not attempt to cure people. . . . Homes provide opportunity and example whereby residents can learn to do those things for themselves.[34]

It should be clarified that CAARH is talking here about *malpractice* insurance, not third-party payments. But this statement highlights the paradoxical relationship between the process of building respectability *vis-à-vis* the insurance world and the process CAARH has embarked on of fostering a non-medical model. A 1975 analysis of the California state-funded alcoholism program caught the irony inherent in present MediCal (the health care plan for needy and low income residents in California) requirements: "on the one hand the state is encouraging non-hospital based detoxification programs and on the other hand only reimbursing hospital detoxification." [35] Further irony lies in the fact that social setting detoxification programs operate at a cost between $25 and $35 a day as compared to hospital detoxification at $150 a day. Obviously, the recovery homes would like to see third-party payments extended to non-hospital detoxification, as recommended in the above report, and to recovery homes as well. But CAARH is understandably wary of MediCal reimbursement, lest it entail the application of medical judgments and medical criteria.

Few insurance policies cover drinking problems.[36] Nevertheless, it is accepted wisdom in the arena that insurance companies are paying for alcoholism symptoms anyway, that "between fifty to eighty percent of the beds in all hospitals are alcohol connected," that "fifty percent of all fracture cases are alcohol connected" (estimates vary between these figures among respondents). From a doctor: "the diagnosis is pancreatitis, gastritis, hepatitis, convulsions, cirrhosis—sometimes we 'forget' to write down due to alcohol." It has not been very long that hospitals have even admitted patients with a diagnosis of alcoholism—open ward acceptance by Mt. Zion Hospital (San Francisco) in 1957 was considered revolutionary at the time, and is still looked upon as a landmark in treatment.[37] Service providers have difficulty understanding the insurance logic. As one industrial counselor put it:

> I can show you the records from my own insurance company that treating alcoholism once and calling it that is a lot cheaper than treating gastrointestinal disorder twice for five straight years, at $5000 a crack against $2500 to treat alcoholism once.

The question for the insurance world is whether utilization would shoot up if alcoholism were openly covered. Even when the state of California proposed to pick up all the premium and administrative costs for a pilot demonstration project for state employees, insurance compa-

nies entered reluctantly. NIAAA has similarly offered incentives—for instance, a $206,000 contract with Blue Cross Association in 1976 for a
"feasibility study" designed to develop "a workable benefit package as
well as the administrative, marketing and educational systems needed to
provide effective alcoholism care." [38]

Guesses from respondents were that insurance companies are ready to
do what somebody else will pay for, and that the best hope lies in employers, e.g., if *they* want alcoholism covered, then the insurance company can work out a rate. However, in a time of economic strain within
the health system, the answer may await national health insurance,
which may turn out to be the real test of just how visible this area has
become.

In the meantime, another curious juxtaposition of worlds has occurred, and NIAAA appears to be finding itself with a new ally. In
keeping with present attempts to cut costs and buy expertise by contracting with private corporations to provide specific services (e.g., laboratory,
emergency room, food operation), a private firm, Comprehensive Care
Corporation, is providing an alcoholism program in a number of hospitals throughout the country (detoxification and a twenty-one day program based on a didactic model). In areas like the San Francisco Bay
Area, where hospitals have overbuilt, filling beds with alcoholic patients
looks much more attractive than in the past—one advantage of "Comp-
Care" programs is that unlike hospitals they can advertise. As this corporation grows (and others copy its format), this segment of the business
world may turn into an effective lobby for third-party payments. Of
course, this would not satisfy the needs of the recovery homes which,
since they are providing much cheaper care, should be entitled to part of
any insurance pie.

Further Attempts to Redefine

In light of the now perceived inadequacies of the disease concept, it is
not surprising to find efforts directed toward moving on to another more
comprehensive, and useful, definition. Thus did NIAAA, through a grant
to the World Health Organization (WHO), help support an interna-
tionally constituted group of investigators charged with developing "Criteria for Identifying and Classifying *Disabilities* Related to Alcohol
Consumption" (emphasis added).[39] Potential rewards were twofold: a
clear-cut disability definition would facilitate buying-in to not only the
health insititutions, but the social disability system (federal disability,
workmen's compensation); drawing on the prestige of the WHO would
hopefully give added legitimation to a disability definition.

Viewed from the above, the work of this group can best be seen as a

beginning. While retaining the concept of a discrete "alcohol-dependence syndrome as a diagnosable condition of great importance," the
final report side-stepped NIAAA's agenda for a definition that is all
encompassing, by pointing out that "many individuals who experience
disabilities related to alcohol consumption are not suffering from the
dependence syndrome, and will not necessarily progress to that syndrome." [40] Nor did the report fully meet WHO's agenda for a definition
valid in all countries, in its emphasis on the culture-specific quality of
definitions of alcoholism: "The relative importance of syndrome-related
disabilities and of disabilities in persons who are not alcohol-dependent
will vary from country to country, and indeed between sub-groups
within a country." [41]

Nevertheless, struggling with a disability definition has implications
for the two perspectives discussed in the previous chapter: the report
takes issue more with the designation of a "problem-drinker" segment of
the alcoholismic population than with the "addicted" segment. Drawing
upon a WHO document on rehabilitation of the disabled,[42] the report
defines disability as "an existing difficulty in performing one or more
activities which in accordance with the subject's age, sex and normative
social role, are generally accepted as essential, basic components of daily
living, such as self-care, social relations and economic activity." [43] Most
salient is the fact that disability may be "short-term, long-term or permanent." Thus the arguments which stem from a problem-drinker perspective (the imprecision of determining the causal role of alcohol, the
sporadicity and unpredictability of problems associated with drinking)
are turned back upon this perspective. The report argues that when a
person cannot be diagnosed confidently as suffering from a dependence
syndrome, one should not take too fixed a position on the *person* as
opposed to the *disability,* asserting that it is unwise to attach a predictive
label such as "problem drinker" to that person.

Notwithstanding this family fight over fine points, the guiding motivation is a more humanitarian approach—the assumption being that the
word "disability" invites a more sympathetic and person-directed appraisal than the word "problem," and that a disability definition moves
beyond distinctions between dependent and non-dependent drinkers in
favor of the position that disabilities are experienced by both groups.
One quotation will suffice to impart the sense of this report:

> In assessing alcohol-related disability, one is never dealing with a condi-
> tion existing in vacuo, but with a disability produced by interaction with a
> unique person; that person's mental pathology or mental health provides
> essential components of the interacting uniqueness.

The generalization extends to physical and to social disabilities: Depression may lead to excessive drinking which may exacerbate the depression; excessive drinking may impose social isolation which may lead to more drinking; heavy alcohol intake may cause painful gout which may induce more alcohol intake; any disorder or event that interferes with ability to work may lead to heavy drinking which can result in further impairment of working capacity. Thus a classificatory system that allows only psychiatric diagnosis, or only physical diagnosis, or both but making no provision for what might be called "social diagnosis," is inadequate to describe and classify disabilities related to alcohol consumption.[44]

Apparently the WHO efforts have lent renewed credence to the orthodox disease definition. The "alcohol dependence syndrome" is written into the current revision of the *International Classification of Diseases* (a prestigious compilation for classifying illnesses) as:

A state, psychic and usually also physical, resulting from taking alcohol, characterized by behavioral and other responses that always include a compulsion to take alcohol on a continuous or periodic basis in order to experience its psychic effects, and sometimes to avoid the discomfort of its absence; tolerance may or may not be present.[45]

However, evidence of a broadening of definition is to be found in a contribution from the legal world, in court decisions that alcoholism is a disease which can prevent gainful employment and entitle its victim to disability insurance benefits under the Social Security Act. Previously, HEW regulations setting forth guidelines for determining disability stipulated as one of the impairments "addictive dependence on alcohol . . . with evidence of irreversible organ damage." A 1976 decision in the District Court for Maryland (supported by similar findings elsewhere) established that impairment need not be medically specific to qualify for Social Security benefits—the disability need only prevent the individual from engaging in gainful employment.[46]

It is significant that the WHO report's statements, even regarding the "alcohol-dependence syndrome" contain qualifications such as "Science is in no position to classify alcohol dependence as a condition of known etiology, established pathology, and determined natural history."[47] (This is not inconsistent with the clinical perspective—most diagnosis is based on inference.) Running as a leitmotif through the report are phrases such as "considerable gaps in present knowledge," the need for "agreed methods of recording and analyzing national alcohol consumption, and for epidemiological studies of risks in relation to quantities of alcohol consumed." Thus, what may have started out of the needs of the bureaucratic world for legitimation, ties in to and further supports the enhanced position of the research world.

One more development emanating from another world of victims, the handicapped, appears to be a windfall for this arena's drive for respectability. After a twenty-five day sit-in in April, 1977, by the disabled in San Francisco, Secretary of Health, Education and Welfare (HEW) Joseph Califano signed new federal regulations banning many forms of discrimination against the country's estimated thirty-five million disabled persons. Again demonstrating a reliance on the disease concept of alcoholism, the definition of the disabled was broadened under an opinion by Attorney General Griffin Bell to include persons suffering from alcoholism and drug addiction. Bell, in a letter to Califano, maintained that the statute does not require that recipients of federal contracts and grants ignore all the behavioral and other problems that may accompany a person's alcoholism or drug addiction if they interfere with the performance of his job or his effective participation in a federally assisted program—a position that would be unrealistic. But he stipulated:

> At the same time, the statute requires that contractors and grantees covered by the act not automatically deny employment or benefits to persons solely because they might find their status as alcoholics or drug addicts personally offensive, any more than contractors or grantees could discriminate against an individual who had some other condition or disease—such as cancer, multiple sclerosis, amputation, or blindness—unless its manifestations or his conduct rendered him ineligible.[48]

The regulations apply only to HEW-funded programs, but "are expected to be the basis for similar regulations to be developed by other federal agencies."[49] That they have precedent-setting significance is evident in a directive which followed from the Labor Department, asking companies doing business with the government to launch aggressive "affirmative action" plans for the handicapped, including alcoholics and drug addicts. According to one report, whose title, "Fair Play For Drunks,"[50] would suggest that respectability is still an unreached goal, the government rationale (as expressed by a Labor Department spokeswoman) is that after the government's investment in rehabilitation and training, it would make no sense to turn around and say "you can't have a job." On the other hand, asking that a work candidate's worth be considered "without regard to personal habits, addictions or impairments"[51] seems at odds with NIAAA's partiality toward occupational programs designed to coerce the alcoholic/problem drinker into treatment using the job as an inducement (discussed in the next chapter). Suffice it to say here that employers may be hard put to know which government guideline to follow.

Controversy over the reading of the law is far from resolved. For instance, the Labor Department, through its Office of Federal Contract Compliance Programs, could, finding federal contractors and subcontractors in violation, debar them from government contract work, have contracts terminated, or take such violators to court. Representative Henry J. Hyde was prompted to ask his colleagues:

> Is the public safety to be sacrificed to attaining goals and quotas of unre-habilitated alcoholics and drug abusers? Are schools which received federal funds now mandated to seek such persons for employment? Will the Federal Reserve System, Federal Deposit Insurance Corporation and the Treasury Department have its quotas of such employees? Will mass transit systems be required to accept such applicants as bus drivers and motormen? [52]

Lengthy discussion of Attorney General Bell's reading of the law has ensued, urging some who might otherwise never have questioned the concept to ask, "what hath the disease/disability definition wrought?"

Notes

1. Robert Straus and Selden Bacon, "Alcoholism and Social Stability: A Study of Occupational Integration in 2,023 Male Clinic Patients," *Quarterly Journal of Studies on Alcohol,* Vol. 12 (1951), pp. 231-60.
2. Robert Straus, "Problem Drinking in the Perspective of Social Change," in W.J. Filstead et al. (eds.), *Alcohol, New Thinking and New Directions* (Cambridge, Mass.: Ballinger, 1976), p. 47.
3. Mark Keller, "Problems with Alcohol," in W.J. Filstead et al. (eds.) *Alcohol, New Thinking and New Directions* (Cambridge, Mass.: Ballinger, 1976), p. 22.
4. Robin Room, "Comment on 'The Alcoholologist's Addiction,'" *Quarterly Journal of Studies on Alcohol,* Vol. 33 (1972), p. 1050. *See also:* S.D. Bacon, "The Administration of Alcoholism Rehabilitation Programs," *Quarterly Journal of Studies on Alcohol,* Vol. 10 (1949), pp. 1-47.
5. N.R. Kurtz and M. Regier, "The Uniform Alcoholism and Intoxication Treatment Act," *Journal of Studies on Alcohol,* Vol. 36 (1975), pp. 1421-41.
6. Robin Room, "Comment on 'The Uniform Alcoholism and Intoxication Treatment Act,'" *Journal of Studies on Alcohol,* Vol. 37 (1976), pp. 113-43.
7. Terrence O'Flaherty, *San Francisco Chronicle* (February 25, 1977) p. 40.
8. *See: San Francisco Sunday Examiner and Chronicle* (May 9, 1976) Section A, p. 2. *The Alcoholism Report,* Vol. 4 (May 14, 1976), p. 2.
9. *The Alcoholism Report,* Vol. 5 (March 11, 1977), p. 8.
10. John W. Fisher, Associate Director of Bay Area National Council on Alcoholism, as heard on KQED-FM radio, "High and Dry," November 12, 1976.
11. *See:* Maurice Weil, "Social Setting Alcohol Withdrawal Leading to Referral," paper researched under a Special Services Contract from the National Institute on Alcohol Abuse and Alcoholism, Yale University, 1974, p. 1.

12. See Chapter 5.
13. Senate Report 94-705-2, p. 6.
14. Jay Lewis, "Washington Report," *Journal of Studies on Alcohol,* Vol. 2 (1974), p. 1385.
15. *The Alcoholism Report,* Vol. 4 (October 24, 1975), p. 4.
16. See Chapter 4.
17. Press announcement released by the National Institute on Alcohol Abuse and Alcoholism, October 13, 1977.
18. *The Alcoholism Report,* Vol. 5 (December 10, 1976), p. 8.
19. See Chapter 5.
20. Testimony before the Subcommittee on Alcoholism and Narcotics of the Senate Labor and Public Welfare Committee, 1976, p. 18.
21. *American Psychological Association Monitor,* (September/October, 1973), p. 17.
22. See Chapter 4.
23. Testimony before the Senate Alcoholism and Narcotics Subcommittee, February 3, 1976, p. 76.
24. *The Alcoholism Report,* Vol. 5 (December 26, 1975), p. 6.
25. *The Alcoholism Report,* Vol. 3 (September 26, 1975), p. 3.
26. *The Alcoholism Report,* Vol. 5 (October 22, 1976), p. 6; *The Alcoholism Report,* Vol. 5 (December 10, 1976), p. 7; *The Alcoholism Report,* Vol. 5 (March 11, 1977), p. 4; *The Alcoholism Report,* Vol. 5 (April 22, 1977), p.7.
27. *The Alcoholism Report,* Vol. 5 (December 24, 1976), p. 7.
28. Telegram from NIAAA to organizations bidding on the proposal, as quoted in *The Alcoholism Report,* Vol. 7 (May 11, 1979), p. 9.
29. *The Alcoholism Report,* Vol. 4 (October 8, 1976), p. 5.
30. *The Alcoholism Report,* Vol. 4 (September 24, 1976), p. 6.
31. *The Alcoholism Report,* Vol. 5 (November 26, 1976), pp. 5-6.
32. See Chapter 3.
33. Robert O'Briant, "Some Thoughts on Evaluation," *The Hearth* (January, 1976).
34. " 'Counseling' and Insurance," *The Hearth* (January, 1977).
35. Steve Thompson and associates, "An Overview of State Alcoholism Services," report submitted to State Health and Welfare Committee, California, 1975, pp. 33-34.
36. *See:* R. Shore and J. Luce, *To Your Health* (New York: Seabury Press, 1976), pp. 193-96.
37. *See:* Jack D. Gordon, Robert I. Levy, and Charles B. Perrow, "Open Ward Management of Acute Alcoholism," *California Medicine,* Vol. 89 (1958), pp. 397-99; and Jack D. Gordon, "The Alcoholic Patient," *Hospitals,* Vol. 44 (1970), p. 63.
38. *The Alcoholism Report,* Vol. 4 (June 25, 1976), p. 4.
39. Griffith Edwards, Milton M. Gross, Mark Keller, and Joy Moser, "Alcohol-Related Problems in the Disability Perspective," a Summary of the Consensus of the WHO Group of Investigators on Criteria for Identifying and Classifying Disabilities Related to Alcohol Consumption), *Journal of Studies on Alcohol,* Vol. 37 (1976), pp. 1360-82.
40. Ibid., p. 1361.
41. Ibid.
42. World Health Organization Working Document for the United Nations Ad

Hoc Inter-Agency Meeting on Rehabilitation of the Disabled, Annex 1, Geneva 16-22 (June, 1975).

43. Edwards et. al., "Alcohol Related Problems in the Disability Perspective,", p. 1361.

44. Ibid., p. 1367.

45. Mark Keller, "A Lexicon of Disablements Related to Alcohol Consumption," in G. Edwards, M. M. Gross, M. Keller, J. Moser and R. Room (eds.), *Alcohol Related Disabilities* (Geneva: World Health Organization, Offset Publication #32, 1977), p. 33.

46. *The Alcoholism Report,* Vol. 4 (June 25, 1976), pp. 5-6.

47. Edwards et. al., "Alcohol-Related Problems in the Disability Perspective," p. 1364.

48. *The Alcoholism Report,* Vol. 5 (May 13, 1977), p. 4

49. Ibid.

50. Eliot Marshall, "Fair Play for Drunks," *The New Republic,* Vol. 177 (July 23, 1977), pp. 7-8.

51. Ibid.

52. *The Alcoholism Report,* Vol. 5 (July 22, 1977), p. 5.

9.

Maintaining a Separate Identity

There remains one more element of the legitimizing process to be examined, one which is crucial to the visibility already achieved—*maintaining a separate identity* for alcohol programs. That this concern should guide the thinking of many of the actors in this arena comes as no surprise when one considers the hard-won fight for autonomy and status, as related in previous chapters. It is a dollar-based concern, for any talk of combining alcohol use with other problems brings an attendant fear that funds will be swallowed up. Corresponding examples are close at hand. Moves to combine programs within the mental health arena have been opposed by parents of the mentally retarded for the same reason; similar reactions surface when there are suggestions to combine services for the blind and deaf under the umbrella of "sensory disabilities." What is more, there is ample evidence that these concerns, especially about funding, are justified.

In this chapter, we look at the rationale behind the separate identity process and examine two consequences: the divisiveness over the issue of "straight alcoholism" versus "broad brush" occupational programs; and the thwarting of the California plan to combine the Office of Alcoholism with the state Department of Alcoholic Beverage Control.

One Stigma Is Enough

As explained earlier, when NIAAA was established, alcohol programs in many states were (and still are) under the jurisdiction of Public

Health, Human Resources or Mental Health Departments, where alcohol people felt they were last in line for funds. Thus the desire for a separate institute equal in status to the National Institute of Mental Health and the National Institute on Drug Abuse stemmed not only from ideological differences over the chicken-and-egg question of mental problems/alcohol problems, but from resentment over diverted dollars.

Maintaining this separation requires eternal vigil. For example, toward the close of President Ford's term, the administration proposed a health block grant plan calling for the consolidation of sixteen health programs, including alcoholism. The move was opposed by Senate Alcoholism and Narcotics Subcommittee Chairman William D. Hathaway, who saw the plan as "forcing alcoholics to compete head to head at the state level with politically far stronger health providers for considerably fewer total federal dollars," adding:

> Discriminated against by hospitals and physicians, unacceptable to many private health insurance companies, forced to fight tooth and nail each year at the federal, state and local level for miserly scraps of the public health care dollar—if alcoholism is in this state, it is small wonder many middle class alcoholics prefer to suffer in silence.[1]

In some cases, the vigilance borders on paranoia, as when the appointment of Ernest Noble, a research scientist, to be director of the institute was viewed by some as signaling changes within NIAAA—a cut in budget, a change in priorities. There *has* been an undercurrent of federal pressure on NIAAA from the start to conform to the pattern of other comparable institutes and concentrate on research and prevention, but Noble consistently supported maintaining a separate identity for alcoholism which reflects *all* constituencies in the arena.

Other examples of this concern abound: optimism over the possibility of coverage under national health insurance is tempered by the threat of being relegated to a psychiatric classification; the move in California to use "recovery homes" in preference to "half-way houses" was explained by respondents as stemming from the consideration that "half-way houses exist for all kinds of other problems." Even the drive for certification of personnel is affected: respondents expressed anxiety lest codification follow a mental health model. Indeed, there is a strain between this process and that discussed in the previous chapter, building respectability: in part, opposition to NIAAA's proposal that the Council of State and Territorial Alcoholism Administrators (CSTAA) set up the national certification board derived from concern over turf rights; but equally important was the recurrent fear of mental health domination. To quote

Matthew Rose, executive director of the National Association of Alcoholism Counselors and Trainers (NAACT):

> The standards of performance for serving clients and families with alcohol problems would be established and maintained by people who report to directors and administrators. The certifying board would tend to be composed of people representing programs rather than the service providers. . . And this is particularly important because most of the agencies operating in the field are controlled by the mental health professions.[2]

When the 1975 North American Congress on Alcohol and Drug Problems tried to get a consensus on certification, fifty organizations were represented at the outset, dwindling to about twenty-five at adjournment. "Most of the divisions tended to split along lines of those plugging for separate consideration of certification of alcoholism counselors, and those supporting assessment of a broader range of credentialing, embracing drug abuse, mental health and human service workers."[3]

As can be seen from the quotation above, the mental health arena does not constitute the only threat; fear of being subsumed surfaces whenever there is talk of combining with drug abuse. When the Council of State and Territorial Administrators Association (CSTAA) found itself cut off from funding,[4] an invitation came from the National Association of State Drug Abuse Program Coordinators (NASDAPC) to make CSTAA a sub-unit of the drug association. CSTAA opted instead to align itself with the Alcohol and Drug Problems Association (APDPA), which while ostensibly addressing itself to both problems, has remained essentially in the alcohol use arena. ADPA's history is itself indicative of the strain between the two problems of alcohol and drug abuse. Originally an association for state alcohol program administrators, it struggled to remain afloat during the early years of low visibility, surviving through the assistance of benefactors such as the Smithers Foundation. When there was a resurgent interest in drugs during the 1960s, the name and the vista of the organization were changed in the hopes of enlarging financial support. But support from the drug people was not forthcoming, as one respondent put it, "They didn't in any way relate."

Nor do the alcohol people "relate" to drugs. Even though NIAAA was established in December, 1970, equal status with mental health and drugs was not achieved until the reorganization setting up the superstructure of an Alcohol Drug Abuse and Mental Health Administration (ADAMHA) in 1973. At that time there was talk of combining drugs and alcohol in a "substance abuse agency" away from NIMH, since, to quote one bureaucrat, "It's tough enough to have the stigma of alcoholism; alcoholic people don't need to carry a stigma of mental illness too."[5]

However, "for many middle class veterans of alcoholism's battle for respectability, the stigma of the drug addict seems worse still." [6] (These veterans have a ready ally on this issue—the alcoholic beverage industries world is not anxious to have public attention drawn to the fact that alcohol is a drug.)

Nevertheless, combining these concerns is a theme that emerges periodically.[7] Sometimes the issue arises in regard to research, as when it was reported that the president's Biomedical Research Panel, convened to review the policies and organization of HEW's biomedical and behavioral research programs, contained members who were in favor of moving the research functions of the three institutes making up ADA-MHA to the National Institutes of Health, HEW's research conglomerate.[8] Similar suggestions appear periodically from elements within the scientific world who would prefer that federal money support "basic" rather than "targeted" research, i.e. research geared toward specific diseases—on the premise that all scientific discoveries pyramid and the scientist should not be constrained by narrow funding limits. However, if one compares a 1978 alcohol research budget of $15,474,000 to the early days in the arena when alcohol use was an *ad hoc* problem topic—as characterized by Bacon, one emerging from a concern about a condition labeled by action groups, not by researchers [9]—it is easy to understand the tenacity with which NIAAA clings to a separate research identity.

More often this issue is tied to concerns over efficient use of limited financial resources. In such an instance, the 1976 legislative proposal by Senator Paul Laxalt to merge NIAAA with the National Institute on Drug Abuse (NIDA), elements discussed in previous chapters were brought to bear. Third-party payments were used as an argument, with NIAAA Director Noble telling Laxalt that no change should be made in the status of NIAAA until such time as alcohol abuse and alcoholism treatment and rehabilitation are fully integrated with the mainstream of this country's health care system.[10] (An observation by the former director of the California Office of Alcoholism, Loran Archer, suggests the merit of the position.[11] When California instigated a demonstration insurance project for state employees, it was initially conveyed in a separate pamphlet; subsequently, after information on coverage for alcoholism was added to the regular health insurance packet, utilization doubled.) Also drawn upon by Noble and the NIAAA Advisory Council is the relationship of the process of maintaining a separate identity for alcohol programs to the process of redefining alcoholism as a disease:

> . . . drug abuse is still heavily cast in the criminal justice climate. And we sure don't want the alcohol problem cast back in that when we fought for half a century to get it out of there.[12]

Former NIAAA Director Morris Chafetz, speaking with the luxury of one no longer forced to be concerned with visibility, said (at the time) that the arena should be "committed enough to the totality of the problem to be willing to set aside our territorial prerogatives, and see if we can make greater progress in the alcohol and other drug issues by combining our knowledge and resources." [13] But combining is no more attractive to the drug agency than it is to NIAAA. NIDA Director Robert DuPont told Laxalt that the strength of the drug and alcohol programs might be diluted if such a merger took place. One statement of DuPont's must have sounded alarming in some quarters. The NIDA Director said consideration of the substance abuse issue:

> could extend beyond the administration merger of the two Institutes at the federal level to focus on those behaviors that are reasonably subsumed under the concept of addiction: cigarette smoking, obesity, drug taking and alcoholism. A true substance abuse agency could encompass aspects of current federal efforts in tobacco, nutrition, poison control, prescription practices, as well as those areas now the concern of NIDA and NIAAA.[14]

Reprint of an editorial from the *Sacramento Bee* in the California Association of Alcoholic Recovery Homes newsletter indicates just how far Dr. DuPont's suggestion would go. Calling the phrase "substance abuse" a prime case of "medical obfuscation," the editorial goes on:

> The phrase could mean anything from someone who breaks a window, drops hot ashes on an upholstered chair, or overloads a plastic garbage can. In our view, persons who coin and use such terms are language abusers. For them, no cure is in sight.[15]

Separate But Equal

Agitation around two quite different issues illustrates the ramifications of this process of maintaining a separate identity, and the tie-in to processes already discussed. The first issue pertains to occupational programs aimed at ferreting out the alcoholic, using the club of job performance and the carrot of treatment.

It is noteworthy that the original suggestion for occupational programs presented them as a means of *avoiding* the labeling of alcoholics as sick.[16] Terming such programs "constructive coercion," Roman and Trice saw their proposal as "early, early intervention," positing that since the employer possesses legitimate authority, rewards may be legitimately withdrawn based on inadequate or inappropriate job performance. Nevertheless, it has taken the process of redefining (i.e., promulgation of the disease concept) to convince management to instigate these programs, and advances are still hard won. Acceptance by management also ties in to building respectability, in that such programs require that management contract for third-party payments. In addition, occupational programs have led to an enlargement of turf rights for the National Council on Alcoholism, which carved out this particular interest for a large part of its programming, aided by a substantial grant from NIAAA, one of those which survived examination by Congress.[17] NIAAA support of occupational programs has in turn led to a developing constituency, abetted in California by the rehabilitation antecedents of the Office of Alcoholism, which funds the program in various counties. Some counties hire their own staff, others contract with NCA, others with private organizations—thus, a growing constituency of occupational alcoholism consultants, all employed to encourage industry to provide in-house counseling for referral. Indication of the rapid growth of this portion of the arena, which is only about five or six years old, is to be found in the parallel growth of its professional association, the Association of Labor-Management Administrators and Consultants (ALMACA).[18] In the San Francisco Bay Area, representatives of ten counties have joined together in an informal, *unorganized* association called County Occupational Alcoholism Consultants (COAC), county and private consultants meeting out of a felt need to share expertise and obtain advice regarding the vanguard situations they are encountering.

Primarily, problems arise over intersections with the worlds of labor and management. A marked cleavage separates those who would maintain the identity of "straight alcoholism" programs and those who would extend them to early, early identification of "troubled employees," or "broad brush programs" (a tacit acknowledgment that the problem perspective is making inroads). For example, the Alcohol and Drug Problems Association (ADPA) has argued that "the 'troubled employee' approach shifts the focus from a single 'alcoholic' hunt with all its stigma . . . to a program concerned with helping citizens effectively on the job."[19] NCA, on the other hand, while as concerned as ADPA with stigma, maintains its watchdog stance:

> The most effective method of counteracting the social and moral stigma associated with alcoholism is to forthrightly identify it by names in all preventive, educational and program activities, rather than substituting such catch-all phrases as substance abuse, chemical dependency, problems of addiction, mental health problems and troubled employee or broad brush problems.[20]

NCA asserts that most unions have only taken positions on alcoholism. Therefore, a broad brush approach would require union approval—

unions respond negatively to talk of medical records, behavior patterns, any indication that employers will be given a license to deal with employees inequitably or to get into aspects of an employee's life beyond work. Conversely, the troubled employee approach is based on two arguments: one, that an employee who has a problem with drinking always has attendant financial, marital and/or emotional problems; and two, a straight alcoholism program excludes employees "unlucky enough to have the wrong problem." [21] Said one industrial consultant, a recovered alcoholic himself:

> Once you open the door for the alcoholic, you've got to take what comes in. The guy coming in and saying I'm really not a drunk like my boss says, I'm bombed on valium—I've got a choice of saying sit down, or get out and start drinking, buddy, so I can help you.

Without ascribing motives, it is safe to say that NCA's position is reinforced by the experience of arena veterans within its ranks who are recovered alcoholics, and the fear that any broad brush program will give alcoholism only token attention.

Straight alcoholism/broad brush aside, the recovered alcoholic experience has at least united both sides of this issue on the value of occupational programs. Steeped in the knowledge that most people seek treatment only after they have been arrested, lost their families and/or their jobs, both sides agree that "the best motivation tool we've found so far is the paycheck." [22] But a crucial question is raised by one industrial consultant, responding to the official NCA position:

> Private industry carries the full burden of their program costs, thereby earning the right to call it an "Employee Assistance" Program or anything else they desire. If the unions are totally committed to solving this problem, expenditures from union coffers could help achieve those ends. Private industry isn't waiting for government funds. Why should the unions? [23]

Some respondents suggested that union leadership is not pursuing alcoholism benefits as assiduously as it has, for example, dental plans, since conscientious attention to alcoholism problems on the job could ultimately result in a loss to the union coffers.

"Who's paying?" may turn out to be the crucial variable. 1977 legislation that would have authorized $100 to $120 million for a federal occupational alcoholism program—keyed to a 2.5 percent share of the federal alcohol taxes—was opposed by HEW and NIAAA Director Noble on the grounds that *extra* money for occupational programs was not warranted. (It had been expected that as part of this effort, alcoholism programs would also be started within professional organizations, such as the one already underway within the California State Bar Association.) Following the lukewarm reception given this proposal and a previous bill which would have set up a trust fund in the Treasury to fund occupational programs, Senator Hathaway, chairman of the Senate Alcoholism and Drug Abuse Subcommittee, was reported to be considering introduction of an amendment to the Occupational Safety and Health Act which would require businesses to have occupational programs.[24] Such congressional persistence may force the bureaucratic world to devote increased attention to this concern and its attendant straight alcoholism/broad brush issue. Like the juxtaposition of third-party payments with non-hospital detoxification and recovery homes, NIAAA involvement in occupational programs may be the catalyst for a confrontation with the definitional conflicts previously discussed.

A second issue which ran up against the process of maintaining a separate identity was the short-lived plan of California's Governor Brown to combine the Office of Alcoholism with the Department of Alcoholic Beverage Control (ABC). When the California Senate Select Committee on Laws Relating to Alcoholic Beverages released the results of a two year study in 1974, its chairman, Senator Alan Short, was quoted as follows:

> The alcoholic beverage industry in California has had its own way over forty years. The liquor lobby is all-pervasive. The ABC is simply an extension of the industry it is supposed to regulate. It is significant that since 1933, when Prohibition ended, nine out of every ten bills considered by the State Legislature have been sponsored by the industry. We have not found any major legislation that was sponsored by the department.[25]

That a governmental regulatory agency should be entirely dominated by the industry it is supposed to regulate is not a situation unique to the alcohol use arena, nor to the California ABC as differentiated from those of other states. Nevertheless, the alcoholic beverage industries in California do have the distinction of having enjoyed a long period of power under the guidance of the man whose name became synonymous with lobbying scandals, Artie Samish.[26] As Bunce reports:

> Actually, political activity in their (the industries) behalf relied very little on persuasion of legislators at times of critical votes. Rather, the industry was a covert and heavy bankroller for selected candidates of both political parties, who upon assuming office proved eager to legislate according to the industry's interest. The State Board of Equalization proved to be a friendly and contented tax collector for many years as the industry pushed

through the legislature frequent salary increases for its members. And the development of an independent state alcohol beverage authority (now the ABC) was promoted by the industry to assist in policing their marketplace.[27]

In the 1950s, largely through the efforts of then Assemblyman Caspar Weinberger, reforms were imposed on the state ABC and on the industry lobbyists. Nevertheless:

> Today, the alcohol beverage industry still retains a powerful, if somewhat less overwhelming, influence over state lawmakers and lawmaking. Generally speaking alcohol taxes are lower and retail prices are higher in California than in many other states. The Department of Alcohol Beverage Control still sees itself as the guarantor of order and legal respectability in the alcohol marketplace. And the ABC's friendly relations with the industry seem undisturbed by reformers' zeal—over the past forty years, every state ABC director, with one exception, has left the ABC only to begin employment with the industry lobby.[28]

Room has pointed out that the ABC has functioned very much as a trade association protecting the market of those already in the industry, seeing its basic job as the referee between the various competing vested interests of the industry, and as the preserver of the moral tone (e.g., campaigning against topless waitresses).

The state policy of alcohol regulation, supporting and legitimizing the interests of the alcoholic beverage industries, has operated totally divorced from the state policy on alcoholism and drinking problems. In this regard, California is following a national pattern. Bacon recalls a gathering called by the federal division then responsible for alcohol-alcoholism problems to which were invited all the leading professions, academic disciplines, government and voluntary agencies, religious educational, and industrial-commercial groups possibly related:

> It was pointed out to the organizers of the conference that one group of agencies had been omitted—a group existing in every state of the union, a group whose official, major, and only purpose was to control the problems of alcohol, a group whose annual administrative budget alone amounted to hundreds of millions of dollars a year (more than all the others combined). Perhaps the significance of this omission lies not in the failure to include this group (the alcoholic-beverage control boards and commissions), but the following: (1) the organizers had "never even thought" about it; (2) many of the groups involved literally did not "know about" this category; and—this is my own understanding, based on many years of relevant experience— (3) representatives of that category would have been surprised to have been invited.[29]

The preceding details have been spelled out to emphasize the historical precedent of Governor Brown's 1976 proposal to merge the state ABC with the Office of Alcoholism. To be sure, this proposal came on the heels of the governor's veto of a bill which would have increased the tax on liquor as a means of increased funding for treatment and prevention of alcoholism. The governor's position had greatly angered the arena constituencies, and some respondents felt this sudden interest in the ABC stemmed from his desire to demonstrate he was not in the pocket of the liquor lobby. Others report that the governor had held a meeting of all the arena's agencies and then innocently asked the question never before addressed (see Bacon, above): where is the ABC representative? He was referred to a study requested by the state Director of Finance as a reappraisal of California's role in the regulation of the alcoholic beverage industry. The report had approached its final recommendations from the following policy perspective: How do and/or should controls imposed on the alcoholic beverage industry contribute to the total State effort in dealing with these problems? Evincing the influence of the sociological branch of the research world by drawing upon the work of Room [30] and Wilkinson, [31] the report recommended that regulation of the alcoholic beverage industry should contribute to the minimization of alcohol-related problems while maximizing consumer and business freedom; that the control laws should be viewed in a common framework of state programs directed at alcohol abuse problems; and that "at a minimum" the Department of Alcoholic Beverage Control should establish liaison with the Office of Alcoholism (then the Office of Alcohol Program Management), "to examine means by which the Department's policies might be enhanced in light of recent research, the emerging data based on alcohol abuse, and complementary programs administered by other State agencies." [32]

Hence, there was logic behind the governor's proposed merger. In fact, such thinking was consistent with a national interest in reversing the "uncritical perpetuation of alcoholic beverage control policies" [33] which had characterized the fifty-year period since repeal. (NIAAA had commissioned a similar national study.) [34] But respondents reported that this logic was overwhelmed by the fear that their newly won Office of Alcoholism would be consumed by the older and more powerful policing agency. And these fears were exacerbated by the semantic obstacles the governor encountered. Changing the name of the Department of Alcoholic Beverage Control would require a change in the state constitution, and so it was proposed that the new superagency retain this title in name only, with OA and the old ABC retaining equal status under that umbrella. The governor's proposal died when this final threat to a separate identity for alcohol problems resulted in the united opposition of the alcoholic beverage industries and the volunteer action/recovery service worlds.

Strange as it may seem to find the interest of these worlds converging, the merger defeat demonstrates the relationship between redefining the problem (as a disease) and maintaining a separate identity for it. Room, delineating the factors which inhibit analysis of the relation between drinking laws and drinking behavior, makes a significant observation. As we have seen, the disease concept of alcoholism, in defining the "problem" to be an attribute of the affected individual, has also often carried the implication that there are two entirely different classes of phenomena, "normal drinking" and "alcoholic drinking," each irrelevant to the other. Therefore, "If 'loss of control' is the salient issue, the actual amount and context of drinking are essentially immaterial." [35] Reynolds, too, has emphasized this relationship, pointing out that the disease model of alcoholism, by providing consumers with such a clear-cut operating distinction, left each drinker to his own diagnostic devices—each drinker is the sole arbiter of whether or not he is an "alcoholic." Consequently, the alcoholic beverage industries have profited from the disease concept. Freeing drinking of moral approbation meant social legitimation of commerce in alcohol, as Reynolds puts it, paving the way "for the social acceptance of more occasions to drink and of drinking more on these occasions." [36] Seen in this light, alliance between seemingly diverse worlds becomes understandable.

Reorganization: Another Threat

Threats to the separateness of alcohol programs came to the fore again with President Carter's announced intention to assert more control over the federal budget. When the president was reported to have said at a closed White House meeting that his reorganization plan may include federal alcoholism programs, the warning signal could again be heard throughout the arena. Senate Human Resources Committee Chairman Harrison Williams was quick to ask HEW Secretary Joseph A. Califano for his views on any possible reorganization involving NIAAA and the drug agency, the National Institute on Drug Abuse (NIDA).[37] And very shortly thereafter, Peter Bourne, special assistant to the president for health issues, announced his support of a White House Conference on Alcohol Abuse and Alcoholism for the Fall of 1977. Addressing the Board of the Council of State and Territorial Alcoholism Authorities (CSTAA), Bourne said of this proposal:

> I think it is a way of maybe overcoming any misgivings people in the field may have about alcohol not being treated on an equal basis with mental health and drugs. I would like to give it whatever kind of status or boost to demonstrate parity that I can in whatever way you and other people in the field feel that can be accomplished.[38]

Such a conference was not held. Given the feelings of past neglect which have motivated the thrust for a separate identity, NIAAA's constituencies are unlikely to judge any reorganization plan solely on the merits of a more manageable organizational chart. Although they do not have the clout of, say, the constituencies of the Veterans' Administration or the Department of Transportation, the NIAAA constituencies would have been tested for strength and visibility by President Carter's reorganization vision. Nevertheless, as James T. Lynn, former director of the Office of Management and Budget, has pointed out, any talk of reorganization also cuts across the normal authority of the congressional committee chairman, "whose enthusiasm for sharing control over such subjects is not unbounded." [39] The merits of reorganization notwithstanding, Franklin Roosevelt at the height of his power, with a House of Representatives that was three-fourths Democratic, could not pass his reorganization bill.

On a state level, the separate identity process runs up against countervailing forces. Not only, as already explained, are alcohol programs in many states under the jurisdiction of Public Health, Human Resources or Mental Health departments, but in a majority of states alcohol and drug programs are combined in a single department. This prevalence of combined programs has led to reconsideration of merging the Council of State and Territorial Alcoholism Administrators (CSTAA) and the National Association of State Drug Abuse Program Coordinators (NASDAPC) in a proposed affiliation with the Alcohol and Drug Problems Association—henceforth to be the ADPA Council of State Authorities. In California, Senator Gregorio, in March, 1977, proposed breaking up the Department of Health, the biggest department in state government, into a number of smaller departments "designed to be more visible and more accountable." [40] Despite the fear expressed by arena participants that Senator Gregorio's plan included combining alcohol and drugs—certainly not the alcohol arena's notion of visibility—commencing in July, 1978, one of the five departments operating under the Health and Welfare Agency became the Department of Alcohol and Drug Abuse.[41] Thus, the drive for a separate identity for alcohol problems has encountered the drive for more scrupulous accountability for all government expenditures. In Part IV, we turn to the philosophy behind this closer scrutiny of support for present programs.

Summary

As explained in Chapter 2, my concern is with the movement of events, as differentiated from the ascription of motives. Nevertheless, in discussing the legitimizing process, it is clear that some action (the use of prominent people and the softening of language to project a respectable image for alcohol problems; the attempts to buy into the health insurance and social disability institutions; the resistance to any blurring of alcohol problems with mental health or drug problems) are clearly in the nature of *tactics*. Some action (the establishment of a clearinghouse for information, an epidemiology division and research centers—indeed, even the promulgation of the disease concept) *may* be tactics for *some* people, but have other equally salient purposes as well. Still other action (the divisiveness over straight alcoholism/broad brush occupational programs, the thwarting of the merger of the Department of Alcoholic Beverage Control with the Office of Alcoholism) occurs as a *consequence* of the legitimizing process. Again it must be stressed: tactics, conditions, consequences are of import as they contribute to the flow of the identified processes. It is the interlocking of the processes *and* the intersecting among alcohol worlds (as well as with outside worlds such as insurance and law) that propels the momentum of the major process—building an arena by increasing its visibility.

Notes

1. *The Alcoholism Report,* Vol. 4 (February 13, 1976), pp. 1-2.
2. *The Alcoholism Report,* Vol. 3 (October 11, 1974), p. 4.
3. *The Alcoholism Report,* Vol. 4 (October 24, 1975), pp. 2-3.
4. See Chapter 4.
5. Kenneth Eaton, NIAAA Deputy Director, as quoted in *American Psychological Association Monitor* (September/October 1973) p. 11.
6. Ibid.
7. *See:* David J. Pittman, "The Rush to Combine," *British Journal of Addiction,* Vol. 62 (1976), pp. 337-43. Robert E. Popham, Jan E. E. Delint, and Wolfgang Schmidt, "Some Comments on Pittman's 'Rush to Combine,'" *British Journal of Addiction,* Vol. 63 (1968), pp. 25-27.
8. *The Alcoholism Report,* Vol. 4 (November 28, 1975), p. 3.
9. Selden D. Bacon, "Fragmentation of Alcohol Problem Research," paper delivered to the Congress on Alcoholism and Drug Dependence" in L.G. Kiloh and D.S. Bell (eds.), 29th *International Congress on Alcoholism and Drug Dependence* (Australia: Butterworths, 1971), pp. 481-95.
10. *The Alcoholism Report,* Vol. 5 (December 10, 1976), p. 1.
11. Remarks made at a Round-Table Discussion on "Relationship of the NIAAA and the State-Funded Alcoholism Program," San Mateo, California, December 8, 1976.

12. Dr. Edwin J. McClendon, as quoted in *The Alcoholism Report,* Vol. 5 (December 24, 1976), p. 2.
13. Interview in *The Alcoholism Report,* Vol. 5 (December 10, 1976), p. 3.
14. *The Alcoholism Report,* Vol. 5 (December 10, 1976), p. 2.
15. *The Hearth* (January, 1977); *Sacramento Bee* editorial (November 22, 1976).
16. P.M. Roman and H.M. Trice, "The Sick Role, Labeling Theory, and the Deviant Drinker," *International Journal of Social Psychology,* Vol. 14 (1968).
17. See Chapter 4.
18. See Chapter 3.
19. *The Alcoholism Report,* Vol. 3 (July 25, 1975), p. 7.
20. Resolution of the Labor-Management Committee and the Labor-Management Council of Alternates of the National Council on Alcoholism, June 11, 1975.
21. Scott Lynch, unpublished "Comments" on a letter from Leo Perlis in the *Labor-Management Alcoholism Journal* (July 28, 1975). Quoted by consent of author.
22. A. J. Sullivan, Director of Special Health Services for Standard Oil Corporation, as quoted in *Standard Oiler,* (March/April 1975).
23. Lynch, "Comments."
24. *The Alcoholism Report,* Vol. 6 (October 28, 1977), p. 7.
25. *San Francisco Chronicle* (December 4, 1974), p. 57.
26. *See:* Elmer Rusco, *Machine Politics, California Model; Arthur H. Samish and the Alcoholic Beverage Industry* (Ph.D. dissertation, University of California, Berkeley, 1968).
27. Richard Bunce, "An Overview of California and Alcohol: Products, Problems, Programs, Policies," paper prepared for the Expert Conference on the Prevention of Alcohol Problems, Berkeley, California, December 9-11, 1974, p. 5.
28. Ibid., p. 6.
29. S.D. Bacon, "Concepts," in W.J. Filstead et al. (eds.), *Alcohol, New Thinking and New Directions* (Cambridge, Mass.: Ballinger, 1976), pp. 72-73.
30. Robin Room, "Regulating Trade Relations and the Minimization of Alcohol Problems," a Statement to the California Senate Committee on Governmental Organization Hearing on the Tied-House Provisions of the California Alcoholic Beverage Control Act, San Francisco, November 26, 1973.
31. Robert Wilkinson, *The Prevention of Drinking Problems* (New York: Oxford University Press, 1970).
32. Mark E. Clark and Larry L. Owsley, "Alcohol and the State: A Reappraisal of California's Alcohol Control Policies," report prepared for the Department of Finance, State of California, 1975, p. 62.
33. Ibid., p. 59.
34. *See:* Medicine in the Public Interest, Inc., "A Study in the Actual Effects of Alcoholic Beverage Control Laws," Washington, D.C., 1975.
35. Robin Room, "The Effects of Drinking Laws on Drinking Behavior," paper presented at the annual meetings of the Society for the Study of Social Problems, Denver, Colorado, August, 1971, p. 3.
36. Lynn Reynolds, *The California Office of Alcohol Program Management* (Ph.D. dissertation, University of California, 1974), p. 85.

37. *The Alcoholism Report*, Vol. 5 (April 22, 1977), p. 1.
38. *The Alcoholism Report*, Vol. 5 (May 13, 1977), p. 3.
39. Quoted by James Reston, *San Francisco Examiner/Chronicle*, January 9, 1977, Sunday Punch Section, p. 3.
40. *San Francisco Chronicle* (March 2, 1977), p. 11.
41. Subsequently changed to the Department of Alcohol and Drug Programs.

Part IV:

Demonstrating the Problem

A persistent question for the sociological pursuit is: under what social conditions does the behavior under examination take place? A number of conditions have already been identified as exerting impact on this arena—New Deal programming and its relationship to the growth of associations; the temperance movement and its effect upon the concept of addiction; the pragmatic impulse which influenced a clinical perspective; the twentieth-century moral relativism which contributed toward a drinking-problem perspective. To these, one more must now be added; the less-is-better political philosophy of the 1970s.

On the heels of the utilitarian thrust of the welfare state, and in many ways in reaction to it, there has occurred in the United States a shift in ideas away from big government. Whatever conceptual and funding explosions are taking place within the alcohol-use arena must also be viewed as happening against an era-of-limits, lowered-expectations philosophy for which California's Governor Brown has become a visible symbol.

In its reversion to an anti-government argument for self-reliance, this social movement reflects the nineteenth-century mood from which the disease concept grew. Although nineteenth century liberals shared a belief in representative government, civil liberties and religious tolerance, the movement split into two wings: one, the utilitarian wing, providing the intellectual rationale for social reform and the welfare state; the other based on the principle of the natural laws of the market and *laissez faire*. Brown, who developed his political consciousness in the New Left times, reflects this

Janus-faced character of liberalism, uttering the unutterable from a clinical perspective, i.e., saying, "Maybe some problems can't be solved." In the post-mortem of the poverty programs, Moynihan had detected an alliance between conservative Republicans and radical reformers, "a certain coming together in opposition to, in distaste for, bigness, impersonality, bureaucratized benevolence, prescribed surveillance" [1]—a movement on which Watergate put the seal. With the very notion of government intervention being questioned, President Carter has felt encouraged to sell economy as a political ideal, and Governor Brown senses political support when he makes pronouncements such as, "Every group wants a little more, and it's my job to give them a little less."

Faced with this condition, constituents of the alcohol use arena have a *demonstrating* job to perform. In part, the demonstrating process lies in saying "me too" in regard to whatever resources remain to be distributed—thus, the sub-processes of competing for attention while at the same time attempting to form alliances. Equally important is selecting supportive data with which to demonstrate that the problem is being attacked. Demonstrating is also ideological in nature—the convincing sub-process in which arena participants engage. And last, we shall examine the various facets by which responsibility for the problem of alcohol use is enlarged (the opening up of careers, the community involvement inherent in the concept of prevention, and the expansion of the bounds of responsibility to include the alcoholic beverage industries).

Note

1. Daniel Moynihan, *Maximum Feasible Misunderstanding* (New York: The Free Press, 1970), p. 160.

10.

Competing for Attention and Combining for Strength

Amidst a tightened economy and a public demand for more effective government, two paradoxical impulses become manifest. Although there is a growing understanding by arena participants of the need to combine forces to demonstrate strength (thereby demonstrating the problem and increasing visibility), running counter to this is the process of competing, demonstrating strength at the expense of others. First we shall look at the forms the *competing* process takes; the relationship of this process to the history of the arena and the processes previously discussed. We shall also look at one consequence of the competition: the clash of worlds surrounding dollar rivalry as it pertains to the public inebriate. Finally, we look at attempts which are not equal in weight to the competing process, but are notable efforts nevertheless: endeavors to form alliances and to foster cooperation, the process of *combining* for strength.

Politics As Usual

NIAAA Director Noble's observation that any arena is going to have some divisiveness, "People are going to compete for funds; people are going to compete for attention," [1] probably is quite as *under*stated as the characterization of one respondent is *over*stated: "Everyone in this arena suffers from the 'crab syndrome'—they're all clawing at each other." Instances of competition have surfaced in previous chapters, e.g. among associations over the issues of credentialing and accreditation, between the Rutgers Center and the National Clearinghouse for Alcohol Information over duplication of effort. A closer look at this competing process reveals that it centers mainly around jurisdiction, funding, eminence and the attention of the public eye. For the most part, these are not discrete but overlapping purposes.

Competition for jurisdiction is a natural outgrowth of the two processes discussed in Part II, establishing turf rights and developing constituencies. For an instructive illustration, take the situation in California. County administrators do not want too strong a county board, and vice versa; each is fighting to establish "who's in charge." Correspondingly, the strain between state and county jurisdiction over programs predates the passage of legislation in 1975 giving the counties express power of approval, and as with all such resolutions, legal settlement does not ensure ideological agreement. Moreover, the other side of the coin in the state/county strain is the fear of voluntary associations that the county administrators association, by virtue of its membership within the bureaucratic world, will be given disproportionate power *vis-à-vis* the state Office of Alcoholism. In fact, the county administration is far from autonomous—compliance to state standards is required. What is more, the county administration is operating within a larger county structure, where it not only has to contend with a Mental Health or Public Health administration, as explained earlier, but also with a Board of Supervisors. Typically, county alcoholism administrators must justify accounting procedures and programming decisions within that larger county administration, which further explains the tenacity of the separate identity process discussed in the previous chapter. Ideally, the state is supposed to set priorities, but based on a composite of all the county priorities. Often these stem not from the needs of the community, but from the fiscal needs of the county. When the probation department says it needs more money, it is not necessarily based on a county-wide assessment of needs.

Regarding the right of the county administration to approve all programs, one respondent asserted:

> I don't know why someone doesn't instigate a civil suit to do away with that provision—it's against civil rights, the right to organize. County administrators don't have the expertise, and the decisions are made on the basis of politics, on who they like and so forth.

"Politics," in an accusatory sense, is the byword of jurisdictional competition, with the ultimate arbiter, the state Office of Alcoholism, the usual target. Some accused the OA of, as one respondent put it:

> . . . playing a divide and conquer game, purposely dealing with each entity separately, and in some instances secretly—kind of handing out plums in order to keep everyone relatively satisfied while at the same time moving ahead with their own design.

Another suggested that the game is not so much divide and conquer as "please and placate," the bureaucratic attempt to be even-handed. Yet another respondent offered his opinion that what others see as a state design has occurred more out of accident, lack of knowledge, misunderstanding, and what he called "the over-reactive process":

> It is not unusual for an action (in the arena) to cause an over-reaction among opposing constituencies, and for the Office of Alcoholism to accomodate that over-reaction prematurely, and change things on that basis.

These statements are presented for just what they are, opinions, the salient point being not their merit but rather the spirit of advocacy they represent, a sense capped in one further quote:

> I go to many meetings from a defensive standpoint, because I know if I don't go somebody will stab me in the back.

As Don Cahalan has observed wryly, "What do people mean when they charge 'politics'—they mean *we* got the money and *they* didn't." For the most part, the competing process is related to carving the pie, a predictable outgrowth of the funding structure. In addition to project grants, discussed earlier, NIAAA was authorized by its enabling legislation to confer formula grants to the states on the basis of the relative population, financial need, and "need for more effective prevention, treatment, and rehabilitation of alcohol abuse and alcoholism." [2] Such thinking was in line with the "New Federalism" of the Nixon years, expressed by the first NIAAA director, Morris Chafetz, as "keeping power by giving it away." Although based on the principle that imposing more accountability on officials in states and localities would result in closer attention to community needs, experience in other arenas has demonstrated that this approach has fallen short of its goals. [3] Because of the previous low position accorded alcoholism programs within the states, Senator Hughes had opposed formula grants, and NIAAA in its early years gave them relatively little attention in favor of project grants.

This has created planning problems at the local level. If NIAAA establishes priorities, and a local private provider presents a grant proposal to meet those priorities, the resultant project *may* not be of the highest priority in the community. But, in effect, NIAAA has pre-empted the future use of local monies, for when the federal funds are no longer available, the project will turn to the county to pick up the costs. This explains why private providers have an interest in the federal/state, state/county competition—it is vital to their *continued* existence.

The scramble among grantees for the dollar is obvious enough to require no more than the mention. Seen from the perspective of a federal bureaucrat who faces the ultimate decision, it is described as follows:

> The National Advisory Countil approves all grants but we may not have enough money to cover all they approve. We then judge each on technical merit, institute priorities, but mix the two in a way only known to God.

Unfortunately, no divine intervention exists to help the state coordinate its planning with national planning. The California Office of Alcoholism was displeased when it discovered the federal Department of Transportation conducting a study similar to its own. Or more to the point, eyebrows were raised by those outside the bureaucratic world when the OA funded the Social Research Group to do a literature survey on alcoholism and minorities and NIAAA funded Stanford Research Institute to do what appeared to be the same. In some cases, duplication of effort could be intended for verification ("competitive analysis" in the language of the Defense Department). NIAAA, when confronted, can fall back on this explanation, which, nonetheless, does not satisfy the state bureaucracy. State authorities have review, but no veto, power over all project grants coming within the respective states. In cases where NIAAA has funded a project despite a negative state review, it is particularly irksome to have the onus put on the state when the federal funds are depleted. As vexing as these problems have been for the states and in turn the counties, the problems have increased since the decree emanating from the federal level in December, 1976, denying any future monies not matched with local funds. The California Department of Finance met this challenge by stating that existing projects faced with federal withdrawal of dollars would henceforth have to compete on an equal basis on the state level with all new grant proposals.

Thus is the situation set up for demonstrating the value of one's own program at the expense of others. Most often this takes the form of small snipes which create large responses, such as the statement attributed to Robert Dorris, president of Counselors on Alcoholism and Related Disorders (CARD). Dorris' consulting firm has helped develop several municipal court diversion programs in southern California, so it is not surprising to find him advising Senator Hathaway that these efforts, rather than the Hathaway favored occupational programs, afford the best opportunity for intervention in alcoholism.[4] Or the vying may center not around specific programs, but rather larger concepts of where the money should be spent, as expressed by Cahalan:

> ... Since such a mammoth part of the total alcohol problem expenditures is expended in treatment of those who are already alcoholics, the national, state and local authorities are inundated with merely meeting the vocal demands for more and more treatment funds; and thus prevention always gets the short end of the budget. This chronic state of affairs is further perpetuated because some powerful groups concerned primarily with treatment either actively or passively resent any expenditure of funds for prevention which might have been spent for treatment.[5]

Even within NIAAA itself, this competition exists. For instance, one bureaucrat charged with jurisdiction over prevention programs told me, "I'm still working on educating the people right here, and most of them haven't sat as long as you have to listen."

In other cases, the vying for funds is exacerbated by the separate identity issue. There is a jealous feeling among some people within the arena that both the "discovery" about alcohol being a drug and that a "polydrug problem" (alcohol taken in combination with other drugs) exists coincided with the drop in drug funds, as the Nixon administration announced it had "solved" the drug problem. (Bitter fights had ensued over changing the North American Association of Alcoholism Programs to the Alcohol and Drug Problems Association of North America.) Nevertheless, when one gets past the rhetoric, it is evident that any merit that might be found in looking at drugs and alcohol together, is overshadowed by the funding competition. At a public meeting in California, one county administrator pointed out that many physicians prescribe tranquilizers out of a lack of understanding of alcoholism. He expressed the displeasure of the county administrators association with the state Office of Alcoholism's inattention to "poly-abuse." To which the OA Director replied, realistically from his perspective, "We are not willing to have the dollars go for drug problems."

Bacon nicely captures the destructive aspects of the competitive spirit:

> I suggest that both a general anti-social-science attitude and also an "anti-any-other-alcohol-program except-my-own" attitude surrounds the social science approach in this field. Nor is it a one-way street; the social scientists, whether through defensiveness, arrogance, ignorance or other unfor-

tunate traits, have managed to provide their own significant contribution to the divisiveness of the conceptual aspect of alcohol phenomena. The nonchalance exhibited by some social scientists about their ignorance of biologic, psychologic and even legal and economic aspects of alcohol phenomena is at times rather disheartening to their more alcohol-oriented fellows.[6]

Bacon's observation is not only applicable to the social scientists, for it is an unfortunate truism that the singlemindedness of purpose which is required of dedicated careerists, especially those dependent on problematic funding, results in an exaggerated sense of the import of one's own work to the exclusion of others.

Competition for Eminence and the Public Eye

To some extent, competition for funds also entails competition for eminence. Alcoholism's low position in the federal funding scheme is often used in the drive for respectability suggested in Chapter 8, as when Dr. Chafetz termed "scandalous" the differential between the 8 percent of the funds provided to NIAAA for research and the approximately 25 percent provided other institutes.[7] A more recent update of this argument is the letter from four senators to President Carter apprising him of the disparity between the $750 million spent on cancer, and the $350 million on heart disease, to the $10 million spent in 1976 on alcoholism research.[8] An illustration is Table 1, published by *The Alcoholism Report* [9] when the Ford administration requested $13,179,000 for alcoholism research for 1978.

Another comparison is offered: the drive for an ever-widening military led by James Schlesinger, when serving as Secretary of Defense, was explained at the time as stemming from the desire, not simply to achieve a kind of parity or advantage that could be measured by statisticians and other analysts, but to sustain the kind of activity—research, development, production—that would be perceived everywhere as proof of a nation's resolve. It is this element that bears on comparisons between NIAAA and other institutes. Eminence (i.e., visibility that is *really* enhanced) is as much a factor in the competitive process as the earnest desire to buy a safe and permanent place in the federal funding picture. (I assert this in light of the arena's major drive for increased public visibility.)

It should be noted briefly that competition is also clearly geared toward the public, since the ultimate goal obviously is clients. Newspaper articles which appear to be informational about the general problem, often end on a note of special pleading for a specific mode of treatment. Furthermore, competing at the level of care ties into the re-

TABLE 1
Federal Outlays for Health Research and Research Facilities
(in millions of dollars)

	Outlays		
	1976 actual	1977 estimate	1978 estimate
Cancer	657	664	757
Cardiovascular	327	298	339
Mental health	125	120	126
Neurological and visual	205	174	211
Population and family planning	65	61	71
Environmental health	465	536	664
Aging	61	69	78
Metabolic diseases	194	179	203
Child health	104	93	102
Infectious diseases	170	204	201
Pulmonary	58	58	61
Dental	56	51	61
Health services research and development	52	84	85
Other research and development	556	710	631
Research facilities	44	28	20
Total	3,138	3,329	3,612

defining process. People have stakes in the varying definitions. A hospital administrator, faced with keeping the beds full, does not wish to be distracted by arguments over "medicalizing a social problem."

The Squeaking Wheel

The clash of worlds surrounding the issue of public inebriety provides an opportunity to examine the larger ramifications of the question: where should the money go? Allusion has been made to the Uniform Alcoholism and Intoxication Treatment Act of 1971,[10] the national effort to decriminalize alcoholism, and to the lag between passage of this legislation and implementation. A look at the competing process reveals, not a slackness at the state/local levels, but a very real concern over dollars. In San Francisco, a source of contention for the county advisory board was the allocation of approximately two-thirds of the county budget ($3.6 million in 1976) to "public inebriates," who were estimated to make up only four or five percent of the alcoholic population. Two-thirds of the budget was still not enough—"getting the public drunk off the street can be so expensive that it can sop up all the money, leaving very little for anything else." [11] Contraposed against the public pressure (from merchants, for instance) to put more dollars into removing the public inebriate from sight, is the drive for a respectable image for the middle-class alcoholic, as discussed earlier. An idea of the competition between these two populations is suggested by the following quote from the director of a hospital treatment clinic:

> Our facility is geared to the middle-class person—a publisher, the chief librarian, a university professor, something like that. He has no place to go. He will not go to the county hospital unless he has lost everything he has. We are interested in people who have a family, a job . . . they can be salvaged. And you say, well that's pretty damn snobbish. What about all those poor people? Those poor people are only 5% of the alcoholic population. Maybe 3%, and they have been absorbing about 80% of the time, the talent, and the money.

To assume that all public inebriates are exclusively skid row habitués is a jump in logic that is often made. The distinction seems rather to be that the middle- and upper-class person who becomes a public nuisance while drunk is often put in a taxi and sent home. As one respondent reported:

> I talked to an officer out of the chief's office, and he told me if they had to prove legally that these people were intoxicated (under law, a danger to themselves and others) they couldn't prove it with any more than 10 to 20%. These people are really picked up because they don't conform in dress or behavior to the area that they happen to be in when the patrol happens to come around.

Nor should it be assumed that all inhabitants of the skid row area are chronic inebriates. The important point for our purposes is that *within the arena* itself the term "public inebriate" signifies the skid row chronic drinker, and that decriminalization, (i.e., the redefining of alcoholism as a disease), intertwined with urban redevelopment, has further dichotomized skid row problems from other alcohol problems in the competition for resources. Except when used as an argument for increasing services for the middle-class ("Unless something is done at this end, skid row is going to get worse"), services for skid row are looked upon as a tremendous drain on the dollar.

What began in the 1960s as concern on the part of civil libertarians over involuntary incarceration of alcoholics [12] has grown in the 1970s into a loosening of attitudes toward "victimless crime"—a sense that the police and the courts have more serious offenders to pursue than drunks, drug addicts and prostitutes. All over the country, court rulings have challenged the precept that public drunkenness is a crime, and, as explained earlier, public detoxification facilities have grown out of this development. Room has noted the lengthy history of the failure of expectations that one solution to a problem will entirely replace another, citing as just one instance the closing of alcoholism treatment facilities at the onset of Prohibition in the expectation that they would no longer be needed.[13] Similarly, one bureaucrat from a county adjacent to San Francisco complained that his one non-medical detoxification unit was faced with an impossible burden to totally eradicate the public inebriate, out of the unrealistic optimism of the courts, business and police. In a reversal of the civil libertarian intent out of which decriminalization has grown, pressure was put on this bureaucrat to convert the facility to involuntary treatment, when it appeared that the problem was not being solved quickly enough.

Use of the term "skid row" began in the nineteenth century. Originally denoting streets down which logs were skidded, it described the squalid neighborhoods of itinerant loggers in the Pacific Northwest.[14] Wiseman notes that not only are these neighborhoods to be found in every fairly large city in the United States, but the area and its culture are strikingly similar from city to city and from time period to time period:

> . ... the majority of Skid Row residents are men alone, without families, whose heavy drinking orientation outweighs efforts toward maintaining steady employment or improved living standards.[15]

These men are known as the "revolving door population" [16] for two reasons. One is that they tend to re-use public resources; the other is that they go from resource to resource ("making the loop," as Wiseman reports the street language) because the resources do not meet their needs. So long as they were contained within a specific geographic area, this population did not constitute a "problem." It was urban redevelopment, the tearing down of the hotels that housed them, that moved the skid rowers into adjacent areas, creating *too much* visibility for business, the police, the courts, and arena participants who fear the depletion of their newly won funds.

On a more positive note, urban renewal also brought the sociologists into the arena (some people may not consider this a plus—I admit a bias), and led to the development of the half-way house. (For example, Rubington's rediscovery of Philadelphia's skid row and his recommendation that facilities should be located away from the "action of the city" to effect dispersion, was supported by the Greater Philadelphia Movement, a civic organization concerned with the real estate problems of redevelopment and the need to provide services.) [17] However, even those most deeply concerned with the urban public inebriate problem, while praising social setting detoxification and social model recovery homes, admit that fiscal limitations prohibit providing enough facilities to cover this entire population. And they admit other obstacles. To quote a lawyer:

> My clients fear detox facilities run by professionals almost as much as jail, because they fear the people running them will not be sympathetic—for example, you can't get a tranquilizer from a non-medical detox facility, whereas if you're going through the DT's in jail, sometimes they'll give you a shot of whiskey.

Nostalgic reference to county jails as "rehabilitation centers" was made by one respondent (admittedly not a habitué), and by a policeman formerly charged with supervision, who described the jails as "their home, where we fed them, gave them fresh clothes, tobacco, nourishing food, and brought them up to shape." The public inebriate had been viewed as a model prisoner, "docile in custody, and, if health permits, willing to work . . . the backbone of the inmate work force." [18]

Glowing accounts of jail aside, detoxification facilities have not met expectations. In some cases, blame can be placed at the door of the center. As explained earlier, just calling a center "non-medical" (particularly when staffing is low and hampered by civil service restrictions on rotating jobs) does not ensure the ideal social setting, as originally envisioned.[19] In addition, agencies want clients who are redeemable: ". . . staffs will often discourage or refuse particular clients or classes of clients. In two of the four California centers evaluated, the staff for a time maintained formal 'Do-Not-Admit' or 'Undesirable' lists." [20] Room found two additionally salient reasons why detoxification centers have fallen short. One is that a substantial proportion of center clients do not accept or follow through on referral for further treatment on a voluntary basis. The other is that the client is often back on the street more quickly than under criminal justice procedures, replacing the "revolving door" with a "spinning door." [21] What is more, the uneven adoption among counties of decriminalization statutes placed an impossible financial burden on those counties that were attempting to substitute detoxification for jail. Santa Clara County, a community to the south of San Francisco, responded to the realization that it was becoming "Santa Claus County" (providing detoxification services to clients flooding in from other counties where jail is the prevalent procedure) by proposing a return of the arrest option to the police. David Hampton, the county's director of Alcoholism Services, was quoted as follows:

> In the two months of September and October (1976), 85 of the problematic drunks each averaged 16 admissions to detox facilities. This is 35% of all admissions. In terms of dollars, of a $1.7 million annual operation, 40% of this or about $700,000 is spent on these people. This amounts to about $10,000 per person. We hope to be able to give back the arresting power, but still have police use the health care system when applicable.[22]

In suggesting legislation at the state level that would allow thirty-day arrest on a civil rather than a criminal basis, so that a person could be held legally within the health care system (seventy-two hours is the present limit), Hampton pinpointed one element that is usually overlooked by those who fear involuntary treatment—the month in jail drying out *did* in the past produce some physiological reversal, such as liver regeneration. Hampton expressed the frustration of the bureaucratic and recovery service worlds:

> Just recently two of the people, whom we have seen many times, have died. They are out there killing themselves, and we are helping them.

To which Kurtz and Regier would answer, the sense of futility was predictable, and has its roots in the very redefining process out of which decriminalization grew:

> In part, the incongruence is implicit in the disease concept, which embodies the notion that those who are labeled as ill should be treated with some compassion and excused from routine responsibilities, while also assuming that the sick will actively seek help and cooperate in promoting their recovery. The Skid Rower is likely to be guilty of flagrant and repeated violations of this assumption. He cannot satisfy the expectations of the sick role just because he has been labeled "sick." And the importance of "proper" role performance cannot be overlooked, for it is questionable whether repeated violations of the role prescriptions will be tolerated by professionals within the health-care system. Moreover, poor role performance will be exacerbated by additional violations of expected standards for personal hygiene, dress, appearance and social behavior. Most likely, through decriminalization the Skid Rower will be freed from the threat of being punished for not satisfying the role of "person on the street" only to have it replaced with that of failing in the role of "sick person." [23]

Transmuted into the competitive dollar, this frustration is increased. Acceptance of the Uniform Alcoholism and Treatment Act is subject to state option. California is not among the states complying, although as mentioned above, California has its own legislation by which the police *may* take the public inebriate to a facility for evaluation and treatment in lieu of jail. Any discussion of conformance with the Uniform Act's proviso that police may not arrest a person unless he is incapacitated entails discussion of the cost of providing alternative services. Former director of the California Office of Alcoholism, Loran Archer, graphically expressed the major impediment: "Implementing the Uniform Act would cost the state $40 million a year. It would mean diverting all present programs into that expenditure." [24] Some federal money is available, providing *all* discriminatory statutes have been repealed. In California, individual county statutes still exist under which drunkenness is the gravamen of a petty criminal offense, such as loitering, vagrancy or disturbing the peace. Regardless, as Senator Gregorio's administrative assistant, Peter Herman, stated at the time, even with repeal of these statutes, California would "only" be eligible for $1.1 million, "which would be inadequate to fund *one* county." [25]

California chose to launch a pilot program in two counties, at $2 million for a two-year period, providing the full range of services deemed necessary for genuine decriminalization—a social model detoxification program, recovery homes, and twenty-four hour-a-day drop-in centers. Of these, the drop-in center may prove to be the balm for all concerned, placating the merchant by decreasing public visibility, decreasing the load on the jails, and leaving the detoxification services for more willing clients. What is to be hoped is that such demonstration projects will lead to a more realistic adjustment of the *total* program to the client needs, and a heightened sense of the different needs of different populations. As expressed by Shore and Luce:

> The residents of skid row need nutritional meals, dietary supplements, occasional detoxification, health screening, medical attention, real beds, and warm clothing. They require a place to wash their clothes and to cash welfare checks without having to pay the same surcharge they must meet at local restaurants and grocery stores. Those few residents who want to stop drinking can profit from involvement in "dry" living groups whose members are also attempting to abstain. Other residents who wish to continue drinking should be allowed to do so in "wet" hotels.

> These and other services can be furnished at a much lower cost than they now are in most cities. For example, although some public inebriates require intensive medical care, most who request routine detoxification can be cared for at non-hospital drying out centers in the community. Similarly, health screening, public showers, washing machines, recreational opportunities, and counseling services can be made available at inexpensive drop-in centers. Given the availability of relevant services, some skid row residents may cycle out of 'the loop'. Most will stay on skid row but their lives will be less destructive. Expensive public resources, such as jails and hospitals, will not be misused by the skid row population, which instead will use facilities that are better suited to their needs and do not function as revolving doors.[26]

Presenting a United Front

Counterbalanced against the diverse manifestations of the "crab syndrome," is the growing sense among arena constituents that, after all, they are swimming in the same ocean. Thus, a mirror image of the competing process is the reflection of the scattered efforts to coordinate activities. Over and above tenuous coalitions like that between the volunteer action world, recovery service world and the alcoholic beverage industries world on the issue of combining the California Office of Alcoholism with the Department of Alcoholic Beverage Control,[27] attempts have been made to form more permanent alliances in order to demonstrate strength. Of course, coalitions will continue to shift as issues shift. Nevertheless, it is important to take note of the enhanced effectiveness *(and* visibility) of alliances such as the National Coalition for Women's Alcoholism Programs (NCWAP), composed of fourteen NIAAA-funded women's treatment programs, testifying before Congress; or the San Francisco Alcoholism Consortium, composed of eleven recovery service agencies, petitioning the Criminal Justice Planning Officer *en bloc* for a drop-in center for "street drinkers." A clear contrast to the competition evident when four organizations were fighting over three seats on the accreditation board,[28] is the Coalition for Adequate Alcoholism Programs formed at the instigation of the National Council on Alcoholism in December, 1975. In addition to NCA, this alliance attracted nineteen organizations at origin, as varied as the AFL-CIO, American Indian Commission on Alcohol and Drug Abuse, United States Brewers Association, Volunteers of America, The Salvation Army, Christopher D. Smithers Foundation, National Council of Community Mental Health Centers, Association of Labor-Management Administrators and Consultants on Alcoholism (ALMACA), National Association of Alcoholism Counselors and Trainers (NAACT), The Rutgers Center of Alcohol Studies, Association of Halfway House Alcoholism Programs (AHHAP), Distilled Spirits Council of the U. S. (DISCUS), and Council of State and Territorial Alcoholism Authorities (CSTAA). Initial efforts were directed toward continuation of NIAAA as a separate institute backed by adequate appropriations, and toward encouraging states to adopt the Uniform Alcoholism and Intoxication Treatment Act (i.e., decriminalization). By 1977, the Coalition was projecting enough of the unified image to appear, from press accounts, to have had an impact on the early Carter administration discussions of combining alcohol and drug interests.[29] In a later development, the private treatment sector of the recovery service world has seen fit to transcend individual differences regarding treatment approaches not only to form yet one more organization, the National Association of Alcoholism Treatment Programs (NAATP), but to hire a Washington lobbyist, former Senator Frank Moss, the first former legislator to represent the arena at the national level on an official basis.

A similar development is the formation of a National Committee of State Advisory Councils for Alcohol and Drug Abuse. (As explained earlier, despite the strong separate-identity thrust on the part of alcohol arena constituents, alcohol and drug programs are still combined in a single department in a number of states.) Twenty states were represented at the first meeting of this group, which explored the creation of a formal organization to provide a forum for exchange, and dialogue among states and with policy makers. Discussion around the formation of this group points up another contributing factor in the advisory board/director authority issue discussed in Chapter 4: the rapid turnover of state alcoholism program directors. At the Alcohol and Drug Problems Association meeting from which this new group evolved, Leonard Boche, outgoing President of ADPA, expressed the opinion that "the newly coalesced group of state advisory chairs could provide the field with a 'level of continuity which we have not been able to obtain with professional staff directors.' " [30]

Room has commented on the astonishing variety of federal agencies which deal with "or potentially impinge on" alcohol problems in the course of their activities. He cites as examples:

- drinking and the selling of drinks on airliners are governed by federal civil-aviation regulations;
- drinking on military bases and by service people is subject to military regulations, and drinking in National Parks to Interior Department regulations;
- advertising of beer and wine on TV and radio is subject to the rules of the Federal Communication Commission;
- Internal Revenue Service rules govern the deductibility of buying drinks as a business expense;
- drinking places which discriminate among customers by race or sex are outlawed under federal equal-protection rulings.[31]

Although the federal legislation which established NIAAA also called for an Interagency Committee on Federal Activities for Alcohol Abuse and Alcoholism to provide for the exchange of information necessary to coordinate federal programs, this Committee did not begin to meet until 1976. Estimates obtained from the various agencies represented on the Committee indicate more than $1.1 billion as the total federal expenditure on alcoholism programs from fiscal year 1974 through fiscal year 1977, as indicated in the Table 2:[32]

TABLE 2
Summary of Expenditures of Federal Departments for Combatting Alcohol Abuse and Alcoholism

FEDERAL DEPARTMENT	FY 1974	FY 1975	FY 1976	PROJECTED FY 1977	TOTALS (INCLUDING FY 1977)
Department of the Treasury	$ 60,671	$ 86,279	$ 138,765	$ 178,044	$ 463,759
Department of Transportation Nat'l Hwy Traffic Safety Admin.	42,936,206*	38,044,872	42,078,469	47,017,177	170,076,724
Veterans Administration	32,420,000	46,332,818	54,315,075	54,675,075	187,742,968
Civil Service Commission	172,900	195,900	194,300	194,300	757,400
Department of Labor	270,809	269,484	76,248	4,700**	621,241
Department of Interior	No Dollars Provided --	--	--	--	--
Department of Defense	29,682,000	33,380,000	33,848,000	33,305,000	138,261,000****
Department of Justice (LEAA)	5,585,183	3,010,827	1,086,896	No Data Provided	9,682,906***
Department of Health, Education, and Welfare:					
NIAAA	199,975,000	167,569,000	151,305,000	152,491,000	671,340,000
HSA – Bureau of Medical Services	788,189	1,304,173	1,471,651	1,665,948	5,229,961
HSA – Indian Health Service	47,500	47,500	48,500	52,500	196,000
SSA – Div. Personnel	142,284	104,173	90,362	66,439	423,265******
SSA – Bur. Disability Insurance	7,500	7,500	7,500	7,500	30,000
Social Rehabilitation Service	No Data Provided	--	--	--	--
FDA	N/A	--	--	--	--
HRA	25,000	25,000	25,000	25,000	100,000
Subtotal – HEW	$200,985,473	$169,057,346	$152,948,013	$154,308,387	$ 677,319,226
TOTALS	$312,113,242	$290,377,526	$284,685,766	$289,682,683	$1,184,925,224

*Including $2,457,724 internal;   **Training only;   ***No FY 77 data;
****Including $8,046,000 for FY 76 transition quarter;   *****Includes $20,007 for FY-76 transition quarter.
****Includes $8,046,000 for FY 76 transition quarter;   *****Includes $20,007 for FY-76 transition quarter.

It would be naive to assume that the mere establishment of such a panel represents a guarantee of coordination between agency interests as diverse as health, welfare, rehabilitation, highway safety, law enforcement, and economic opportunity, particularly in light of "the low policy level of officials of the interagency group." [33] Nevertheless, that this panel had begun to function is a significant indication of the increasingly preceived need to consolidate efforts.

Other attempts have emanated from the bureaucratic world to bring about better communication among the arena's constituents. It was, in fact, a grant from NIAAA that enabled the Alcohol and Drug Problems Association (ADPA) to be the secretariat for the San Francisco Congress which pulled 64 organizations together.[34] Task forces and forums, both on a state and national level, provide another avenue. In California, Senator Gregorio scheduled public hearings and roundtable discussions away from Sacramento, successfully attracting wider participation. For a select few within the research world, international conferences provide the opportunity for a wider prospective on alcohol problems. This ties in with our discussion of building respectability, since possible recognition at international conferences makes the arena a more prestigious career opportunity; the enhanced status reverts back on NIAAA and on the entire arena in terms of visibility.

There are yet further indications of a felt need for more exchange of information and perspectives, and for unified expression. In 1976, the California Association of Alcoholic Recovery Homes (CAARH), in planning its annual meeting at Lake Tahoe, convinced other groups (the State Advisory Board, the Women's Commission, the Black Commission, the County Alcohol Administrators Association) to meet there at the same time. Each group held a separate meeting, but respondents reported valuable personal interaction. The following year, joint sponsorship heralded the Second Annual California Conference on Alcoholism in Santa Barbara. By 1979, eighteen groups were listed as endorsing and cooperating in the Fourth Annual California Conference on Alcoholism organized by CAARH.

To some extent, these groups should thank Governor Brown for providing them with a greater sense of community. A huge victory had been attained with the passage in 1975 of a new liquor tax, with a vote in the California Senate of 26 to 9, and in the Assembly of 65 to 8. The added tax would have cost drinkers two cents on a six-pack of beer, seven cents on a quart of whiskey and a penny on a gallon of wine, and was expected to raise approximately $35 million a year to support treatment and prevention efforts. Success was attributed to: (1) the establishment in California of a clean campaign act governing reporting of contributions, which caused a decline in financing from the alcoholic beverage industries; (2) press support; and (3) the increasingly vocal and visible arena constituents, particularly the recovered alcoholics. In spite of this, the governor vetoed the bill, based on his oft-announced opposition to any new taxes and especially to inflexible special tax funds. Nor did the governor endear himself to the arena constituents when he suggested in typical Brown-ese, "Not every disease has a cure."

A new group, Friends of Senate Bill 204, was formed, and the most organized political activity in the state arena's history was mounted. Although the state senate failed to override the governor's veto, falling seven votes short of the two-thirds needed, out of the Friends of Senate Bill 204 grew the California Citizens Action on Alcoholism Public Policy (CCAAPP). As mentioned earlier, Alcoholics Anonymous members are prohibited from exercising political activity in the name of the fellowship. Furthermore, under Internal Revenue rules, a non-profit charitable corporation (such as the National Council on Alcoholism) may not use an "appreciable amount" of its time and resources to influence legislation. This has roughly been taken to mean ten percent, and the California NCA has had no trouble with the ruling. Now, however, having tried their wings in an almost successful override attempt, arena constituents with a separate lobbying organization are ready to fly wider at the next opportunity. A sagacious observation was offered by one respondent:

> As I participated, I enjoyed seeing the unifying force that developed. But I dreaded the result if it had passed. The nature of the issue was such that the major forces could unify to accomplish the goal, but if it had passed, and that amount of money had become available, the splits would again occur. Maybe the process is what we have to go through—maybe *the unifying nature of that process* needs to jell before we're ready for all that money. (Emphasis added.)

That *any* unification was possible indicates the arena had moved on to a stage where establishing turf rights was not the sole concern. As one pioneer expressed it:

> We had little opportunity in the past to get together. And as my own philosophy regarding recovery from alcoholism was evolving, I was busy bringing my own staff along.

The defeat on the tax bill was eventually mitigated when the governor signed a 1976 alcoholism budget one-third higher than the previous year, providing more funds than the tax bill he vetoed would have gleaned. But finances continue to influence the demonstrating process, as we shall see in the next chapter.

Notes

1. Jay Lewis, "Washington Report," *Journal of Studies on Alcohol,* Vol. 2 (1974), p. 1392.
2. Title III, Comprehensive Alcohol Abuse and Alcoholism Prevention Treatment and Rehabilitation Act of 1970.
3. *See, for example:* Carroll L. Estes, "New Federalism and Aging," *Developments in Aging,* Report of the Special Committee on Aging, U. S. Senate; June 24, 1975, pp. 150-57.
4. *The Alcoholism Report,* Vol. 4 (September 24, 1976), p. 8.
5. *The Alcoholism Report,* Vol. 5 (October 22, 1976), p. 8.
6. S.D. Bacon, "Concepts," in W.J. Filstead et al. (eds), *Alcohol, New Thinking and New Directions* (Cambridge, Mass.: Ballinger, 1976), p. 103.
7. Morris Chafetz, speaking to the National Academy of Sciences, January 10-11, 1975, Washington, D.C., as reported in *Physician's Alcohol Newsletter,* Vol. 10 (February, 1975), p. 1.
8. Letter from Senators Harrison A. Williams, Jacob K. Javits, William D. Hathaway, and Richard S. Schweiker, as reported in *The Alcoholism Report,* Vol 5 (February 11, 1977), p. 1.
9. *The Alcoholism Report,* Vol. 5 (January 18, 1977), p. 6.
10. See Chapter 7.
11. Don Cahalan, as quoted in the *San Francisco Examiner* (February 12, 1976) p. 6.
12. See Chapter 7.
13. Robin Room, "Comment on the Uniform Alcoholism and Intoxication Treatment Act," *Journal of Studies on Alcohol,* Vol. 37 (1976), p. 134.
14. See: J.P. Wiseman, *Stations of the Lost* (Englewood Cliffs, N.J: Prentice-Hall, 1970); and R. Shore and J. Luce, *To Your Health* (New York: Seabury Press, 1976), pp. 197-200.
15. Wiseman, *Stations,* p. 4.
16. *See:* David Pittman and C. Wayne Gordon, *The Revolving Door: A Study of the Chronic Police Case Inebriate* (Glencoe, Ill.: The Free Press, 1958).
17. E. Rubington, *What To Do Before Skid Row Is Demolished* (Philadelphia: The Greater Philadelphia Movement, 1958). *See also:* H.M. Bahr, "The Gradual Disappearance of Skid Row," *Social Problems,* Vol. 15 (1967), pp. 41-45; Leonard Blumberg, Thomas E. Shipley, Jr., and Irving W. Shander, *Skid Row and Its Alternatives* (Philadelphia: Temple University Press, 1973); D. J. Bogue, *Skid Row in American Cities* (Chicago: University of Chicago, 1963); J. P. Spradley, *You Owe Yourself A Drunk: An Ethnography of Urban Nomads* (Boston: Little Brown, 1970); and S.E. Wallace *Skid Row as a Way of Life* (Totawa, N.J.: Bedminster Press, 1965, reprinted as a Harper Torchbook, New York: Harper & Row, 1968).
18. Steve Thompson and associates, "Drunk on the Street: An Evaluation of Services to the Public Inebriate in Sacramento County," report to the Sacramento County, California Department of Mental Health, 1975.
19. See discussion of the expectations for social setting detoxification in Chapter 7.
20. Room, "Comment," p. 135. *See:* Thompson and associates "Drunk on the Street"; Arthur Young and company, "Final Report Evaluation of the Santa Clara County Alcohol Facility (Evaluation and Referral Unit,"

Sacramento, California, 1975); Ronald W. Fagan, Jr. and Armand L. Mauss, "Padding the Revolving Door: An Initial Assessment of the Uniform Alcoholism and Intoxication Treatment Act In Practice," *Social Problems,* Vol. 26 (1978), pp. 232-46.

21. See: D. Lockhart and Desrys M., "Detoxification Center Evaluation Report: Sacramento County: June 1973–April 1974" (Sacramento: State of California, Office of Alcohol Program Management, 1975).
22. *The Alcoholism Information Distiller,* No. 76-10 (December, 1976).
23. N. Kurtz and M. Regier, "The Uniform Alcoholism and Intoxication Treatment Act," *Journal of Studies on Alcohol,* Vol. 36 (1975), pp. 1434-35.
24. Remarks made at a Round-Table Discussion on "Relationship of the NIAAA and the State-funded Alcoholism Program," San Mateo, California, December 8, 1976.
25. Ibid.
26. Shore and Luce, *To Your Health,* pp. 199-200. *See also:* Thomas L. Jones, "Drop-In and Referral Centers for Public Inebriates," discussion paper prepared for the California Office of Alcoholism, 1976.
27. See Chapter 9.
28. See Chapter 8.
29. *See: The Alcoholism Report,* Vol. 5 (January 28, 1977), p. 2.; *The Alcoholism Report,* Vol. 5 (March 11, 1977), p. 3.
30. *The Alcoholism Report,* Vol. 6 (October 14, 1977), p. 7.
31. Robin Room, "Draft Position Paper: Policy Initiatives in Alcohol Problems Prevention," Social Research Group Working F48, prepared for National Institute on Alcohol Abuse and Alcoholism, 1978, p. 31.
32. *The Alcoholism Report,* Vol. 5 (November 12, 1976), p. 6.
33. Remarks of Senator Hathaway, as reported in *The Alcoholism* Report Vol. 5 (November 26, 1976), p. 8.
34. See Chapter 2.

11.

Selecting Supportive Data

Nowhere is the "social construction of reality" more evident than in the *selecting* of data to demonstrate the alcohol problem. Students of the arena, as seen from the clients' perspective, have noted the selective process of self-reporting exhibited by these clients, in order to get into or out of treatment.[1] However, this strategy is by no means confined to the client population, or to would-be grant recipients, as suggested earlier. The universal human tendency to select out that which enhances a desired position manifests itself in a variety of ways. For instance, it is evident in the use of language: even the most vehement anti-psychiatric members of the recovery service world readily use psychiatric terminology ("the whole arena suffers from the denial syndrome") as rhetorical weapons. Similarly, arena participants select definitions of alcoholism which have utility for them—in a sense engaging in special-purpose borrowing, drawing on definitions of the American Medical Association or the American Psychiatric Association to suit selective needs. However, it is in the selective use of figures, the configuring of information, that this process is most extravagantly used.

Gouldner pinpoints a utilitarian thrust behind the programming emerging from New Deal days:

> Increasingly, the Welfare State's strategy is to transform the sick, the deviant, and the unskilled into "useless citizens," and to return them to

"society" only after periods of hospitalization, treatment, counseling, training, or retraining. It is this emphasis upon the reshaping of persons that differentiates the Welfare State's disposal strategies from those that tended to cope with the useless primarily by custody, exclusion, and insulation from society. The newer strategies differ from the old in that they seek to be self-financing; the aim is to increase the supply of the useful and to diminish that of the useless.[2]

Faced with the challenge of providing programs that are self-financing, "evaluation" of these programs succumbs to "the vitality of mythical numbers." [3]

Statisticians are the first to admit that figures are only as trustworthy as the use to which they are put—in that sense a borrowing process is at work here too. Just as the choice lies with television weather forecasters between predicting "partly cloudy" or "mostly fair," just as social scientists have been known to color their reporting by qualifying "as little as 50%" or "as many as 50%," so too arena participants can be found justifying Mark Twain's famous observation: "There are three kinds of lies—plain lies, damn lies, and statistics." And, as Irving Kristol, has pointed out, the magic of figures is impressive:

> The fact is that the partisan use of statistics in the modern world seems to have outdistanced the ability of even well-informed and educated citizens to cope with them. . . . One can do quite marvelous things with statistics, and the sad truth is that most of us are utterly defenseless against their inherent persuasive power.[4]

No one questions the need for accountability—it is the form that accountability takes, the problems it avoids and the problems it creates, that are at the focus of this chapter.

The Audiences

Increased visibility has brought in its wake increased oversight. It is important to understand that there are multiple audiences demanding proof of efficacy. Providers must answer to the bureaucracy that is funding them: the county bureaucracy to its advisory board and to the state; the state to the state advisory board and the state legislature and the Department of Finance; NIAAA to the national advisory council, the Congress, the General Accounting Office and the Officer of Management and Budget (OMB). Of these, the last epitomizes the threat hanging over all government programming. OMB performs an accounting function for the president—it is expected to be a watchdog agency, ready to trim the budgets of any departments that appear to be spending excessively. In a

systematic study which probed the immortality of government organizations by comparing lists of federal agencies in 1923 and 1973, Herbert
Kaufman, the principal investigator, found these agencies to be enjoying
an "indisputable hardiness." [5] Nevertheless, Kaufman stressed his correlate finding that agencies can and do die. And, as a bureaucrat-respon-
dent told me, the hatchet of OMB is the final *bête noire:*

> This is what we saw happening under Ford—they were saying we'll com-
> bine you with health block funding, take a million out here, a million out
> there, then OMB cuts another million. That way you don't have to cut a
> program out, just disguise it.

In reality, as Kaufman points out, federal agencies are protected by a
fortuitous element: the size of the federal budget. The budget is now so
huge that Congress cannot treat it as a new document each year:

> Rather, the record of expenditures in the recent past is taken as a base, and
> attention is focused on whether to exceed the base by some fraction (which
> is what agencies typically request), reduce it by some fraction (which is
> what agency critics and economy-minded people urge), or leave it as is.
> Total elimination of funds for an established agency or even massive
> slashes approaching total elimination are unknown, for all practical
> purposes.[6]

It is perhaps more likely that a new Bureau of Lowered Expectations
will be established than that NIAAA will be totally eliminated. Nevertheless, it is the threat of extinction, not the reality, that is the governing
principle. As a *Washington Post* editorial summarized the consequences,
Congress tends to fight the bureaucratic aging process by "heckling
agencies, poking at them, issuing more directives and demanding more
reports—while voting them more money to pay for more personnel and
more activities." [7] OMB, Congress, state legislatures are looking for
proof of efficient expenditure—increasingly so, as the tighten-the-belt
philosophy of the 1970s takes hold. As Senator Gregorio told the alcohol
arena constituency in California:

> Legislators are faced with the nagging problem of the educator who tells
> them, "you can't evaluate learning by just giving a test," and the probation
> officer who says, "you can't just look at the record." They all say, "we're
> providing intangible services that can't be measured. Everyone says just
> give us the money and trust us." But we've come to the end of that line—
> we need tangible, measurable things to look at.[8]

Just as the Russian menace increases commensurate with the Defense
Department budget needs, the administrative and legislative mandate

for show-and-tell is read as a mandate to devise easily translatable demonstrations of the worth of alcohol programs.

This explains the selling power of the industrial alcoholism programs discussed earlier: they provide the easiest means of demonstrating benefits over costs, and, especially in California, fit nicely with the vocational rehabilitation orientation of the state Office of Alcoholism. For example, it is possible to calculate the increased taxes and purchasing power of those who remain employed and useful to society, balancing variables such as rates of absenteeism, growth of income of the national product, inflation, depression etc., and come up with figures to equal program costs. Of course, issues are sidestepped in the process. For instance, the assumption that the worker lost is not replaceable; the fact that most of the taxes go to the federal government, while the state bears most of the cost of programs; the sensitivity of absenteeism to economic conditions, e.g., recession.

Such deflections can only obscure the purpose at hand: the obligation on the part of the legislature and the governor to require accountability, and the obligation on the part of the bureaucracy to provide the proof. In California, the governor's veto of the longed-for tax bill to increase alcohol funding impressed this need on all, causing a tightening up of measurement strategy, but increasing the risk, as one respondent put it, of "measurement becoming the tail that wags the dog." What is more, this is a risk that is likely to increase in direct relation to the drive for third-party payments for alcoholics, as presaged by James Isbister, former administrator of the Alcohol, Drug Abuse and Mental Health Administration (ADAMHA):

> It is my personal belief that major health policies are going to be set in an operational sense largely through accounting and reimbursement procedures, both with respect to the kind of services which will be reimbursed and with respect to costs . . . (And most important) is the unflagging attention to the gathering of actuarial data so that we are able to meet the actuaries on their own ground. . . .[9]

In other words, the insurance criteria for reimbursement and accounting procedures stand to distort further the emphasis on highly measurable programs to the neglect of the less measurable ones.

The Prevalent American Illness

To date, the easiest way to communicate effectiveness of programs has been to submit to what Griffith Edwards has called "the prevalent American illness—the belief in standarized guidelines, the magic of the word 'monitoring,' and a belief in something called evaluation." [10] An editorial in *The Hearth* poignantly expresses the predicament:

> Elected public officials demand demonstrations of cost effectiveness; the state and counties embark on a variety of program evaluation activities; the legislature sponsors its own evaluative studies; private programs and associations assume defensive postures—knowing well what the paperwork game does to programs; arguments rage back and forth about what we all basically know to be true: California has good alcoholism programs that are generally quite effective. The question is, *how do we demonstrate it*—to everyone's satisfaction? [11] (Emphasis added.)

Much faith was put into a computerized system set up by Stanford Research Institute (SRI) to monitor and evaluate NIAAA-funded treatment programs, by measuring such items as scores of quantity-frequency of alcoholic beverage consumed, and impairment (shakes, blackouts, quarrelsomeness or aggressiveness while drinking). Interviews were designed to occur at client intake, 30 days later, and again in 180 days. NIAAA Director Chafetz stressed the importance of uniformity of data on program planning and on judging effectiveness: "A profile of monthly project activities in the following areas is reported each month: initial contacts, intakes, total terminations (and number completing treatment), pre-intakes served active clients, 90 days caseload and full time equivalent staff involved in direct and indirect services." [12] Regardless of criticism of, as one respondent put it, "politics by capitation—head count credibility," the SRI system, as a *recording* system, did yield some useful data. NIAAA found at the first readings that the utilization of the services was enormously low; the centers had failed to reach their primary target population, the mainstream middle-class population; very little dent was being made in "early intervention," and the ratio of staff time to patients seen was very high. Based on this information, a shift was made in 1973 away from NIAAA funding of in-patient medical care and toward "more cost-effective outpatient services offering group therapy." [13] Similarly, the state of California's Management Information System, the form for which was eventually redesigned down to a single page, is expected to yield basic demographs, such as distribution of special target groups, i.e. women and minorities.

Despite the use to which such figures are put—as in oversimplifying conclusions or expecting an information system to double as a means of evaluation—in practice, genuinely accurate evaluation is very difficult. Of course, as one bureaucrat sardonically expressed it:

> You have the same problem if you don't have the data—people will still do the interpretation, will tell you what the nature of the problem is by what

they saw as they walked down the street. I feel it is less of a problem, if you have *some* data.

The difficulties in measuring results of programs are manifold. Most crucial is the unreliability of the figures, reliant as they are on self-reporting. Not only do clinicians have an obvious interest in reporting high census figures, but at intake ". . . there is often a strong material incentive for the potential client to create a particular impression, which may well be that of a person with a host of problems." [14] As to follow-up inquiries, most alcoholics can control their drinking to the point of stopping for a period of time.[15] Consequently critics note an additional bias in the reporting system: "the respondent fills out the form in the clinic—he can complete the form and go out and get drunk." Follow-up is also hindered by the stigma of alcoholism—once a person is out of treatment, he wants to blend with the rest of society. Another problem lies in comparison of data. Most people are likely to enter treatment in a time of crisis. If the history immediately before treatment is examined, 30-day follow-up is likely to look like an improvement. Also, the criteria for admission vary from program to program; those with a wider admission policy will suffer from comparison with centers that will only accept highly motivated clients. Furthermore, successful outcome has been found to be directly related to the extent of impairment before treatment. Thus comparison between success rates of programs presents a distorted picture (e.g., chances of improvement are far better in an industrial program than in a program for chronic alcoholics with multiple problems). Comparisons made between counties on the basis of cost-effectiveness also present a false impression. One county may have a client population of predominantly public inebriates while another is servicing clients with less than a year of drinking problems. Costs vary greatly: one county alcoholism office may be housed in a rent-free facility, its services integrated with other services, while another bears the full brunt of these costs.

Yet another hindrance to evaluation is the difficulty in converting what is going on in treatment into measures of success. O'Briant has summarized the complexity of this issue:

> . . . we assume that if an alcoholic person participates in a recovery program and then stays sober, the program was successful and therefore valuable. This assumption may or may not be true. This same alcoholic may have participated in several programs over a period of years and perhaps gained something from each experience necessary in his final commitment to recovery. Without their previous experiences, the last program might not receive the credit for success.

We must also consider that as "treatment people" or "counselors," we like to believe that what we did in the name of treatment or counseling was the reason for a successful recovery. That is another assumption. The alcoholic may have recovered, not because of us or what we did, but because he found a comfortable place to make a decision, benefited from his association with other residents, or attended Alcoholics Anonymous outside the recovery program . . . the point is we just don't know why some people get sober or which factors are timely for their recovery. . . . It is conceivable in other words, that some alcoholics recover for reasons unknown to the staff or even in spite of what the staff did to them in the name of treatment.[16]

As stated above, the problem lies in the form evaluation is expected to take. Again, as with insurance carriers, the government, as a funding source, is legitimately asking for a return on its investment. However, the bureaucratic world of this area is caught in the cost-benefit thrust that started in the 1960s in the Kennedy Defense Department under Robert McNamara, an impetus that became manifest in the Pentagon's obsession with a Vietcong body count and the FBI's head count of captured lawbreakers. As one researcher observed:

That started the computerization of *everything*. Contracts all asked for chi-square, as if that were all that was needed. It fit with government statisticians' requirements—never mind anything else. The result is more time is spent preparing the report than is spent on the research.

Furthermore, to use an information system to judge cost-effectiveness is to risk making evaluation the determination of program content, i.e., an emphasis on services that "look good" on audit at the sacrifice of others, perhaps more meritorious, that do not. For an industrial contract to require reporting on how many firms were contacted, size of the firms etc., or for a grant to NCA to ask how many phone calls came in, how many spouses of alcoholics were seen in the office, how many radio spots were broadcast, is not only to sidestep the basic question—are you really making inroads into helping people—it is to reinforce a sense that only through numbers can we deal with our problems. That is the basic stance of the critics of "the prevalent American illness."

The Numbers Game

Thus far we have looked at the difficulties of demonstrating the value of programs. An even greater numerical misrepresentation occurs because of the need to demonstrate a more global picture of the problem of alcoholism and alcohol abuse. Room has caught the essence of what happens as research figures are transferred into the bureaucratic world:

Bacon's early estimate that 20% of alcoholics were on skid row was gradually eroded by common tendencies to inflate policy-relevant figures and the expansion of the meaning of alcoholic until the current figure of "probably less than four percent" was reached. Although the original research report on which the argument is based was by two sociologists, the argument soon became primarily the property of clinically-oriented policy advocates, and left the realm of research.[17]

Such bureaucratic transformation of research figures is not always lacking the tacit approval of participants from other arena-worlds. Room subsequently reported the following:

Following the "discovery" of the fetal alcohol syndrome in the last few years, in an era of "problem maximization," governmental and alcoholism movement organs have vied with each other in overreaction and overextension, culminating in the National Council on Alcoholism's recommendation that pregnant women abstain entirely from drinking. Challenged about biologists' responsibility for correcting the overinterpretations of their data, a leading alcohol biomedical researcher replied blandly that biological scientists could use any extra resources resulting from the public attention to the fetal alcohol syndrome.[18]

Regardless of the political usefulness of figures, alcoholics do not stand up to be counted, and demonstrating their numbers must rely on estimates. However, just as the disease concept obscures the ambiguities and complexities surrounding problem-drinkers/alcoholics, so too do estimates take on the status of authoritative facts, disguising their equivocal nature. A glance at four cases reveals how the desire to demonstrate the problem by quantifying it can distort rather than illuminate.

Problem Drinkers,[19] based on a survey of male adults living in households, was a landmark study of drinking in the general population, as differentiated from previous work on treatment clients or skid row habitués. Cahalan was able to establish categories for types and numbers of problems according to age, sex, region, economic and social status etc. Nowhere does the author define or count *alcoholics.* Yet when alcoholism was still under the jurisdiction of NIMH—prior to the establishment of NIAAA—the Cahalan score for a certain number of problems in relationship to the entire sample was projected by the NIMH staff to the adult population in the United States, and the figure of nine million emerged. Although NIAAA later qualified this by dividing the figure into five million who suffer from alcoholism and "perhaps" another four million who abuse alcohol,[20] the total became the established figure, to be drawn upon *as needed.* Typical of the use to which this figure is put is an article in a publication emanating from the temperance world, which divides the total NIAAA budget for fiscal year 1975 by nine million, and reports that this will provide roughly $16 per alcoholic.[21] This example demonstrates the disjunction between imperatives within the research world and the needs of the bureaucratic world. As Room has observed, the size of the sample and the cut-off points for problem categories in the original study were set, as in all such research, by balancing the competing demands of the need for respectable numbers and the need to have some inherent plausibility. Room speculates. "It is only half joking to say that if Cahalan's sample had been twice the size, there would be half as many alcoholics in the U.S. today." [22] Despite protestations from Cahalan, the nine million endured as dogma until the Second Report to the U.S. Congress, *Alcohol and Health New Knowledge,* was being prepared. At that time, Room was pressed by NIAAA for a figure and, influenced by the previous experience, gave an answer based on subsequent surveys, estimating that if one talked of people in treatment, one could *guess* in the upper hundreds of thousands; if one talked of those who have had some problem with their drinking, his estimate would be in the order of ten million. The first page of the first chapter in *Alcohol and Health New Knowledge* reads:

> The number of Americans whose lives alcohol has adversely affected depends on definition: those under active treatment for alcoholism by public or private agencies are probably in the upper hundreds of thousands, but there may be as many as ten million people whose drinking has created some problem for themselves or their families or friends or employers, or with police.[23]

Room had thought he was suggesting an order of magnitude, but the subtlety was lost when "in the order of" was transformed to "as many as." Moreover, NIAAA's qualifying "may be" was dropped as both the private and the public sector picked up ten million. An anecdote, related to me by a respondent, is indicative of the reaction:

> At Congressional hearings after the release of *Alcohol and Health New Knowledge,* one of the congressman was heard to express great alarm at the severity of the problem of alcoholism based on the fact that the number of alcoholics had gone up from nine million to ten million in just three years.

The number of alcoholics thereby became enshrined, albeit sometimes appearing as nine million, sometimes as ten million—figures henceforth to be often used and little questioned.

A somewhat different aspect of the selecting process is highlighted in the attempt to calculate costs to the nation of alcoholism. In this case, an expensive study was undertaken in order to simplify the message for legislators and the public.[24] The result was a new "public fact"—alcoholism costs the nation $25 billion a year.

The investigators took six known sources of "potentially significant economic cost," analyzing each for fiscal year 1971, to come up with the following dollar values:

Lost Production	$ 9.35 billion
Motor Vehicle Accidents	6.44 billion
Health and Medical	8.29 billion
Alcohol Programs	.64 billion
Criminal Justice System	.51 billion
Social Welfare System	.14 billion
	$ 25.37 billion

A scathing critique has been prepared by Donald Light, specifying the methodological and theoretical shortcomings which reduce this study to a hodge-podge of mismatched figures as specious as the *New Yorker* cartoon which showed the following highway marker:

Entering

HILLSVILLE

Founded	1,802
Altitude	620
Population	3,700
Total	6,122

For example: utilizing figures from the Social Research Group surveys, the investigators make the gross assumption that the difference in average income between moderate-drinking and problem-drinking males is due to the difference in their drinking behavior. For another: the total expenditure for the social welfare system did not include transfer payments, i.e. direct benefits to support persons whose jobs may have been lost due to alcoholism.[25] Two criticisms offered by Light deserve special note. The first is the distinction between the problem of causation versus correlation:

> As any social scientist knows, it is one thing to say that event A (alcohol abuse) is often associated with event B (motor vehicle accidents), but quite a different thing to say that event A causes event B.[26]

Although this statement is self-evident, the wider implications of this distinction are examined at the conclusion of this chapter. A second major difficulty examined by Light is the failure to weigh the costs against the economic benefits of alcohol use. It is a noteworthy aspect of the selecting process that this factor receives conscientious attention from the alcoholic beverage industries world. The Distilled Spirits Council of the United States (DISCUS) publishes a Fact Book containing graphs depicting for example "Growth of the Industry's Contribution to the Economy" (e.g., employment, contribution to other industries, payroll and earnings, taxes). The cost study, on the other hand, makes brief mention of the value of alcohol consumed in 1971, as $15 billion. Light protests:

> Scattered throughout this study and *Alcohol and Health* are references to situations in which the use of alcohol may have benefits in job performance, health and other areas. When one considers the impressive statistics that 57 percent of all adult Americans drink at least once a month; that 29 percent of all prescriptions in the United States are for psychotropic drugs; the amounts of illicit drugs including amphetamines and barbiturates; and the consumption of nicotine and caffeine, one begins to suspect that a major source of social and economic cohesion in this country is the ubiquitous use of mood-altering substances. It is interesting to speculate on the effects of the complete elimination of alcohol abuse; what would be the economic cost of the consumption of alternative substance and/or the antisocial behavior which would then occur? [27]

The summary point is that the concept of economic costs is not applicable. As Room has suggested, what is the cost of a wife getting angry; or as Norwegian criminologist Nils Christie asks, how do we know how many marriages are held together by alcohol and where would such marriages belong on the balance sheet? [28] In addition, the financial slant of this approach detracts from more important human needs—the study "does not place a price tag on death or on the physical and psychological suffering of problem drinking patients and their families." [29] Room has maintained there are pitfalls in selling health and welfare programs on the basis of money saved in the long run, instead of on the basis of humaneness. By lessening the need to make an argument for the intrinsic and inherent worth of the program, a pitch made solely on dollar value decreases the opportunity for building a constituency based on ethical and moral reasons. Furthermore, a program justified by an economic argument is likely to direct its attention primarily to the clients who can provide the greatest economic payoff, who are not necessarily those most in need of, or most able to make use of, assistance.[30]

Although the original study contained caveats, some of which survived publication in *Alcohol and Health New Knowledge,* the sum total remained $25 billion for the press and for public pronouncements like President Ford's message to the North American Congress on Alcohol and Drug Problems in 1974. As with the nine to ten million alcoholics, it is the figure that has persisted and taken on a life of its own, disguising the complexity of the problems it is supposed to represent. (A new study commissioned by NIAAA in 1977, produced a cost-to-the-nation figure of $42.5 billion, a recalculation based partly on inflation considerations.)

Yet another twist in the selecting process occurred over an examination into the correlation between alcohol and mortality. A researcher at the Social Research Group, working on data from general population surveys, found that the mortality rate for abstainers was higher than for moderate drinkers. The finding coincided with NIAAA's preparation of *Alcohol and Health New Knowledge,* and the consequence was an article in that document entitled "Alcohol and Mortality," [31] which was interpreted by segments of the press and television as indicating that moderate drinking is better than abstention. (One respondent suggested that this was quite possibly to rationalize the drinking of those doing the reporting!) Dissemination of the Room-Day findings was given a giant boost by NIAAA Director Chafetz, who was then championing his concept of "responsible drinking." Chafetz's views on the appropriate use of alcohol had been summed up five years before his appointment in his *Liquor: The Servant of Man,* to wit: alcoholism is a major public health problem, *liquor is not.*[32] His position on the safe drinking of alcohol had been a factor in Chafetz' appointment, where it was expected he would place an emphasis not only on treatment but on education and prevention. The "responsible drinking" credo was spelled out in NIAAA documents—in the Second Report to Congress on Alcohol and Health and in the accompanying Task Force Report, which stated:

> The decision as to whether or not to use the drug alcohol is properly a personal and private choice to be made by each individual. However, should the choice be to drink, that individual assumes a responsibility not to destroy himself or others. That in the broadest sense, is responsible drinking.[33]

Educational material from the National Clearinghouse for Alcohol Information (NCALI) promulgated this concept, which was also central to the prevention activities of the National Center for Alcohol Education (NCAE). Chafetz's philosophy fit nicely with the agenda of the alcoholic beverage industries world, which could point to the social responsibility

of moderation messages such as "if you choose to drink, drink responsi-
bly." To a large segment of the alcohol use arena, especially those ascribing to an addiction concept of alcoholism, this advertising remained
anathema. As one respondent told me:

> Alcohol is a drug. We don't talk about responsible drugs. If there is such a
> thing as addiction, if as we know withdrawal can be fatal, a little alcohol is
> also dangerous.

Or as the case was presented to a representative of the liquor industry at
an ALMACA meeting:

> You're just feeding a myth. Most alcoholics think they are drinking re-
> sponsibly. It's like the banks urging people to go into debt, to buy more
> and more, *irre*sponsibly.

Nevertheless, Chafetz continued to stress the importance of sipping
slowly, combining food with drink, not drinking alone etc. In an article
with the intriguing title "How to Drink Without Becoming a Drunk,"
published after he had left his post, Chafetz engages in some selecting of
his own.[34] He reports how elated he was with the discovery, while preparing the second report to the Congress on Alcohol and Health, that
researchers from all over the world were all, independently, using the
same level to determine safe or moderate drinking. That was the equivalent of 1.5 ounces of absolute alcohol per day; three one-ounce drinks
of 100-proof whiskey, which should be drunk diluted; four eight-ounce
glasses of beer; or half a bottle of wine taken with food. As Chafetz
himself points out, this level had its origin in the 1862 publication by a
British psychiatrist, Sir Francis Anstie, called "Anstie's Law of Safe
Drinking." Considering the controversy in the arena concerning even a
definition of alcoholism, such a "law" more accurately can be assessed as
a carrying forward of conventional wisdom rather than, in Chafetz'
words, "a known safe level of drinking."

As mentioned above, the Room-Day data was picked up by the press
and television, achieving the dubious notoriety of a reference on the
Johnny Carson Tonight Show in the form of jokes lauding drinking.
Room and Day had suggested not only that further study might reveal
an overlap in "explanations" of early death, but had cautioned against
extrapolating findings from clinical populations to the alcoholic population at large. As with the "costs to the nation," such caveats were sub-
merged in the attendant publicity. The "news," after all, creates its own
reality. In the meantime, Day was re-working her data, having formed
the hypothesis that separating life-long abstainers and current abstainers

might yield additional insights. After discovering that, indeed, the mortality rate of life-long abstainers more closely resembled that of moderate drinkers, (suggesting that the more recent abstainers may have been heavy drinkers who had altered their drinking habits due to health problems), Day speculated that her dissertation, then in progress, could eventually be entitled "Death Warmed Over." [35]

The Search for More Sophisticated Figures

NIAAA is under eternal pressure to devise a more sophisticated means of convincing its audiences of the continual, or better still, increased need for funding. This was underscored once again when Congress added a directive to the 1976 Alcoholism Act Amendments calling for a methodology to measure the incidence and prevalence of alcohol abuse within individual states, for use in determining formula grants. Until that time, formulas for each state had been computed on the basis of relative population and financial need, or per capita income, with two-thirds weight going to financial need. In the desire to devise a formula that was defensible, NIAAA again pressed figures into service in a manner that proved inappropriate. Working in conjunction with the National Center for Health Statistics, and employing data from the Social Research Group on frequent heavy drinkers and tangible consequences, NIAAA averaged out the figures and projected them for every state. Population, financial need and need for services were now to be given equal weight. One problem with the new formula became evident immediately: the poorer states would receive less money than before, while a state like California would enjoy an increase. Another difficulty is more subtle, but no less important. What the Social Research Group has measured in the general population is far from what one sees if one walks into a treatment center. As indicated in Chapter 7, studies support the conclusion that there is wide gulf between alcohol-related behavior in the general population as against the clinical population.[36] Any attempt to assess needs by selecting estimates of how many alcoholics are "out there" runs into the definitional dilemma already discussed. Definitions such as general population problem scores and the NCA Criteria,[37] as Room remarks, "cast a fine net but catch many small fry"; definitions such as classical disease concepts of alcoholism "cast an open-weave net and yield only a small catch in the general population." To explain:

> On the one hand, it is clear that projections of the number of "alcoholics"
> on the basis of results for the population at large are gross overestimates, *if*

the term "alcoholics" implies "persons like those in treatment for alcoholism." On the other hand it is clear that the search for the "hidden alcoholic," and the increasing emphasis on casefinding and "secondary prevention," are doomed to failure *if* these efforts are predicated on the existence of a large hidden population many times greater than the number in clinics but resembling clinical populations in every way except that they are not hospitalized.

... But there are so many more "problem drinkers" in the general population than there are clinical cases that "problem drinking" cannot be a very good prediction of clinical alcoholism.[38]

The disjunction between the two populations, and a tie-in to the labeling process, is evidenced in Cahalan's observation that even survey respondents reporting a high consumption of alcohol and a high problem incidence, still seldom answer affirmatively when asked if they consider themselves "alcoholic." Similarly, Roizen et al. when preparing their paper on "spontaneous remission" [39] attempted to separate the self-ascribed alcoholics not in treatment, in order to follow them in Time II—only to find the sole self-ascribed alcoholics were those who had had treatment.

The U.S. Senate met the initial obstacle to a new formula for grants (the decrease in funds for the poorer states) with an additional amendment holding all allotments at (at least) the fiscal-year-1976 level. At the same time, Senators Hathaway and Javits "agreed to press NIAAA for a more sophisticated methodology in determining a state's need for alcoholism services based on the prevalence and incidence of alcohol abuse:

> Hathaway told the Senate that when the Human Resources Committee framed the directive to NIAAA to come up with a new formula last year, "it was not anticipated that the state of the art of needs assessment was as primitive or that the available data was as old and based on such small samples." [40]

NIAAA, sufficiently mindful of the need to convince Congress, allocated a sizable portion of its grants and contracts to studies geared toward publication in the Third Report to the U.S. Congress on Alcohol and Health, scheduled for 1978 release. Sensing that reliance on figures like nine to ten million alcoholics, or costs-to-the-nation figures, would no longer suffice, NIAAA, for example, engaged M. Harvey Brenner of the Johns Hopkins University School of Hygiene and Public Health to employ his econometric techniques as a further demonstration of alcohol problems. Brenner's method of "detrending" (separating long and short term effects) had proven useful to the arena even prior to the publication of the third Alcohol and Health report. In a study done for the Congressional Joint Economic Committee, Brenner had attempted to measure the impact of economic variables on seven indicators of stress—total mortality, homicide, suicide, cardiovascular-renal disease mortality, cirrhosis of the liver mortality, total state imprisonment, and state mental hospital admissions. Each indicator was evaluated to determine its sensitivity to changes in real income, rates of inflation and rates of unemployment, with unemployment emerging as having the most impact on the stress indicators.[41] From the data available, Brenner concluded that cirrhosis mortality showed substantial increases one to two years following national economic recession. He was quoted as saying:

> It is clear from the long period of time apparently necessary to acquire (chronic) cirrhosis of the liver, that the short-term economic trauma did not initiate the cirrhotic condition, but once present tended to hasten mortality.[42]

In addition, Brenner commented on the importance of the inverse relationship between consumption of distilled spirits and the state of the national economy, based on his findings regarding alcohol-related admissions to mental hospitals, arrests for drunkenness, and for driving while intoxicated. A hint of the manner in which such data fills the Congressional agenda is provided by the reaction of the late Senator Hubert Humphrey, Chairman of the Committee, and also co-author of the Humphrey-Hawkins employment bill. Commenting that the study "reveals that unemployment has a strikingly potent impact on society," Humphrey concluded that the 1.4 percent increase in unemployment during 1970 alone was:

> *associated directly* with some 1,500 additional suicides; 1,700 additional homicides; 25,000 additional strokes, heart and kidney disease deaths; 5,500 added mental hospital admissions and 800 additional deaths from cirrhosis of the liver—all in the last five years.[43] (Emphasis added.)

It is the direct association that continues to be an unproven problem for those with audiences to convince. As attractive as well-defined causal relationships would be, the *extent* to which alcohol is involved in a specific situation or condition is difficult to pinpoint. As Room has expressed it:

> We know that the role of alcohol is likely to be underestimated in many situations, for instance in many chronic illness conditions. But in a society like the USA, where drinking alcohol does potentially carry a moral onus

which differentiates it from drinking water or soft drinks, there is also a strong tendency to assume alcohol is the primary cause if it is present in any problematic situation, resulting in *overestimations* of the role of alcohol.[44] (Emphasis added.)

With a skepticism so clearly expressed, it is indicative of NIAAA's interest in coming to grips with this barrier that a contract was let to the Social Research Group, for which Room was the study director—the goal, to reanalyze existing data in order to determine the relation of alcohol to various casualties: accidents, crime, suicide and family abuse. Scheduled to appear in the third report to the Congress on Alcohol and Health as "Physiological and Psychological Costs of Alcohol Consumption," the study took a turn away from the implications of that title, by examining each problem category separately and taking the position that events in which alcohol is present do not necessarily signify the existence of a condition called "alcoholism."

To explain, the alcoholism literature has tended to suggest that behind every event there is a condition. Room explains the connection of this blurring of concepts to the disease definition:

> It of course makes sense to treat an event that occurs all the time as a condition. But often we interpret sporadic events as conditions—as in the assumptions that any driver with a blood-alcohol content of .25 or more, or one who is arrested twice for drunk driving, must be an alcoholic. The disease concept of alcoholism has resulted in a strong tendency to interpret events as conditions, since the concept treats a variety of events in the drinking history as symptoms of an underlying condition.[45]

Diversion programs based on this principle had limited success, since, as the Rand Report (discussed in the next chapter) found, the behavior of the drunk driver resembles that of problem drinkers in the general population more than it does that of the treatment population. Thus, the stance of the Social Research Group was to focus on the nature of the relation of alcohol to the event and to emphasize the complexity in establishing causal relationships. For instance, in regard to suicide, the researchers pointed to indications in the literature that one cause of suicide among alcoholics may be enforced abstinence from alcohol; that drinking may buck up one's courage for the suicidal act; or conversely, cheer up the potential suicide such that the act proves to be no longer desirable.

This is not to deny the involvement of alcohol in serious events. As the researchers emphasized, their data search suggested that in at least some events the involvement of alcohol helps precipitate the event; for some times and places and circumstances the proportion of events which can be attributed to alcohol has been quantified. The Social Research Group report acknowledged that "for purposes of public information and persuasion on the importance of alcohol issues, this may be enough: publicists have available a more than adequate collection of studies from which to pick and choose percentages of particular crimes and casualties which are 'due to alcohol.' " [46] Their argument, however, was that while such single percentages may be programmatically useful, they are often misleading. "More importantly, they are inherently meaningless: alcohol's involvement in casualties or crimes is not a matter of immutable constants like a law of physics, but varies with time, place, actors and circumstances." [47]

This endeavor highlights once again the difficulty of meshing the bent of the research world with the policy needs of the bureaucratic world. Despite the realization by elements within NIAAA of the need for a more sophisticated scrutiny *and* communication of alcohol problems, the institute, with a Congress to convince and an enlarged constituency to satisfy, was caught between whether to treat the Social Research Group report as a research document or a policy statement. Subject to successive levels of review within NIAAA, the Alcohol Drug Abuse and Mental Health Administration, and the Department of Health, Education and Welfare, the ambiguity of causal connections between specific casualties and alcohol was not viewed as a useful message for demonstrating the problem. Out of the report was *selected* that which was compatible with the policy statement NIAAA was making in its Third Report to the U.S. Congress—the need for program, where program emphasis should be placed, etc. The Social Research Group had conscientiously avoided giving a single modal figure which could be interpreted as the proportion of, for example, homicides "due to" alcohol, giving instead the range of figures on the *association* reported in the literature. Filtered through bureaucratic needs, not the least of which is to maintain an alcohol-specific institute, such obscurities were transformed into another "exercise in problem magnification." [48] The official government report based on this review reported the results throughout in terms of "up to," giving the high end of the range.[49] The new magical figures were dutifully relayed by the press:

> An estimated ten million Americans are problem drinkers or alcoholics, and drinking may be to blame for as many as 205,000 deaths a year, federal health officials claimed yesterday.
>
> The risk of death from disease, accident or violence is two to six times

greater for the problem drinker than for the population at large, the National Institute on Alcohol Abuse and Alcoholism said in its third special report to Congress.

. . . Alcohol may be involved in up to one-third of all suicides, half of all murders, half of all traffic deaths and a fourth of all other accidental deaths, the report said.

Furthermore, alcohol is now suspected to be a major factor in child abuse and marital violence as well as such crimes as rape, the report said.[50]

Thus do research figures become "public facts."

In the next chapter, we turn to further illustrations of the conflicting agendas of the research world and other segments of the arena.

Notes

1. *See, for example:* Bigus, *Becoming Alcoholic* (Ph.D. dissertation, University of California, 1974); and Wiseman, *Stations of the Lost* (Englewood Cliffs, N.J.: Prentice-Hall, 1970).
2. Alvin Gouldner, *The Coming Crisis of Western Sociology* (New York: Basic Books, Inc., 1970), p. 77.
3. Max Singer, "The Vitality of Mythical Numbers," *The Public Interest*, No. 23 (1971), pp. 3-9.
4. Irving Kristol, "Taxes, Poverty and Equality," *The Public Interest*, No. 37 (1974), p. 4.
5. Herbert Kaufman, *Are Government Organizations Immortal?* (Washington, D.C.: The Brookings Institute, 1976), p. 65.
6. Ibid., p. 7.
7. *The Washington Post* (November 23, 1975), p. 74.
8. Remarks at a meeting called by Senator Gregorio, Foster City, California, October 30, 1975.
9. *The Alcoholism Report*, Vol. 5 (November 12, 1976), p. 6.
10. R. Room and S. Sheffield (eds.), *The Prevention of Alcohol Problems:* Report of a Conference (Sacramento: California State Office of Alcoholism, 1976), p. 246.
11. *The Hearth* (February, 1976).
12. M. Chafetz, "Monitoring and Evaluation at NIAAA," *Evaluation*, Vol. 2 (1974), pp. 50-51.
13. *American Psychological Association Monitor* (September/October 1973), p. 17.
14. Robin Room, "Measurement and Distribution of Drinking Patterns and Problems in General Populations," G. Edwards et al. (eds.), *Alcohol-Related Disabilities* (Geneva: WHO, 1977).
15. *See:* Roizen, Cahalan, and Shanks, " 'Spontaneous Remission' Among Untreated Problem Drinkers"; and Emrick, "A Review of Psychologically Oriented Treatment of Alcoholism II."
16. *The Hearth,* (January, 1976).

17. Robin Room, "Comment on the Uniform Alcoholism Intoxication and Treatment Act." *Journal of Studies on Alcohol,* Vol. 37 (1976), p. 115.
18. Robin Room, *Governing Images of Alcohol and Drug Problems: The Structure, Sources and Sequels of Conceptualizations of Intractable Problems* (Ph.D. dissertation, University of California, Berkeley, 1978), p. 194.
19. Don Cahalan, *Problem Drinkers* (San Francisco: Jossey-Bass, 1970).
20. National Institute on Alcohol Abuse and Alcoholism, *First Special Report to the U.S. Congress on Alcohol and Health,* from the Secretary of Health, Education, and Welfare (Washington, D.C.: U.S. Government Printing Office, 1971).
21. *The American Issue,* Vol. 82 (January/February, 1975), p. 2.
22. Robin Room, "Measurement and Distribution of Drinking Patterns and Problems in General Populations," p. 27.
23. National Institute on Alcohol Abuse and Alcoholism, *Second Report to the U.S. Congress on Alcohol and Health New Knowledge,* from the Secretary of Health, Education, and Welfare (Washington, D.C.: U.S. Government Printing Office, 1974), p. 1.
24. Policy Analysis Inc., *The Economic Cost of Alcohol Abuse and Alcoholism.* Boston, Mass.; *See*: NIAAA, *Alcohol and Health New Knowledge,* p. 137.
25. Donald Light, "Costs and Benefits of Alcohol Consumption," *Society,* Vol. 12 (1975), pp. 13-24.
26. Ibid., p. 18.
27. Ibid., p. 19.
28. Discussion at the North American Congress on Alcohol and Drug Problems, San Francisco, California, 1974.
29. R. Shore and J. Luce, *To Your Health,* (New York: Seabury Press, 1976), p. 184.
30. Robin Room, "Saving Money Vs. Reducing Suffering," *Surveyor,* No. 7 (1973).
31. Based on R. Room and N. Day, "Alcohol and Mortality," Special Report to National Institute on Alcohol Abuse and Alcoholism, 1974.
32. Morris Chafetz, *Liquor: The Servant of Man* (Boston: Little Brown & Co, 1965).
33. National Institute of Mental Health, "From Program To People," Research on Alcoholism, Task Force Report #6; DHEW Publication No. (ADM) 75-155, 1974, p. 29.
34. Morris Chafetz, "How To Drink Without Becoming A Drunk," *The National Observer,* (August 7, 1976), p. 18. *See also:* M. Chafetz, *Why Drinking Can Be Good For You* (New York: Stein & Day, 1977).
35. Nancy Day Asher, *Alcohol and Mortality: Separating The Drink From The Drinker* (Ph.D. dissertation, University of California, Berkeley, 1978).
36. *See:* Robin Room, "Measurement and Distribution of Drinking Patterns and Problems in General Populations," pp. 81-83; Harold Mulford and Ronald Wilson, *Identifying Problem Drinkers in a Household Health Survey,* Public Health Service Publication No. 1000, Series 2, No. 16 (Washington, D.C.: U.S. Government Printing Office, 1966), pp. 28-29; David J. Armor, Michael Polich, and Harriet Stambul, *Evaluating Alcoholism Treatment* (Santa Monica, California: The Rand Corp., 1976); and Robin Room, "Amount of Drinking and Alcoholism," paper presented at the 28th International Congress on Alcohol and Alcoholism, Washington, D.C., 1968.

37. See Chapter 7.

38. Room, "Measurement and Distribution of Drinking Patterns and Problems in General Populations," p. 82.

39. See Chapter 7.

40. *The Alcoholism Report,* Vol. 5 (May 13, 1977), p. 8.

41. M. Harvey Brenner, "Estimating the Social Costs of National Economic Policy: Implications for Mental and Physical Health and Criminal Aggression," a study prepared for the use of the Joint Economic Committee, Congress of the United States, 1976.

42. *The Alcoholism Report,* Vol. 5 (November 26, 1976), p. 5.

43. Ibid.

44. Room, "Measurement and Distribution of Drinking Patterns and Problems in General Populations," p. 76.

45. Robin Room, "The Prevention of Alcohol Problems," Social Research Group Working Paper F63, 1977, p. 7.

46. Marc Aarens, Tracy Cameron, Judy Roizen, Ron Roizen, Robin Room, Dan Schneberk, and Deborah Wingard, "Alcohol, Casualties and Crime," report prepared for the National Institute on Alcohol Abuse and Alcoholism, 1977, p. 577.

47. Ibid.

48. For discussion around this point, see Robin Room, *Governing Images of Alcohol and Drug Problems,* pp. 196-202.

49. National Institute on Alcohol Abuse and Alcoholism, *Third Special Report to the U.S. Congress on Alcohol and Health,* from the Secretary of Health, Education, and Welfare. (Washington, D.C.: U.S. Government Printing Office, 1978), pp. 61-66.

50. *San Francisco Chronicle* (October 18, 1978), p. 2.

12.

Convincing Opposing Ideologists

We have seen how the selection of data often occurs in order to convince an audience or audiences—defending the expenditure of program monies in terms of cost-analysis. Another aspect of demonstrating the problem of alcohol use by *convincing* deserves special consideration, however, because it strikes at the very heart of this arena—the demonstrating that occurs around evaluation of "success rates," or outcome measures as they are seen both within and without the recovery service world.

In Chapter 6, we examined the eclectism of this arena, the variety of treatment approaches and the growing understanding that people with problems of drinking have different needs—not only for different levels of care but for different environments in which to deal with their problems. In Chapter 7, we looked at the manner in which "alcoholism" has been redefined—the conditions leading to a disease concept and the conditions which undermined that concept, contributing toward a problem-drinking perspective. I have alluded to the vast spectrum of definitions given by respondents: alcoholics have a genetic predisposition and/or physiological dependence and/or specific psychological traits and/or are affected by sociological and cultural factors. However, while this variation may suggest liberality and tolerance, differences are sharpened when it becomes necessary to measure goals of treatment and to evaluate success. Around the evaluation issue, convincing moves beyond funding considerations, involved as it is with the ideological positions which separate participants in the arena. In spite of the impression that may have been created by some of the discussion in previous chapters, everything is not tied to the dollar.

The dichotomy between those who believe there is a definite alcoholic syndrome, and those who do not, is central to the process of demonstrating the problem of alcohol use. In this chapter, we look at this intra-arena debate and the turn this debate has taken regarding the issue of "controlled drinking."

How Does a Cucumber Become a Pickle?

The concept of addiction as originally formulated by Jellinek has, in spite of transmutations over the years, remained a divisive issue among the worlds of this arena. Jellinek initially defined "disease alcoholism" as loss of control over drinking, either the inability to abstain, or the inability to stop when started, i.e., addiction in the pharmacological sense.[1] Keller has made numerous attempts to clarify this formulation by acknowledging that no evidence of physiological addiction has ever been produced, but explaining his own interpretation of addiction as follows:

> I hold that the only logical inference, from the behavior of a man who is continually dependent on alcohol, drinks in an undisciplined way and in contravention of all society's rules, and suffers damage from his drinking in his personal relations, or in his economic welfare or in his health—the only logical inference is that the man has lost control; that if he could control his drinking he would. . . . It must be that the immediate rewards of the relief of pain—even, and in my opinion, particularly emotional pain—is sufficiently important to overcome the disadvantages of the delayed punishments of damage to personal relations, economic well-being, and health.[2]

Keller's refinement of the classic definition stresses that one need not distinguish between physiological and psychological addiction: a person who cannot choose whether to take a drink or not, has the specific disablement which constitutes the disease alcoholism. In his distaste for the engineering metaphor of "tolerance," Keller substitutes "adaptation," to signify the need for increased amounts of a drug. But he qualifies the process of adaptation as applying only to "vulnerable people," thus opening up the floodgates to what he admits becomes a complex psycho-physio-sociological orientation. For vulnerable people are:

. . . those who, whether for constitutional reasons or because of being reared in particularly unfortunate ways, or perhaps especially the combination of constitutional and psychic developmental misfortune, find difficulty in achieving satisfactory adaptations to the way of life that they expect of themselves, and that society expects of them.[3]

Loss of control, as Glatt reiterates, does *not* mean that it is necessarily the first drink that is "fatal." "Rather does 'loss of control' mean that a drinker *can never be quite certain* that once he has taken a drink he will be able to stop whenever he wants to." [4]

Varying interpretations still surround the concept of "loss of control." Keller's personal account of the source of the confusion is a significant piece of history for those who would study the tenacity of questionable "public facts." A World Health Organization report had published Jellinek's enlargement on the phenomenon he had first set forth as cited above. In the second statement he explained:

[Loss of control means that as soon as a small quantity of alcohol enters the organism a demand for more alcohol is set up which is felt as a physical demand by the drinker, but could possibly be a conversion phenomenon. . . . This demand lasts until the drinker is too intoxicated or too sick to ingest more alcohol.]

The "loss of control" is effective after the individual has started drinking, but it does not give rise to the beginning of a new drinking bout. The drinker has lost the ability to control the quantity once he has started, but he still can control whether he will drink on any given occasion or not. This is evidenced in the fact that after the onset of "loss of control" the drinker can go through a period of voluntary abstinence . . .[5]

Keller reports that he confronted Jellinek soon after publication, pointing out that the inevitable inability to stop after drinking any small amount was unlike the reality they both knew. Keller continues: "He agreed at once, explained that it was a slip that had passed his notice in the haste of going to press in Geneva, and wished it could be *unsaid*." [6] Consequently, the two men arranged for publication of another version in the *Quarterly Journal of Studies on Alcohol* in which the sentences I have bracketed now read:

Loss of control means that any drinking of alcohol starts a chain reaction which is felt by the drinker as a physical demand for alcohol. This state, possibly a conversion phenomenon, may take hours or weeks for its full development; it lasts until the drinker is too intoxicated or too sick to ingest more alcohol.[7]

The distinction, for Keller, lies in facing up to what Jellinek and Keller had observed, a point verified repeatedly by respondents—alcoholics can have periods of no drinking; can set up their own drinking schedules; and *some* alcoholics report that while institutionalized they do not suffer from being deprived of alcohol. Keller's explanation is that an alcoholic who has started to drink, started the so-called chain reaction, but has not reached its critical end-point, can stop, as he often does, during the hours or weeks before the loss of control in Jellinek's sense achieves "full development." The difference for Keller appears to lie in correcting the impression, still perpetuated by some elements in the arena, that loss of control consists simply of being unable to control the *amount,* once drinking is started. But more important for our discussion, he is insisting on an empirical fact which is incapable of proof: that the addictive property (the loss of control) is lying dormant even when it *appears* controlled, and can always potentially reach full development. The nature of the addiction is that "at some time, under the impulsion of some cue or stimulus which may well be outside his conscious awareness, (the alcoholic) will drink. . . . Addiction, in this conception, is thought of as a form of learned or conditioned response." [8]

Other theorists feel it is important to separate the physiological and psychological components. To quote Milam, a proponent of this perspective, ". . . the obvious and profound psychosocial symptoms of the alcoholic are secondary to his unique physical reaction to alcohol as a drug . . . (the psychosocial symptoms) are rooted . . . in the progressively adaptive, toxic and organic effects of alcohol." [9] Milam goes on to explain that early onset is often so gradual as to go unnoticed, and early symptoms are easily rationalized. Furthermore, there is a gradient of differences in susceptibility to alcoholism: some drink socially for some time before symptoms develop; others have early symptoms at the start of drinking; still others have advanced symptoms when they first drink. This is essentially an allergy concept: one can react to ragweed upon first exposure, or one can cross the allergy threshold after a build-up of exposure. From this standpoint, to paraphrase Roizen, "alcoholism *is* because of special susceptibility, but alcoholism *stays* because of psychology." [10] Thus, for Milam-theorists the "is" is more narrowly stated than for Keller-theorists, but both groups believe in a reaction to alcohol which separates alcoholics from their brethren.

The Search for Scientific Proof

With a large contingent of the arena adhering to an addictive-property theory, it is not surprising to find this group expecting the proof to come out of the biochemistry laboratory (which explains the relative emphasis on hard science experimentation, in contrast to social science research characteristic of this arena).[11] A problem inherent in all research thus arises: the popular interpretation of findings. As explained in Chapter 11, the process of selecting elements in research which enhance a desired position affected the interpretation of findings on alcohol and mortality. Similar experience can be found stemming from the desire to settle the issue of alcohol addiction. Periodically, a new discovery is heralded, enhancing the visibility of the arena in a crisscrossing of the convincing and selecting processes. What to the scientist remains a hypothesis is sometimes taken by some arena participants, and by the press, as providing the yearned-for verification.

A case in point is the research of Shaw, Stimmel and Lieber, which received wide press coverage in 1976. Conducted among hospitalized and ambulatory alcoholic patients and healthy nonalcoholic volunteers, this study found that the ratio of amino acids in the blood of the alcoholics was more than twice as high as in the nonalcoholics. It was found that the ratio is consistently elevated among heavy drinkers and may remain positive for more than a week after drinking is discontinued and all signs of alcohol have disappeared from the blood.

Disregarding Lieber's cautious statement, "At this time, the test is not a predictor of who will become a heavy drinker but a determinant of who is a heavy drinker," [12] *Newsweek* reported that this finding may make it possible to detect alcoholism in its earliest, most treatable stage; [13] the *New York Times* announced the discovery as "the first specific blood test to detect chronic alcoholism," commenting that such a test "is considered an important step toward the eventual scientific unraveling of the mysteries of why many heavy drinkers die of cirrhosis of the liver while others seemingly tolerate the effects of chronic drinking without apparent damage." [14] Despite the eagerness of the press, it is still unclear if the physiological changes these scientists were reporting are the result of many years of heavy drinking rather than a sign of susceptibility to alcoholism.

Another example of the pursuit of an addictive property is the research directed by neurophysiologist R. D. Myers of Purdue University. Dr. Myers' team found that injecting a fluid called tetrahydropapaveroline (THP) into the brains of rats who normally will not drink alcohol, will induce the animals to go on a binge that starts again every time they are given one drink. In this case the researcher, as quoted in a press report, was somewhat less cautious than Dr. Lieber. Speculating that alcoholism may stem from a defect in the brain cells that results in too much THP, Dr. Myers writes, with extravagant enthusiasm or visionary grasp, depending on one's viewpoint:

> If we can reproduce this effect in monkeys, and figure out a way to reverse it, we should be able to come up with a drug that cures alcoholism, or even prevents it.[15]

Periodic research findings such as these rekindle the hope that evidence of differing physical responses to alcohol will eventually prove "loss of control." Respondents spoke of the promise of such findings leading to tests such as the glucose tolerance test for diabetes, to predict the pre-alcoholic. Similarly, faith is placed by some in the search for a hereditary factor that fosters alcoholism.[16] That this would be a far less threatening concept than psychosocial explanations, and may even have a prestige benefit, is evidenced by the remark of one respondent, a Native American alcoholism counselor: "The Blacks have their Sickle Cell Anemia, the Jews have their Tay Sachs—why should the Indians be left out?"

As significant as these research endeavors are to arena participants, it is important to return again to the core of my thesis. Such endeavors become part of the demonstrating process—they are called upon to convince, i.e. to provide the empirical proof that special susceptibility exists in some individuals. Sometimes the meaning of the findings is extended beyond the researcher's intent; sometimes the researcher, quite naturally, is enthusiastic over the possibility that susceptibility has been pinpointed. But the sum total of the attendant publicity is increased visibility for the arena.

Reconciling Problem Drinking With Addiction Theories

Lacking tangible proof, a difficulty arises for those who subscribe to the disease-as-addiction concept in that they must convince those with a drinking-problem perspective (who see all drinking in a continuum) that there *is* a definite syndrome, while at the same time acknowledging the existence of gradients. It is hard to have it both ways, and in the convincing they weaken their argument. Milam, for example, states that potential alcoholics do not differ from nonalcoholics in any initial psychological, social, or cultural factors, and before symptoms develop they drink for all of the reasons other people do. He then says that "perhaps some forty million nonalcoholics in the United States must be classified as irresponsible drinkers because these are the individuals whose drinking is not progressive but who willfully drink and drive their cars, drink to compromise their moral integrity, or otherwise use alcohol in ways that are potentially harmful to themselves or other people." [17] But Milam's claim that "the majority of alcoholics do not come from the ranks of irresponsible drinkers" [18] is weakened by his earlier insistence that some alcoholics drink socially for some time before the first symptoms (that they are in the addictive population) develop.[19] Keller, in a somewhat less judgmental tone, says much the same thing: "Within the total population of drinkers, there is of necessity a pool of potential alcoholics—we may conveniently designate all of them, though we can probably identify several classes, as problem drinkers. They are people who have not yet crossed the line of loss of control." [20] Small wonder that a simple blood test sounds so attractive. On a radio call-in show devoted to alcohol problems, a representative of the National Council on Alcoholism, responded to a caller's question regarding the risk of three nightly martinis, by saying such drinking *could* be progressive, "*could* work toward alcoholism." He then speculated on how nice it would be if there were a medical center where the caller could go to take an amino acid test, and "know once and for all. Then if you found out you do not have the disease alcoholism, you could begin conditioning yourself to use alcohol as a 'euphoriant,' a mild relaxant." [21]

Controlling the Concept of Controlled Drinking

It is the confrontation over goals of treatment and definitions of recovery that makes this intra-arena debate most visible. For those who subscribe to an addiction concept, abstinence is held to be the only cure. But the cure, unlike that for diabetes, is *also* dependent on convincing, i.e. convincing the sick person. Roizen explains why this is so:

> In the classical model, an alcoholic is "diseased," first and foremost, in that his drinking behavior is outside his own volitional control. His troubles with drinking, as Jellinek suggested, stem from the fact that he is ignorant of his own constitutional difference from other people and because he sees no reason to suspect that such a difference exists. Strong rationalizations may surround his drinking behavior, and these may serve to "explain" his drinking to himself to his own satisfaction, thereby making it more difficult for the therapist to convince him that he is different. But it is the education—the convincing of him that he *is* different—that is the major element of the classical treatment ideology . . . In short, alcoholism treatment, as it is seen in the classical model, is largely a didactic and persuasional effort that attempts to treat the alcoholic by getting the alcoholic to accept a particular theory of alcoholism, and his acceptance of that theory is itself the essence of alcoholism treatment . . . *Embracing abstinence is, thus, a sign that the model of alcoholism has been accepted by the client. Measuring whether or not the alcoholic internalizes this theory and makes a commitment to abstinence becomes the only really important outcome criterion.*[22] (Emphasis added.)

Abstinence remained inviolate as a goal for the recovery service world until the last two decades, during which time studies have periodically surfaced purporting to demonstrate that some alcoholics can, after treatment, resume "normal drinking" without relapse. In spite of attack, rejection, and, as some respondents hinted, suppression, this concept of "controlled drinking" has persisted. To a large extent, this is a reflection of the impact on the arena of the world of psychology, specifically its subworld of behavior modification. The goal of this mode of treatment is for the person to gain control over the drinking situation, the frequency of drinking, or the amount of alcohol drunk, using techniques like filming a patient as he drinks in the program's wet bar and later re-running the videotape to show him what he looks like drunk. (As explained earlier, such techniques are usually used in combination with others, i.e., counseling, alternative training, alcohol education.) It is the claims of these programs that have aroused such controversy among the disease proponents. Obviously, if one has accepted the loss-of-control tenet with which this chapter began, no former compulsive drinker can ever trust himself to become a social drinker. As Keller has said, ". . . if I believed that an alcoholic can always choose whether or not to take the first drink, I could not believe in the existence of a disease, alcohol addiction." [23] This is the basis for the AA credo "one drink away from a drunk." Thus, in AA language, there are never ex-alcoholics—they are called "dry" or "sober" alcoholics. Confronted with reports of controlled drinking, AA's answer is "if these people drink normally today, then they were never alcoholics in the first place." [24]

That this is *ex post facto* reasoning makes it no less tenacious. A great deal of intellect can be invested in belief when the need for that belief is deep. No amount of "new knowledge" is going to penetrate beliefs that come out of life experience—especially experience as painful and hard-won as recovery from alcoholism. The following remarks from respondents are representative of the depth of feeling on this issue:

- Abstinence is not only the dividing line in treatment, it's almost a moral issue.

- I don't know why scientists and people are that concerned with wanting people to drink. I wonder if it has something to do with their own feelings.

- What a con job—that this particular drug, a mind altering drug, is a drink. That taking this drug is a norm, that's a hell of a con job.

- Because one or two can do it (resume drinking), you have some clown say it's o.k., and too many people ruin their lives again.

The critical point is that the disease theory (with its abstinence implication) was adopted by AA and by the early alcoholism movement, as

Roizen argues, because "it worked." [25] It has persisted because of its therapeutic utility. From the standpoint of the recovery service world, there is much less risk in telling "an alcoholic whose best friend is the bottle to give it up," as a respondent put it. To quote another, who could see the practicality from a bureaucratic perspective:

> There are people, we found it in our early McAteer programs, who do mature out of problems with drinking. The problem I have is we were never able to predict who they were. So you do them less harm with a goal of abstinence. My experience is it is easier to maintain abstinence than it is to maintain controlled drinking.

Controlled Drinking Revisited: The Rand Report

Release of the Rand Report, in June, 1976, brought this controversy to the fore once again. This episode has added significance in that the attack was so strong as to force the Rand researchers and their opposition into behavior that moved beyond mere convincing toward a more militant stance. Arguments were mustered even before official distribution of this report, since news of its most disputatious conclusion has been circulating within the arena during the previous year.

NIAAA had given a grant to the Rand Corporation to study its comprehensive alcohol treatment centers (ATCs) by evaluating reports on patients compiled through the SRI Monitoring System (described in the previous chapter). Six-month followups in 44 ATCs were examined; eight ATCs were selected for special 18-month followup study. The focus of the contention was the statement by the principal investigator, David Armor, a sociologist, and his colleagues Michael Polich and Harriet Stambul, that the majority of improved clients were either drinking moderate amounts of alcohol—at levels far below what could be described as alcoholic drinking—or engaging in alternating periods of drinking and abstention. Their deduction:

> We cannot overemphasize the import of these findings. Based on the relapse rates for a subsample of clients with followup reports a year apart, it appears that some alcoholics do return to normal drinking with no greater likelihood of relapse than alcoholics who choose permanent abstention. While the evidence here is by no means final, it does support a definition of remission that allows for drinking in normal or moderate amounts. Even through total abstention by definition is a more certain method for avoiding harmful consequences of alcohol, there is no guarantee that those who adopt a total abstention policy will in fact keep to it forever. Empirically, our data suggest that totally abstaining clients are just as likely to return to alcoholism as those who choose to drink at normal levels. Moreover, long-term abstention—defined as abstaining six months at both fol-

lowups—is a relatively rare event, occurring for only ten percent of the sample.[26]

The report was immediately and vehemently attacked as "riddled with scientific shortcomings," "shoddy," and "dangerous."[27] Criticism centered around a number of points. One was the unreliability of self-reporting when it comes to alcohol consumption.[28] Another was the confounding issue of known fluctuations in drinking behavior. If drinking episodes wax and wane, of what value is measurement at a fixed point?[29] In addition, the size of the sample came under heavy attack. The "normal drinking" conclusion had been drawn from a subsample of 161 patients. This was due partly to the fact that there had been a 21% response rate at six months, and a 62% response rate at 18 months, significantly reducing the number of patients in whom change or stability could be evaluated. What is more, in their desire to purify the sample, to include only the "true alcoholic," the researchers had further reduced this number using two additional criteria. First, they included only those clients who were "definitely alcoholic at intake," i.e., those suffering from the classic symptoms associated with loss of control. Second, they had dropped the drinking drivers when they found this group exhibiting closer resemblance in drinking behavior to the general population than to the treatment population. Thus, the table singled out for criticism showed a number of nineteen who had returned to normal drinking.[30] (The turnover table without the purification was also presented, but the critics paid no attention to that.)

Strongly questioned also was Rand's measure of "normal drinking," criteria for which were: 1) daily consumption less than three ounces of alcohol; 2) typical quantities on drinking days less than five ounces; 3) the lack of frequent episodes of at least three of the following symptoms—tremors, blackouts, missing meals, morning drinking, being drunk, and missing work. Emrick and Stilson called this "overly generous," averring that using these criteria, a patient could be labeled a normal drinker and have frequent episodes of any two of the above symptoms.[31] As Pittman and others pointed out, under this gauge, 25% of the clients were drinking normally at the time of intake into the ATCs for treatment.[32]

Some critics also objected to the use of the term "normal drinking," based as it was on statistical comparisons with the general population:

> Had the authors chosen to use the term "improved," "much improved" or "reduced drinking" to describe the group of patients who had greatly decreased their alcohol intake at the time of follow-up, I would have no objection to that section of the report. It is part of common clinical experience that many patients continue to struggle with their drinking both dur-

ing and after treatment. Treatment teaches such patients places to go for help, techniques for cutting short their relapses into drinking and ways of remaining well for increasing periods of time. Such patients are usually still aiming for abstinence and this goal is an important factor in their continued struggle for recovery.

. . . The term "normal drinking" conjures up an image of spontaneous joyful problem-free drinking, or, at the very least, carefully controlled problem-free drinking. The study definition and data do not support either picture.[33]

In other words, failure to remove "controlled drinkers" (those who continue to think of alcohol as a major stress reliever and exert great effort to maintain limited drinking) from the normal drinking group, "probably led to exaggerated normal drinking rates."[34]

The most energetic language, however, reflected the concern that the report would be misinterpreted as an invitation to all alcoholics to resume drinking. Typical was the response of clinical psychologist Mary Pendery, who then chaired the California State Alcoholism Advisory Board:

The alcoholic's wildest hope is that he's going to be able to drink again like ordinary people. And to play on that hope as this study does is shocking.[35]

Again, the researchers' caveats had been obscured in the furor. Armor et al. had warned that alcoholics who had tried to drink moderately and failed should not use the report as a rationale to try again. They also warned alcoholics with physical impairments such as liver disease not to drink again. A crucial admission by the researchers, however, went to the very heart of the most vocal criticism: "we have no evidence whatsoever, nor is there any method at present, that enables us to identify those alcoholics who might safely return to drinking and those who cannot."[36] The Rand Report had once again hit the experiential nerve of the recovered alcoholic. To quote Florette Pomeroy, a former executive director of the San Francisco and Bay Area National Council on Alcoholism:

I have taken some of these "experiments" to the hospital and watched them die . . . There is nothing in the world an alcoholic wants more than to be able to do that (controlled drinking). Somehow they want to be told that. I am a walking example of this. I made nine trips in one year to a recovery facility because I couldn't accept the fact that I could not drink the way other people did.[37]

One noteworthy consequence of this controversy was the manner in which lines were drawn, and the tie-in to the organizational turf carving discussed in Chapter 3. In May, prior to the release of the report, the State Alcoholism Advisory Board passed a resolution stating its unanimous support of the concept of total abstinence, as the only proven continuously successful approach to recovery. Furthermore, it stated its support of the State Office of Alcoholism's policy of not expending state funds to support research or treatment programs that advocate "so-called 'controlled drinking' practices." The following month, the County Alcohol Administrators of California passed a resolution supporting:

> . . . a treatment philosophy encompassing care for all persons with problems of alcohol abuse and alcoholism. Because we recognize that people are individuals our treatment concept must assume that persons will approach the resolution of their drinking problems in different ways, only *one* of which might be total abstinence.

The State Advisory Board countered with another resolution at its June meeting, now specifically citing the Rand Report, calling it "methodologically unsound," "clinically unsubstantiated" and "endangering to the lives of many persons with this disease." Also singled out for criticism and a requested investigation was a previous study,[38] which, prior to the Rand Report, had evoked the anger now transferred to Rand.

As stated above, the heat engendered from this convincing process centers around goals of treatment and definitions of recovery. In a climate of cost-benefit expectations, it is not surprising to encounter skepticism regarding evaluation of programs into which NIAAA had placed a considerable investment. Milam, for instance, offered his opinion that NIAAA, discovering its treatment programs had "failed to produce significant recoveries from alcoholism," was now reverting to a policy that says "since our approach to alcoholism doesn't get alcoholics to stay sober, we will find ways to rationalize their continued drinking."[39] To some extent Milam was right: not as to rationalization, a motive I would hesitate to judge, but as to the belief on the part of some elements within the arena that alternative goals of treatment have to be examined. As one respondent, an NIAAA official and a veteran of the arena, explained:

> Abstinence was okay when we were getting only heavily addicted people, but with earlier identification we are getting people with problems with drinking, so we have to change public understanding.

This was far from a new suggestion. In 1968, Pattison et al. had suggested that the goal of abstinence may be too extreme in some cases—many long-confirmed alcoholics cannot achieve it, and more moderate improvement, such as reduced frequency of intoxications and reduced duration of bouts, should be considered valid gains.[40] In 1974, Emrick had reviewed 271 published studies, and concluded that although abstinence is the most used criterion of improvement, it is not the only, and occasionally not the most reliable, measure.[41] In 1976, Pattison again reviewed the literature, and concluded that abstinence as a single criterion is inadequate, suggesting five possible outcomes: social drinking, attenuated drinking, controlled drinking, and normal drinking.[42] Even the World Health Organization Group of Investigators report on alcoholism as a disability,[43] although still adhering to "duration of abstinence" as the "most practical" criteria, had suggested it might be simplest to speak of "remission of condition, specifying the period of time the subject has been abstinent or drinking socially." [44]

The uproar might not have been so intense if the researchers had been content to have the report released quietly by NIAAA. Armor et al. had, after all, merely suggested "the *possibility* that normal drinking might be a realistic and effective goal for *some* alcoholics" (emphasis added), specifying" . . . it would be premature to endorse or advocate a policy of normal drinking for alcoholics" since the data on long-term feasibility and on identification of appropriate individuals are not adequate as yet.[45] Nonetheless, efforts had been extended to halt release,[46] and the Rand researchers, wanting their day in court, set up their own press conference to announce the report. Immediately, the National Council on Alcoholism countered with a press conference of its own. As picked up by the press, the issue was no longer a research finding to be studied further. (An indication of the emotionalism surrounding this issue is that two equally significant findings—the remission rate for untreated alcoholics was nearly as high as for treated alcoholics, and there was no difference among patients receiving treatment in different settings whether hospitalization, recovery houses or outpatient care—were overshadowed by the abstinence question.)

Armor now set about defending his study by appearing at a series of public meetings. Thus, the focus for Armor became one of convincing others as to the validity of his methodology, the reliability of return (percent of bias in regard to unfound former clients) and the problem of costs (spending taxpayer money to get a larger response). At the meeting I attended, when Armor was asked about the unreliability of self-reporting, he responded sardonically:

> My understanding is that they're all liars. Except when they go to AA and say they've abstained for three months, somehow they're not.

Regarding the semantic problems of "remission" and "improvement," his view (summarized) was that there is a lot of instability between abstention and some drinking, that abstention on a long term basis is a rare thing in alcoholism—there are other reasons why it is the goal of treatment centers. But knowing this should not necessarily change anyone's philosophy or treatment pattern. Normal drinking is also not a common event. It is "stable improvement," some drinking and some abstention, that is a very common event. His claim: 50% of the cases are in that improved category.

The spin-off from this episode was significant for the vitality and visibility of the arena. NIAAA was also put on the defensive, and Director Noble quickly issued a news release stating that until hard evidence is produced to the contrary, "abstinence must continue as the appropriate goal in the treatment of alcoholism." Rand had already been given a grant to do a four-year followup study for which they had devised their own questionnaires. Talk within NIAAA of doing a "study of the study" subsided as it was agreed to name a group of five consultants (two psychiatrists, one social psychologist, and two sociologists) to review the next report. Meetings at which the controversy was the main subject abounded for a number of months and the University of California Berkeley Extension Division offered a summer seminar on "Alcoholism at the Crossroads: Implications of the Rand Report." The announcing brochure stated that the reaction to the study "signals a developing crisis of meaning in the way we think about alcohol problems," and promised to consider the issue of "whether we must begin to look at alcohol use and misuse with a new openness." Caught in the cross-fire was the Rutgers Center, when two articles were published in the August, 1976 edition of the *Journal of Studies on Alcohol*—one on a controlled drinking study performed at the Addiction Research Foundation in Ontario, Canada, and the other a review of the literature by three researchers from the Psychiatry Department of the University of Pennsylvania, who stated that belief in the disease concept was based on the unproven hypothesis of Jellinek. Although the Ontario researchers suggested that a small percentage of alcoholics can return to normal drinking, but also noted that the controlled drinking program had proven less successful than those with abstinence as the outcome measure, the insult was sufficient, coming on top of the Rand brouhaha, for the Rutgers Center to be removed from the will of one of its long-standing benefactors. The Center subsequently issued a statement to the effect that the Journal, as a scientific publication, publishes papers that meet its criteria of standards, reiterating its position in favor of total abstinence as the best available treatment. However, the issue had moved far beyond the point where a rational response was sufficient.

Indeed, the convincing that centers around this issue demonstrates a further link to turf rights. Armor, from the perspective of the research world, was saying, "I'm a policy scientist, and policy ought to be based on science rather than ideology," [47] taking the pure science hard line that the findings have an identity of their own apart from the researcher. And even those fellow-researchers who were initially critical of the report on grounds other than normal drinking (for example, the 70% success rate as viewed against the measurement obstacles discussed in Chapter 11), protested that it was more important to defend the right to publish and the right to "question the faith."

In addition, there is a tie-in to the selecting process. For the bureaucratic world, the 70% success rate provided a new figure, which Dr. Chafetz and his successor Dr. Noble quickly utilized at Congressional hearings. However, the difference in their use of the normal-drinking finding is indicative of the difference between their personal agendas on the subject. Chafetz used this finding with his usual eloquence:

> People with alcohol problems are not static, fixed entities. They are a dynamic: constantly subjected to the physical, emotional, and cultural pulls and pushes that impinge upon us all. Who among us always feels well, strong, physically and emotionally? Who among us does not have moments when we regress to points of immaturity, unreasonableness and inadequate responses and behavior? Yet we demand that alcoholic people in order to wear the badge of recovery, must not have relapses and we now have scientific findings that they do sometimes take alcohol without relapsing into a full-fledged alcohol debauch.[48]

Noble's comments were much more cautious, emphasizing that the Rand study was "only part of the continued search for answers to the questions surrounding the issue of alcoholism" and stressing the need for "widespread reviews by the scientific community before policy is made or changed." [49]

That NIAAA was in a bind is clear. The institute, called upon to demonstrate effectiveness, had put a large amount of money into the research, which then produced elements that proved unpopular to an important part of its constituency. It is not difficult to see why a more liberal criterion for "success" would redound to the credit of the bureaucratic world. (Seen in this light, the position of the County Alcohol Administrators of California, discussed above, has more weight than a simple competition with the State Advisory Board.) Yet without the support of its constituency, or at least under battle from a large quarter, the bureaucratic world's position in this arena is precarious. Similarly, the disease advocates are also in a bind. As Roizen has adroitly demonstrated, advocates of alcohol reform have often used:

a loose definition of alcoholism when drawing attention to the many problems and casualties that came in alcoholism's wake—under the liberal notion that any damage caused by beverage alcohol counted as alcoholism: a portion of traffic accidents, violent crimes, child abuse, physical pathologies. . . . But when, on the other hand, the *treatment* of alcoholics was addressed, it was the tight definition—the one that offered determinate diagnostic symptoms and a rationale for abstinence—that was employed. When pummeling the public or the Congress for funds, protagonists used loose alcoholism; and when counseling the alcoholic in treatment, the tight alcoholism was substituted—thus advocates of alcoholism reform enjoyed the benefits of an expanded territory of problems over which they might establish territorial claims without at the same time diluting the salience of their recommendations about how "the problem" should be approached.[50]

Roizen also pinpoints the historical roots of this dilemma, the relationship to the redefining process. Moving alcoholism from punitive to benevolent social institutions required a dividing line: "institutions of social control do not come in fine gradations, covering at every interval of the way the 'amount' of personal responsibility that should be attached to an act . . . people are either guilty or not guilty, they are either sick or not sick, they are either sinful or not sinful." [51]

More Turf Claimed

The issue of controlled drinking is not about to go away, particularly since a growing band of its supporters is demonstrating this approach to problem-drinking by forming a new self-help mutual-support group, called Drinkwatchers. With local chapters growing in various parts of the country, this organization is offering a low-keyed mode of convincing, an alternative to abstinence and to AA, and to the disease concept. Its founder, Ariel Winters, emphasizes that Drinkwatchers is not trying to lure away anybody who wants to abstain completely from alcohol. But she has found her own experience with AA to be a shared one:

> It was unreal. I felt so much guilt all the time. I wasn't enjoying life at all. I did not want to drink to excess but I sorely missed a drink in the evening. I enjoyed drinking socially. So, with (Dr. Mortimer Hartman's) help, I tried drinking moderately and it worked.

> I am a cured alcoholic. I've regained my self-respect by throwing off the feeling that I was a diseased person. I am not. I have learned to drink moderately and there is now a stability to my life and a joy in living that wasn't there before.[52]

Drinkwatchers' basic stance is the belief in individuality, and the need for not one answer, but many. Members are interested in changing habits and mastering situations which cause abuse of alcohol. Meetings and a newsletter are devoted to the interchange of ideas, advice, trial and error, expert testimony, and tips on how to abstain if that is what one wants to do. The *Drinkwatchers Newsletter* is the only place in the alcohol literature (aside from publications of the alcoholic beverage industries) where one can find recipes for "Red Cabbage in Wine" and "Robert Mitchum's Christmas Egg Nog." But unlike the alcoholic beverage industries world, which is tolerant toward the disease concept since it still leaves a sizable market of normal drinkers, the *Drinkwatchers Newsletter* concerns itself with such concerns as the dangers of the labeling process inherent in the term "alcoholic," the possibility that uniform standards of certification of alcohol counselors will "favor the one treatment syndrome to the exclusion of all else." [53]

Thus, out of the convincing process new territory is being carved by this group, which, as it feels its strength, will confront the issues of concern—bringing more visibility to the arena.

In Summary

Again, before proceeding, it may be necessary to reflect on the twisting and weaving of tributaries that make up what have repeatedly been referred to as the flow of events—now, in relation to the *demonstrating* process. For instance, we have seen the way decriminalization (*redefining* alcoholism as a disease), intertwined with the macrosociological condition of urban redevelopment, has further dichotomized the public inebriate problem from the rest of the alcoholic population, for whom *respectability* is in the process of *being built*. Branching off in quite a different direction, is the intersecting of research and bureaucratic worlds over accountability for the programming described in previous chapters (the *selecting* process). We have seen how, as a consequence of the *selecting* process, a research agenda (investigation of the link between alcohol and mortality) coincided with a bureaucratic agenda (promulgation of a "responsible drinking" theme) to the advantage of an industry agenda (advertising "moderation messages" to signal social responsibility). Also examined was the manner in which *selecting* and *convincing* intertwine around the issue of alcohol addiction. In yet another instance, NIAAA, called upon to demonstrate the dimensions of the alcohol problem, contracted the Rand Corporation, whose findings mobilized the *convincing* process around the issue of "controlled drinking." A consequence for the arena was both an assertion of claims between *competing* associations and boards, and, to some degree, a *combining* in the ranks. And the issue of "controlled drinking" itself has led to the *establishment of turf rights* for a new organization, Drinkwatchers. As disparate as these examples are, they portray the action occurring as worlds and processes intersect—and the resultant growth of the arena's visibility.

Notes

1. E.M. Jellinek, "Phases in the Drinking History of Alcoholics," *Quarterly Journal of Studies on Alcohol,* Vol. 7 (1946), pp. 1-88.
2. Mark Keller, "Some Views on the Nature of Addiction," paper presented at the 15th International Institute on Prevention and Treatment of Alcoholism, June 9-18, 1969; Budapest, Hungary, p. 6.
3. Ibid., p. 11.
4. M.M. Glatt, "The Question of Moderate Drinking Despite 'Loss of Control,' " *British Journal of Addiction,* Vol. 62 (1967), p. 267.
5. Expert Committee on Mental Health, Alcoholism Subcommittee Second Report. Annex 2. "The Phases of Alcohol Addiction," World Health Organization Techn. Rep. Ser. No. 48, (August, 1953).
6. Mark Keller, "On the Loss-of-Control Phenomenon in Alcoholism," *British Journal of Addiction,* Vol. 67 (1972), p. 157.
7. Jellinek, "Phases of Alcohol Addiction," *Quarterly Journal of Studies on Alcohol,* Vol. 13 (1952), pp. 673-84.
8. Keller, "On the Loss-of-Control Phenomen," p. 160.
9. James R. Milam, *The Emergent Comprehensive Concept of Alcoholism.* Kirkland, Washington: ACA Press, p. 3.
10. *See:* Ronald Roizen, "Alcoholism Treatment's Goals and Outcome Measures," Social Research Group Working Paper F61, report prepared for the National Institute on Alcohol Abuse and Alcoholism, 1977, p. 40.
11. *See:* Robin Room, "Priorities in Alcohol Social Science Research," paper presented at Symposium on Research Priorities, Rutgers Center of Alcohol Studies (1977), p. 12. For a review of the literature on the biological effects of alcohol, *see* Henrik Wallgren and Herbert Barry, *Actions of Alcohol* (Amsterdam, N.Y.: Elsevier Publications, 1970).
12. *San Francisco Chronicle,* (November 29, 1976), p. 2.
13. *Newsweek* (December 13, 1976), p. 101.
14. *New York Times* (November 28, 1976), p. 39.
15. *The Wall Street Journal* (August 12, 1977), p. 18.
16. For examples of genetic research see: D. Goodwin, *Is Alcoholism Hereditary?* (New York: Oxford University Press, 1976); and L. Kaiji and J. Dock, "Grandsons of Alcoholics," *Archives of General Psychiatry,* Vol. 32 (1975), pp. 1379-81.
17. Milam, *The Emergent Comprehensive Concept,* p. 9.
18. Ibid., P. 10.
19. Ibid., p. 9.
20. Keller, "On the Loss-of-Control Phenomenon," p. 164.
21. "High and Dry," KQED-FM (March 18, 1976).
22. Ronald Roizen, "Comment on the 'Rand Report,' " *Journal of Studies on Alcohol,* Vol. 38 (1977), pp. 172-73.
23. Keller, "On the Loss-of-Control Phenomenon," p. 160.
24. Sagarin, *Odd Man In* (Chicago: Quadrangle Books, 1972), p. 50.

25. Roizen, "Comment," p. 174.
26. Armor et al., *Evaluating Alcoholism Treatment* (Santa Monica, California: The Rand Co., 1975), pp. 86-87.
27. *The Alcoholism Report,* Vol. 4 (July 9, 1976), pp. 2-5.
28. See Chapter 11.
29. Ibid.
30. Armor, et al., *Evaluating Alcoholism Treatment,* p. 87.
31. Chad D. Emrick and Donald W. Stilson, "Comment on the 'Rand Report,' " *Journal of Studies on Alcohol.* Vol. 38 (1977), p. 156.
32. *The Alcoholism Report,* Vol. 4 (July 9, 1976), pp. 3-4.
33. Sheila Blume, "Comment on the 'Rand Report,' " *Journal of Studies on Alcohol.* Vol. 38 (1977), p. 166.
34. Emrick and Stilson, "Comment," p. 157.
35. *The National Observer* (July 10, 1976), p. 6.
36. Ibid.
37. *Berkeley Daily Gazette* (August 4, 1976), p. 7.
38. Mark B. Sobell and Linda C. Sobell, "Second-Year Treatment Outcome of Alcoholics Treated by Individualized Behavior Therapy: Results," in Sobell and Sobell (eds.), *Emerging Concepts of Alcohol Dependence* (New York: Springer Publishing Company, 1977), pp. 300-35.
39. Letter to the *Seattle Post-Intelligencer* (August 18, 1976).
40. E.M. Pattison, E.G. Headley, G.C. Gleser, and L.A. Gottschalk, "Abstinence and Normal Drinking: An Assessment of Changes in Drinking Patterns in Alcoholics After Treatment," *Quarterly Journal of Studies on Alcohol,* Vol. 29 (1968), pp. 610-33.
41. C.D. Emrick, "A Review of Psychologically Oriented Treatment of Alcoholism: The Use and Interrelationships of Outcome Criteria and Drinking Behavior Following Treatment," *Quarterly Journal of Studies on Alcohol,* Vol. 35 (1974), pp. 523-49.
42. E. Mansell Pattison, "A Conceptual Approach to Alcoholism Treatment Goals," *Addictive Behaviors,* Vol. 1 (1976), pp. 177-92.
43. See Chapter 8.
44. Edwards et al., "Alcohol-Related Problems in the Disability Perspective," *Journal of Studies on Alcohol,* Vol. 37 (1976), p. 1373.
45. Armor et al., *Evaluating Alcoholism Treatment,* p. 140.
46. See testimony of Dr. Chafetz before the House Subcommittee on Health and the Environment, 1976, p. 10; and letter from Joe Takamine, president of the Alcoholism Council of Greater Los Angeles, and chairman of the Alcoholism Committee of the American Medical Association, as reported in *The Alcoholism Report,* Vol. 4 (September 10, 1976), p. 7.
47. *The National Observer* (July 10, 1976), p. 6.
48. Testimony before the Subcommittee on Alcoholism and Narcotics, p. 9.
49. *The Alcoholism Report,* Vol. 4 (July 9, 1976), p. 5.
50. Roizen, "Alcoholism Treatment's Goals and Outcome Measures," p. 28.
51. Ibid., p. 62.
52. *San Francisco Chronicle* (March 31, 1975), p. 14.
53. *Drinkwatchers' Newsletter,* Vol. 2 (December 10, 1976).

13.

Enlarging the Bounds
of Responsibility

We turn now to the last sub-process of demonstrating the problem of alcohol use—*enlarging the bounds of responsibility*. Although occurring under the condition of a less-is-better political philosophy, this sub-process, in effect, runs counter to it, by entailing *more* government involvement in terms of careers, prevention approaches and pressure on the alcoholic beverage industries world.

Career Stakes

As Senator Hughes implied in his allusion to a civilian army, [1] the opening up of territory has meant the opening up of careers. There is now a greatly enlarged "ownership of the problem" to include therapists, evaluators, researchers, bureaucrats, industrial counselors, volunteers, social workers, and so on. As mentioned previously, the most recent history of this arena is marked by a reversal of the early period, when the Classic Temperance Movement borrowed from established professions and disciplines. It is now the alcohol-use arena which is being "used" for grantsmanship and the advancement of careers (for instance, the behavior therapists who built careers in the 1960s around the application of their mode of therapy on alcoholic patients who were conveniently to be

219

found on back wards of Veterans Administration Hospitals). And, in keeping with another recent trend, retirement from any of these careers quite often means a new career as a consultant. Furthermore, NIAAA and the State Office of Alcoholism provide career opportunities for their legislative committees and subcommittees, their appropriations committees and subcommittees, and the committee's staffs.

Thus, the lines drawn over issues discussed in previous chapters, the ideologies defended, have a clear relationship to career stakes. An instructive illustration is provided by Roizen's discussion of outcome measures, the abstinence criterion and the different "preoccupations of mind" with which clinicians and program evaluators approach the *meaning* of remission or recovery.[2] The clinician's decision to regard an alcoholic as recovered, arrested or remitted may have substantial impact on the client's fate: "it may determine release or discharge from treatment, it may carry that tacit or explicit assurance from the clinician to others in the alcoholic's life that 'here is a person who has been returned to responsible and conforming behaviors,' and it may even be a decision that carries considerable emotional significance for both the therapist/counselor and the patient." For the clinician, the designation "recovered" is not a matter of good data collection or clear definitions, "but one in which a great many aspects of the patient's behavior and circumstances— both impressionistic and objective—are likely to be weighed carefully." The evaluation researcher on the other hand "is not responsible for managing the alcoholic, or making decisions regarding his fate, or otherwise affecting his circumstances." The central concern of the evaluation researcher is adequate description from readily available and easily collectable kinds of information. For example:

> One of the important differences between the evaluator's and the clinician's conceptions of remission arises around the problem of time: for the evaluator the outcome measurement must describe a respondent's "state" over a delimited time-span period. But for the clinician, a determination of recovery involves precisely the question of whether a particular state ought to become the basis for anticipating that the patient will continue in an unproblematic condition.[3]

Hence, that separate agendas are career-based partially explains the tenacity with which positions—not only regarding abstinence, but regarding straight alcoholism/broad brush programs, the issue of "responsible drinking," cost-benefit assessment, etc.—are defended.

In addition, some ideological differences reflect disputes within a career world. For example, underlying Dr. Milam's treatise on the physiological aspect of alcoholism is his criticism of those psychiatrists who have neglected the "biological substrates of behavior" and those clinical psychologists "who have in recent years severed relationships with the more basic life science branches of their parent discipline." [4] Equally significant, ideologies are reinforced by the work experience. One of the most judicious comments on the Rand Report came from a Director of Alcoholism Services who said in effect, the scientific proof of addiction may not yet be available, but ". . . the clinical evidence of tolerance and potentially lethal withdrawal syndromes is clearly visible in many patients." [5] Most important, career stakes, by entrenching an ever-widening number of people in an ever-widening progression of perspectives, enlarge responsibility for the problem of alcohol use, not incidentally increasing its visibility.

Recovery as a Career

These stakes become most evident in the growing cadre of recovered alcoholics who have found not only career opportunities, but a life purpose in the expanded arena. Abetted by the rise in the 1960s and 1970s of volunteerism as an entrance to paid positions, recovered alcoholics now constitute a large portion of the arena's personnel. While the stigma of alcoholism is far from erased, there is now, in keeping with the increased demands from the handicapped and the drive for respectability discussed earlier, an enhanced position for the "professional abstainer." As Gusfield has put it, stigma becomes a claim so that the label is no longer punitive, but a designation of expert status.[6] While this career direction bears a resemblance to other arenas (physical and speech therapists often come from the ranks of the afflicted), there is an additional mystique surrounding the recovered alcoholic, a connotation of being reborn, which fits into the American value of self-improvement. Also, unlike the mental health arena, where groups such as the Mental Patients Liberation Front or the Network Against Psychiatric Assault (NAPA) define themselves as counter to the "establishment," the recovered alcoholics represent a large segment of support. In fact, the recovered alcoholics are themselves so arena-establishment as to make it necessary for others in the arena to proclaim their own identity. I was continually struck in my interviews with the consistency with which respondents felt compelled to tell me early on if they were, or were not, recovered alcoholics.

The main distinction from other arenas lies in the philosophy of AA, from whose ranks come such a large number of counselors, directors of recovery homes, and industrial consultants. The Twelfth Step of AA calls upon the recovered alcoholic to carry the message to other alcoholics and to practice the other eleven principles in all affairs. To quote Taylor:

> . . . most veteran members do some form of Twelfth Step work, which includes such things as volunteer work at the local Central Office, taking phone calls, and talking to people who drop in. More traditionally, Twelfth Step work consists of going into homes, jails, or hospitals, in answer to the calls of distressed alcoholics, or their relatives or caretakers. On these visits, the Twelfth Step workers tell their own stories of alcoholic misery and of recovery in AA. They present themselves as living proof of AA's success, and insist that they bring to the sufferer hope and a promise of aid which he can find nowhere else. Twelfth Step workers regard themselves as rescuers, and their work as saving lives.[7]

With an expansion in the recovery service world, these people are now, as one respondent put it, "getting paid for Twelfth Stepping." To the arena they bring a missionary zeal and a belief in the efficacy of action. The explanation of one program director is typical:

> I believe that everyone can recover, everyone can grow, that I am calling forth what is there already. The thing that I don't usually get into when I discuss this because some people are frightened by it, is that this life force you're tapping into, this creativity that everybody's got, is God.

> I am a rebellious individual, but now I am called a pioneer. All my compulsiveness is rechanneled.

It is important to remember that the majority of AA members never get involved with the public. However, the ones who assume leadership positions, those who are most visible, bring with them the kind of dynamism and sense of purpose displayed above. As an amusing illustration, I began all of my interviews with an assurance that no remarks would be for attribution, to which one respondent, a recovered alcoholic, responded: "A lot of people will be disappointed—in this field you have a lot of egocentric people who will want bylines."

While the number of job opportunities has increased due to the funding explosion of the last years, even more noticeable is an increase of professionals, especially in the recovery service world, and especially since the establishment of NIAAA. The disproportion between the two groups, albeit seen differently by each, remains a source of tension. In an article by a clinical psychologist and a clinical social worker, both of whom had worked in an alcoholism program, the non-professionals were described as holding the power, both political and clinical. Conversely, a number of my respondents described the non-professionals in the following terms: "grossly exploited"; "they are dedicated, and will do things for a certain salary level that nobody else will touch"; "very often the social worker receives the salary and the recovered alcoholic is responsible for what happens." What is occurring is a classic confrontation of the old with the new, not surprising in an arena where the veterans were hampered in the past by meager resources, but free to follow their own inclinations. Unlike other health services where the non-professional has been brought in to work under the supervision of the professional, here it is the professional who is looked upon as the newcomer. Moreover, in addition to the inherent anti-professional bias of self-help groups,[8] there exists, as previously identified, the specific antipathy many recovered alcoholics harbor in regard to mental health professionals.

A major aspect of the conflict is nicely caught in the title of the article referred to above, "The Future of Alcohology: Craft or Science?" Kalb and Propper characterize the non-professional as craftsman, learning through the experiences of his teacher, deviating only in style, eschewing critical analysis of the traditions of the craft, establishing loyalty through mutual agreement. By contrast, the scientist-professional they describe as exposed to a broad variety of competing viewpoints, encouraged to exercise autonomy in establishing an independent conceptualization of the issues, and to critically evaluate the work of teachers and peers. The authors suggest that these disparate perspectives make it impossible for the two groups to co-exist to the benefit of the arena:

> Research is not used, as in other fields, as a springboard for developing and testing new hypotheses and abandoning old ones that are empirically disproved. Alcoholism treatment concepts in the overwhelming majority of clinic settings have developed and survive not with the aid of research but in spite of it. Clinical treatment is not the logical outgrowth of scientific discoveries but instead remains an encapsulated body of theories and shopworn slogans that are apparently immune to the outcome of scientific research.[9]

Kalb and Propper have specific reference to the abstinence issue, where, as already indicated here, data must be filtered through experiential understanding and self-esteem: "For the professional, a challenge to traditional beliefs is often an academic issue for debate, but for the recovered alcoholic, it often becomes a threat."[10]

Milam substantiates that recovered alcoholics sometimes refer to non-alcoholics as "civilians" or "earth people" to indicate the futility of attempting to explain the strange transformations they have experienced both in drinking and in the recovery process: "To suppose that the profound biological transformation of recovery can be understood in functional psychological terms or made to occur by strictly psychological strategies and manipulations, is only to prolong the age-old alienation and mutual frustration between patient and therapist." [11] To the status differential inherent in any relationship where the "paraprofessional" is struggling to enter a chosen field, is added an extra fillip which carries the weight of the special historical experience of the alcoholic. One respondent explained:

> What people needed are role models. And you can't believe in a clinical Ph.D. as a role model. When I talk to a client and say I failed high school, and now I teach classes . . . they can look at themselves and say damn, it's possible. Recovery in and of itself is pretty much close to taking a Ph.D. It's a laborious process—to achieve it you learn a great many things, what it's all about.

No wonder that certification and accreditation, the imposition of standards to professionalize non-professionals, is seen as a threat in some quarters. As to staying power, Kalb and Propper place their bets on the dedicated recovered alcoholic. The professional, they say, can flee to more comfortable and less divisive and frustrating clinical pastures: "Those who choose to stay are likely to be the best and the worst." [12]

The Co-Alcoholic: More Responsibility, Fewer Rewards

A slowly emerging development in this arena is the recognition of those who suffer with and around the alcoholic—dubbed "co-alcoholics." Again, AA was at the forefront in the launching of Al-Anon and Al-Ateen—self-help groups for families of alcoholics. Gradually, the bounds of responsibility are being extended beyond the family, in keeping with the social model of recovery, where, as one respondent expressed it, "the whole community represents 'significant others.' " [13] Here, as with the disease concept, there is a wide definitional range. Some of the time the co-alcoholic is explained as encompassing everyone, as when the moderator of a weekly radio program devoted to alcoholism described the term as follows:

> There is no person who is not affected by alcoholism. You can be hit by a car driven by a drunk driver. Your insurance rates are higher because of drunk drivers.[14]

More often the definition is confined to anyone who has a helping, rescuing relationship with an alcoholic—family, doctors, nurses, social workers. As explained by NCA in its launching of Alcohol Action Week for 1977 with a theme of "Alcoholism: The Family Disease," the co-alcoholic, in rescuing the alcoholic from the problems that arise because of his/her drinking behavior, thereby prevents the alcoholic from dealing with the realities of the problem.[15]

In the San Francisco Bay Area, a disheartening effort at organizing was made, stymied by the very factors that had suggested a need for association. Leaders of the Bay Area Council on Co-Alcoholism (BACA) were looking for an association to give co-alcoholics support, to do educational outreach and research into the health and social problems of the co-alcoholic. In a sense, such an organization would be an acknowledgment that they too have careers—explained by one respondent:

> As painful as supporting behavior is, it is at times rewarded. But when the alcoholic starts to get better, nobody rewards the co-alcoholic.

As to social problems, one example will suffice: "if you take the family car away because of drunk driving, it affects the rest of the family members." Nevertheless, leaders of BACA have not been able to form a membership base. As explained by one:

> There are large numbers of co-alcoholics, but nobody knows that word, or acknowledges that the other person has tremendous problems. Nobody acknowledges that they are in a continuous fear state, have low self-esteem. If you look at AA you'll find most of the participants are men, and in Al-Anon most are women. The co-alcoholic state is the women's state— they are programmed to be loving, caring, responsible, and to put their own life second. The problem in organizing was that we got an organization of basically dependent non-assertive women, and those who work a forty-hour week, who could only give it so much time.

Despite aborted organizational efforts, the enhanced visibility of the arena may yet open up this area as it has for other nascent efforts already discussed, e.g., Women for Sobriety and Drinkwatchers. Furthermore, a national effort just getting underway called The Other Victims of Alcoholism, Inc. (TOVA Inc.) may meet with greater success.

The Professionalization of Reform

In spite of the disillusion expressed by Kalb and Propper, one aspect of professional work in this arena requires closer examination. It pertains to the group of professionals who, along with the recovered alcoholics, are carrying forward the pragmatic tradition discussed in Chapter 7—the clinical compulsion that "something has to be done." Moynihan has characterized this phenomenon as "the professionalization of reform." [16] Similarly, McCarthy and Zald note the marked increase in the number of career positions in organizations related to social movements, observing that such careerists "define their opportunities less in terms of the use of professional skills and more in terms of social change objectives." [17] Gouldner looks upon this development much less kindly, averring that the rise of the welfare state has meant the rise of the "uninvolved reformer." He continues:

> It means the rise of reform-at-a-distance. Reform today is no longer primarily the part-time avocation of dedicated amateurs but is increasingly the full-time career of paid bureaucrats.[18]

Gouldner sees a connection between this development and the selecting of data discussed earlier, asserting that social reform has become a kind of engineering job, a technological task to be subject to bland "cost-benefit" or "system-analysis."

In the alcohol use arena, this development is by no means confined to bureaucratic careers. For example, a recovery program may be run by an ex-priest or an ex-teacher, reflecting the shift in career opportunities. Nevertheless, the phenomenon is most noticeable in the NIAAA bureaucracy, largely because NIAAA was formed just as funding was decreasing in the mental health arena, and a carry-over in personnel and philosophy from the Community Mental Health Programs occurred. Kingsley Davis' 1937 portrayal of the mental hygienist as "practicing moralist" rather than scientist [19] is reinforced by Musto's 1975 argument that the impetus behind Community Mental Health Centers was faith in their contribution to social progress through early identification and prevention efforts. Musto concludes that the American mental health professional has believed, and has been supported in the belief, that his expert insight and technology could achieve a better social day.[20]

McCarthy and Zald had wryly speculated that the next step in the professionalization of reform would be the founding of a social movement organizers' association and the institution of formal credentialing procedures. Sure enough, a new organization, the National Association of Prevention Professionals (NAPP) was formed in 1976, comprising "prevention people" from mental health, drug and alcohol abuse, delinquency and health arenas. NAPP promised to address the following concerns: "the inequitable ranking given prevention vis-à-vis other program components, the resulting frustration experienced by prevention workers, the absence of decent benefits and services available to prevention workers, and the scarcity of relevant prevention-oriented training." [21] Not only is NAPP interested in building public and political support for prevention efforts, but it is seeking "greater opportunity for training and credentialing in prevention objectives." [22]

This career development dovetails with the social history already recounted, most notably the growth of the alcohol-program approach. As the worlds of this arena have grown there have arisen "new support publics" concerned with "community and social costs, accidents, family destruction, public disorderliness, traffic deaths, inefficiency in the job world and other problems" [23]—in short, a thrust to narrow the gap between "the ideal and the real," [24] leading to the logical question: how to prevent alcohol problems? During the years when primary concern was for the plight of the individual alcoholic and the adequate provision of treatment, all of the processes previously discussed were brought into play. Now there are increasing calls for a "restatement of objectives" [25] adapted to the enlarged boundaries of the alcohol problem population. Beauchamp had noted that in many social problems a major aspect of social policy in the long run may well be whether the public and its representatives hold the victim as being morally deserving and blameless for his plight. "This is a complex subject, but one key variable is the numbers of victims involved in the problem as compared with comparable groups who do not suffer." [26] Obviously, recognition of the existence of the co-alcoholic could be a force in this direction. But it is the early intervention and prevention efforts of social reformers—making visible a larger number of victims, increasing the public's responsibility for their welfare—that is vital for social policy.

The Many Faces of Prevention

That I have already made numerous references to "prevention" without defining the concept is consistent with the practice in this arena. In 1977, U.S. Senator William D. Hathaway opened hearings before the Alcoholism and Drug Abuse Subcommittee by comparing federal prevention activities to an athletic team composed of "a basketball center, a football halfback, two pole vaulters and a lacrosse goalie—they have a lot of individual ability, but nobody can tell us what they're all doing on the same team." [27] Noting that in 1976 nine different federal agencies spent more than $60 million on alcohol and drug abuse prevention programs, he commented, "They seem to have as many different approaches to education and prevention as they have separate grantees and program administrators." Any semantic discrepancies previously discussed herein pale when compared to the range of understanding of just what constitutes prevention.

For some people, particularly against a background of competitive funding, all treatment is seen as prevention—there is no need to distinguish a separate category, and even the establishment of a separate Prevention Division within NIAAA is seen as a threat. On the other hand, some treatment (or counseling) is clearly based on the theory of prevention, i.e. early intervention, as for instance, ACCEPT (Alcohol Counseling Center for Early and Preventive Training) in San Francisco. Located in proximity to middle and upper class residential districts, this program offers counseling to people who still have their jobs and families, who are just beginning to experience problems with their drinking, and to the families of such drinkers, thereby encouraging people to question themselves (and/or others to question their behavior) much earlier than had been done previously.

Others look beyond the arena, seeing dependency on alcohol as a signal that something is missing in the body social. It has been suggested that rather than concentrate on the perils of alcohol in public school curricula, more would be gained by teaching "values clarification" and "self-actualization," based on the assumption that a "whole person" will not need to drink himself into a problem state. This recourse is attractive to those who no longer hold the victim responsible for his condition, but see him brought to his state by a dysfunctional society. (The pragmatic impulse remains basic in American thought: human happiness can be engineered through treatment of evil, now transferred from a personal to a social evil.)

Also suggested is the promotion of activities intended to substitute for drinking. However, Room has pointed out what a mixed bag substitution strategies present. Although sports and soft drinks were promoted by the temperance movement as alternatives to drinking, "both activities are now associated with drinking as often as not—beer is as much a part of going to the ballgame as hotdogs, and a major part of soft drink sales is as mixes for alcoholic drinks." Nevertheless, "the soft drink industry has made a place in American culture for non-alcoholic drinks acceptable to adults which did not previously exist." [28] Furthermore, although such suggestions seem worthy of trial, they run up against funding problems under the conditions of increased oversight described earlier. How does one measure behavioral changes in the general population, those who are not "yet" in the problem drinker category? In applying for a grant designed to provide alternatives to drinking (e.g. recreation for young people), how can one promise to evaluate the number "saved"?

Another approach is based on the theory that many drinking problems arise from breaches of the insulation around what are considered permissible situations for drinking. Proposals from this quarter have to do with strengthening the insulation: staggered work schedules which would allow a worker to sleep in with a hangover, thereby reducing the labeling process; the provision of taxi service or beds for guests to prevent driving after party-drinking. (Gusfield exemplifies this approach when he says that the problem is not in the foolishness of the driver but in failure to construct an automobile designed to be driven by foolish drivers.) [29] These suggestions run up against a countervailing philosophy: identifying the worker who drinks, or the drunk driver who can be frightened by his first offense, are seen as early case-finding, an alternative means of prevention. Griffith Edwards has compared insulation proposals to "drowning out the cries of the dying by wearing earmuffs" or "suggesting high stepping exercises for sober people so they can walk over the drunks without tripping." [30] Once more illustrated is the wide separation between those who would prevent the personal tragedy of alcoholism and the more nominalist stance of some members of the research world.

Thus, although the new breed of social reformers is unwilling to say with the certitude of a clinician that there is an entity called alcoholism, they are nevertheless willing to examine the notion of intervention. This is consistent with developments occurring outside the alcoholism arena—not only the anti-labeling-anti-psychiatry thrust already discussed, but the more recent development of "holistic" or "humanistic" medicine. When the focus was on classification and identification of disease, the person who contained the disease was an abstraction, an object for clinical appraisal and action. Once disease was seen as occurring outside the tissue (i.e. emotional, affected by stress, by attitudes, by community) the floodgates were open to the medicalization not only of social problems, but of the whole society.

Despite the avoidance by the new social reformers of the moral stance that marked an earlier period (when it was the individual drinker who was being judged and found wanting), there are moral overtones to this mode of prevention insofar as the obligation of the community is a variant of being one's brother's keeper. This is the impetus behind drawing in organizations like the Education Commission of the States, the Parent-Teachers Association, U.S. Conference of Mayors, the General Federation of Women's Clubs, through the awarding of grants, as well as the not-so-hidden agenda of occupational programs—enlisting labor and management as allies is expected to make these people "change agents" in the community. One bureaucrat explained, "When we need political pressure—for alcohol education in the schools for instance, we can call upon these people." As described in Chapter 5, the State Prevention

Coordinator Program was designed around this concept of community organization, i.e. changing attitudes by changing the environment. That these programs turned toward the less ambitious undertaking of public information and education is not unique, since, in spite of all the previously described theorizing, this is where the prevention emphasis is most often placed.

Public information and education generally takes the form of publications and television warnings from the National Council on Alcoholism and/or NIAAA about drunk driving, or checklists of symptoms of alcoholism, or the promotion of alcoholism as a treatable disease. It is in this category that the enlargement of responsibility can be seen most clearly. For instance, the 1974 television presentation entitled "Drink, Drank, Drunk" aimed its questions and its admonitions not at the "diseased" person, but at those around him: do you worry about how much he drinks?; do you complain about how often he drinks?; do you criticize him for the money he spends on alcohol?; don't get mad at him; don't moralize; don't lie and cover for him—a tacit recognition of the role of the co-alcoholic. Alcoholism was labeled a "family disease," a rhetorical device parallel to "a cancer on the body politic." (The disease concept can be expected to persist: illness, after all, despite its negative effect on social worth, is still the only legitimate label by which society is prepared to extend a benevolent hand.)

With respect to enhancing the visibility of the arena, it is important to note that while public information is geared toward drawing new clients into the recovery service world, the image projected to the public is not that more media coverage exists but that there is more alcoholism. Thus a television campaign built around a slogan like "What is a drink? Why does it have to be alcohol? Why not lemonade?" stands more chance of demonstrating the problem to the non-alcoholic than it does of stopping the problem drinker in his tracks. Moreover, in light of the definitional chaos, a media barrage may increase the anxiety of people without affecting their behavior. For some people, the campaign associating cholesterol with heart disease has meant that they continue to eat forbidden food all the while protesting, "I shouldn't be eating this." With the alcohol campaign, anxiety takes the form of, "how does one get from those two drinks I have every night to that disease TV and the newspapers talk about?" Furthermore, popularization of alcoholic symptoms, as a prevention measure, may serve to make people more prone to label as alcoholic others in their acquaintance, thereby *increasing* the "prevalence" of the problem population.

It is obvious that public information campaigns are subject to selective perception: people are more likely to absorb information that coincides with their prior attitudes and will interpret information differently. The experience with seat belts and with smoking has amply demonstrated that there is much more governing behavior than the rational facts. And, barraged daily with information about cancer-producing substances in their food and air, people are likely to decide that their only recourse is to eat, drink and be merry. Nevertheless, the very concept of prevention is predicated on the exaggerated notion of the value of information. Why else put a sign next to the teller's station, as has a California bank, warning "Bank robbers can get 25 years in prison"? It should be noted, moreover, that media programs fill another need: as convincing mechanisms for legislators, nothing can compare to the splash of a television campaign.

A "New Era of Enlightenment"

Despite the failure of the most extreme prevention measure, Prohibition, the philosophy behind this experiment (alcohol is a poison, and its consumption should be limited, or better still, stopped) persists. Prevention approaches based on "little Prohibitions" [31] are again being proposed, forcing a confrontation with the drinking ethos of Americans and a substantial enlargement of responsibility for the social problem of alcohol use. One respondent, a member of the NIAAA Prevention Division grant review committee, quite nicely captured the direction this thinking is taking:

> Regarding getting the community involved, there's the old saw that people get the kinds of elected officials they deserve. I think communities get the kinds of alcohol problems they want. It's clear that alcohol plays such a tremendous role in lubricating society, and has so many positive valuations attached to it, that I think communities generally are willing, even eager, to tolerate casualties from the drug to maintain the use of this social device. I think that unless communities feel that the maintenance of the social device isn't worth the number of casualties that are coming up, I can't imagine that there will be anything like alcoholism programs that they have any major impact. And so I think communities need to address these issues, if they're going to talk about treatment services: do we really want treatment services anyway or would we rather build a place on the edge of town and shovel Joe Blow over there in such a way that we manage to create and identity for him that selects him from us. Even if he was my next door neighbor.

In addition to the obvious role alcohol plays in lubricating leisure activities, Room points to the many ways alcohol and worklife intertwine: taverns were traditionally the hiring halls for many occupations (newspapermen, policemen, court functionaries); in some occupations, (company sales representatives, lobbyists) drinking is virtually a requirement of the job and much of the work is carried on in drinking situations; alcohol is a traditional gift or exchange commodity in our culture where money transactions would be considered unaesthetic or unethical, and qualifies as a business expense for tax purposes.[32] Indeed, the heat generated over controlled drinking as a treatment goal bears on this issue of the place that alcohol enjoys in American society. The study that drew fire prior to the Rand Report [33] was criticized by one bureaucrat on these grounds:

> These people are not just saying it's possible that some people can drink after treatment. Science is never that pure. They feel very strongly that we live in a drinking culture; therefore people should be assisted to get back into that. Being abstinent is deviant. What they fail to realize is that this drinking culture is not a heavy drinking culture—in fact, only about 10% of the people who drink are heavy drinkers. The major portion drink so lightly that most alcoholics can't believe it—they'd never think of that as social drinking.

Regardless of the ratio of heavy to light drinking, the government, asked to reduce problems associated with drinking, cannot help but wonder about the efficacy of its programs so long as its target groups (the young, women and minorities) are the same as those singled out for the alcoholic beverage industries by marketing research.

As was explained earlier, the temperance movement did not become a prohibitionist movement until the 1890s when it combined with the Progressive effort to achieve social reform through government regulation. However, traces of this shift can be found earlier in the nineteenth century when the temperance argument began to be based on social responsibility for the less fortunate. True, some people might be convinced they were able to handle liquor consumption, but it was the example they set for others by not giving it up that was crucial. Thus, not surprisingly, representatives of the alcoholic beverage industries world began nervously calling NIAAA "neo-prohibitionist" when they heard NIAAA Director Noble speak of "a new era of enlightment," of "working to change social mores regarding the use of alcohol" and of the effect control policies and price can have on consumption.[34]

The very choice of Noble for the directorship was considered indicative of a "new era." His predecessor, Dr. Chafetz, was seen as having played "a central role in the visibility the institute achieved in its first five years" due to his "strong talents in the arena of public affairs and publicity." [35] Dr. Noble, who besides being an M.D. holds a doctorate in biochemistry and is a professor of psychiatry, came to the institute as a researcher into the effects of alcohol on the destruction of brain cells and consequently on brain function (memory, concentration, learning new tasks)—certainly a reasonable basis for a conservative attitude toward its use. To quote Noble from an interview held shortly after he took office:

> People are asking many questions which are going to make vested interest groups very uncomfortable. . . . As far as taxation is concerned, we are not a regulatory agency. It is for us to provide information. If, in fact, increased consumption causes more problems, then I think that those in policy-making roles should then begin to make decisions based on fact. If taxation should be the best way of dealing with the issue, I think we should have enough data for the policy makers to make those decisions.

> . . . In Scandinavian countries during World War II, when alcohol was in limited supply, there was a dramatic decline in cirrhosis. Of course, you can attribute many other factors to it, and obfuscate the issue. As a scientist, if you want to, you can take any side of the argument. But if you want to be an honest scientist, and you look at the burden of evidence, then I believe the evidence is more towards the conclusion that the more you drink, whether as an individual or as a society, the more problems you will have.[36]

Hence, Noble's public statements often emphasized the relationship of alcohol to health, e.g., stress on tissues of the main heart muscle, elevation of plasma cholesterol and triglycerides, malabsorption of vitamins and minerals. Moreover, he struck a blow against the slogan favored by his predecessor and embraced by the alcoholic beverage industries—the notion of "responsible drinking," saying:

> I don't think that the concept of responsible drinking is something we should continue because I don't know what the heck responsible drinking means. Responsible drinking for one person may be one glass of wine every second or third day. For another, it could be ten glasses of beer.

> . . . I contend there are people who are so-called "socially" using alcohol in terms of our present definition of moderate drinking, and who are still destroying their lives. . . . This is not to say I believe in Prohibition, but I mean we strongly need to define a clearer role for alcohol in our society.[37]

Declaring the responsible drinking theme to be "inoperative" (this may have been tongue-in-cheek, considering the unfortunate association surrounding this term in post-Nixon years), Prevention Division Director Donald Phelps announced its replacement by a concept of "responsible decision-making" about alcohol—seemingly a fine point, but from the institute's perspective meant to signal a tilt toward legitimizing abstention. Noble tried to explain his dissatisfaction with the simplicity of "responsible drinking," saying, "it is a moralistic term which damns the alcoholic." [38] In truth, it is circular reasoning to replace moral judgment with a disease concept only to imply that alcoholic drinking is irresponsible. Not only is the term often confused with "controlled drinking," a totally different concept, but as social scientists have pointed out, it is in itself a contradiction. Much drinking has its meaning in being irresponsible (letting-go, time-out). To be sure, this fact is an impediment to the early case-finding mode of prevention; a frequent response of those whom others have labeled alcoholic is, "I do my work, so my drinking is no problem."

The newer "responsible decision-making theme" was spelled out in the report of a Task Force convened under one of the grants discussed in Chapter 4. Awarded to the Education Commission of the States (ECS), this $1,626,674 grant (preceded by a $226,272 contract) had supported a three-year study which recommended that government, industry, labor unions, church groups, volunteer organizations, public and private school systems and the media join together "in an integrated effort to help Americans develop rational attitudes about the use and nonuse of beverage alcohol." [39] In terms of visibility, the announcement of this report was significant. The chairman of the Task Force, former South Carolina Governor John C. West and others of the committee were given a White House spotlight, when the press covered a ten-minute meeting with President Carter, an old friend of West's. The message by which responsible decision-making was clarified was that the decision not to drink must be accorded equal respect with the decision to drink in a responsible manner. And conversely, that those who do not drink must be given an opportunity to learn to respect those who do. Question arose, however, over whether the report was to be regarded as a "political" or a "scientific" document. Criticism was addressed to the general lack of substance, direction and specificity; the failure to call for an innovative approach to prevention, but rather to reply primarily on an educational approach; and the "compromising" tone of the report—in short, if "for an investment of $2 million, the taxpayers of America might expect something more than they received." [40] That the Task Force made a special effort to cater to the liquor industry to win their support is adduced from the following account of the official presentation ceremony at the White House:

> West indicated that there could be a limited number of persons to go with the Task Force to meet with President Carter. We understand that space was limited, but when West selected the non-Task Force members to

make the visit to the White House, he chose not only representatives from DISCUS (The Distilled Spirits Council of the United States), the Wine Institute and the U.S. Brewers Association, but also the public relations counsel for DISCUS.[41]

As to the "abstinence" correlate of "responsible-decision-making":

> What seems to permeate the ECS report is the feeling that it is okay for some people to abstain, so long as they not interfere with anyone else's drinking patterns.[42]

The obscurity of a prevention approach based on community change was re-emphasized in the response to the report's recommendation that "public policies that encourage appropriate attitudes and skills must be developed and implemented now." Two weeks after the release of the report, Dr. Noble was telling a National Council on Alcoholism assemblage, "We don't know how to develop skills that would bring about responsible decisions about alcohol." [43]

Such honesty notwithstanding, the term "problem-drinker" implies that there is such a thing as appropriate drinking, making it incumbent upon the institute to come to grips with this issue. As already stated, for its part, the alcoholic beverage industries world was only too happy to have a disease concept which set the afflicted apart, a slogan by which to attract the rest of the population, and attention deflected from regulation of social factors—conditions of sales, taxation etc. In all fairness, former Director Chafetz was mindful that more could be done, and he had been trying to softsell the industries into accountability. In his address to the Fourth Annual NIAAA Conference he asked, ". . . doesn't the liquor industry have a social responsibility to assure the nondestructive use of their product, just as the automobile industry has a responsibility to promote the safety of their automobiles?" [44] Nonetheless, as one NIAAA official put it, "We tried to take a nonadversary role, but I'm not so sure they took us seriously, throwing kickers and cows in our face." *

Little Prohibitions

Numerous references to the beverage world in the plural have no doubt made clear that there is no such thing as the "liquor industry."

---

* The reference is to two products produced by Heublein Inc., and directed to new tastes (youth, women): Kickers, a 30-proof pop-flavored beverage marketed in milk bottle-shaped containers; and Hereford Cows, milkshakes with a 20% alcohol content—i.e. more than wine, but less than distilled spirits.

The interests of the distilled spirits people are quite opposed to those of the beer people, whose interests are quite opposed to the wine people. For example, the distilled spirits industry worries about the trend to lighter beverages, the wine industry about capturing even more of the market than it already has. Coalitions are as tenuous as those among Arab states, and organizations as diverse as the Distilled Spirits Council of the United States (DISCUS), the Wine and Spirits Wholesalers Association of America (WASA), the United States Brewers Association, the Association of American Vintners, the Independent American Whiskey Association, the National Association of Beverage Importers, the National Beer Wholesalers Association of America, the National Licensed Beverage Association, the National Liquor Stores Association, and the Wine Institute express the interests of the various sub-worlds.

Nevertheless, in terms of the dollars this world provides for government, it is clear that any temperance efforts have an uphill battle. Revenues going to federal, state and local government from excise, license and other beverage taxes and fees in 1976 were estimated at $10.1 billion, with corporate and personal taxes estimated at $1.7 billion.[45] Approximately $600 million a year goes back to the federal government from California alone. Government revenue from alcoholic beverages is the second largest source of its income—albeit a big leap, the first being income taxes. (It was this mine Senator Hathaway wanted to tap when he proposed that $100 to $120 million annual funding be earmarked for occupational alcoholism projects.)

In regard to organizational turf claims, the alcoholic beverage industries world obviously represents a formidable force as contrasted with the valiant efforts of the two temperance groups remaining in California, the California Council on Alcohol Problems, (CAP) and the Women's Christian Temperance Union (WCTU). Both of these groups concern themselves with lobbying activity and supplying material to the public schools, with the WCTU also providing radio programs and the Council a monthly newsletter. While they may find some hope in the prevention rumblings emanating from NIAAA, organizations as old as these are accustomed to the tortoise pace of such efforts, and were not surprised to find NIAAA Director Nobel's goal of "stabilization of per capita consumption" immediately encountering the opposition of the National Coalition for Adequate Alcoholism Programs (NCAAP). Chairman of the Coalition, Leo Perlis, Director of the AFL-CIO Community Services Department suggested such a stated objective would "unnecessarily stir opposition from the alcoholic beverage industry" and that while this might be an outcome of an overall plan, "there was no need to spell it out as a goal"; Augustus Hewlett, Director of the Alcohol and Drug

Problems Association (ADPA) called the consumption objective "a red flag and a very difficult thing to explain to the public." [46] (It should be noted that the Distilled Spirits Council of the U.S. is a member of the Coalition.)

Of the mechanisms for reducing consumption, manipulation of prices through increased taxation is one that rises to the fore from time to time. In the discussion over the 1975 proposed legislation for an added tax in California, the argument offered was twofold: increased taxes could reduce the recruitment of new drinkers; drinkers should pay for the problems that drinking causes. A subsidiary argument, one favored by the Scandinavians and the Canadians,[47] is that per capita consumption and cirrhosis are related, and that taxation could have an effect on both. As one respondent explained:

> Cirrhosis is probably the highest ranking cause of death that doesn't have its own foundation! Of course, you can say that cirrhosis isn't always connected to alcoholism, but none of the other disease figures is that pure—the diabetes count includes the elderly in its mortality figures. But cirrhosis still has never been stressed by the alcoholism movement. Perhaps it is seen as fostering the low status image of the public inebriate. When it is referred to, it is used to emphasize disease, and then very quickly the disease aspect becomes loss of control, where the heart of things is.

Of course, there is lay recognition that cirrhosis is a threat, and some public anxiety about safe levels of drinking mentioned in regard to media campaigns is no doubt also related to this fear. But the concept of lowering per capita consumption through taxation implies that affecting everyone's drinking will affect alcoholism. Cisin has expressed the main objection to this stance in his reference to a survey question, "Would you be willing to pay a little more for your alcoholic beverages in order to cut down on the prevalence of alcoholism?":

> It sounds plausible until you try it in a *reductio ad absurdum,* and try a lot of other questions like that. This is where the governmental philosophy leads: "Would you be willing to pay more for your gasoline in order to make it more difficult for those wild drivers on the road to have accidents?" Ultimately, "Would you be willing to pay more for your bread in order to cut down on the prevalence of obesity in this country?" And, after awhile, I, as a consumer say, "For heaven's sake, stop picking on me. If you've got problems go pick on the people who are creating the problems. I'm not one of them." [48]

Cisin's examples are not off the mark. Not long ago, California Health and Welfare Secretary Mario Obledo proposed a tax on soda pop to finance a program for combatting tooth decay.[49]

While taxation proposals wrestle with the issue of responsibility, other proposals place responsibility right at the door of the alcoholic beverage industries world and the world of communication (e.g. the broadcast media). Some take oblique swipes, such as attempts to disallow liquor advertising as a business tax deduction or to require warning labels on containers to prevent the use of artificial flavorings in domestically produced wines. (A measure allowing such flavorings, termed the "Juvenile Alcoholism Promotion Act of 1976" by Senator Hathaway, was successfully blocked in the Senate.) [50] Also in this category was a suggestion from Senator Orrin Hatch regarding President Carter's brother (prior to his entering a recovery program). Characterizing Billy Carter as a folk hero, Senator Hatch called on the media to refrain from showing him with beer in hand, describing Billy as "one of the great philosophers of modern times in a homespun way," but adding:

> I think we sometimes emphasize one aspect of his life more than others. I think he is a folk hero in America, and has a lot to say without opening up a six pack every time he comes on television. I'd like to see some of the responsible leadership in television and movies be encouraged to maybe keep the six pack away from him until he's through.[51]

Much more direct are threats to ban advertising, for example as expressed by Congressman Paul Rogers in conjunction with his criticism of the use of coaches and ex-athletes in beer television advertisements aimed at the youth market.[52] The advertising issue arises periodically, usually surrounding the promotion of a new product. As one respondent explained:

> The distilled industry has a code, and what happens is somebody goes way off base, like Black Velvet—there is a huge outcry either within the industry or without, and there is a move back. They say, "we should have standards," everyone complies for a month or two, and then some bright advertising guy gets a Black Velvet idea, and the whole thing gets going again.

NIAAA Director Noble tried employing the tactic of persuasion, for instance, chastising two brewers, one for the television commercial depicting a bartender asking a youth for proof of legal age, which Noble characterized as "perpetuating the concept of the 'rite of passage' from adolescence to manhood by using alcoholic beverages"; the other for a campus newspaper advertisements depicting the use of beer as a "palliative for frustrating situations." [53] In the case of Heublein's "Kickers," Noble was successful in getting the company to cancel its introductory campaign which featured young people and invitations to join "The Portable Party." [54]

An even greater indication of the extension of industries' responsibility is the goal spelled out by NIAAA in its presentation to the Advisory Council and the National Coalition for Adequate Alcoholism Programs: "establish and implement a national code of standards on alcoholic beverage advertising and the portrayal of alcoholic beverages in all public media." As reported at the time:

> It was stressed that while NIAAA is not a regulatory agency with authority in this area, it could study such questions as the impact of advertising on risk populations, and encourage development of standards.[55]

The shift is even clearer on the Congressional level, where Senator Hathaway held hearings in 1976 on "media images of alcohol," saying:

> All in all, many millions of American youth are bombarded every day with many thousands of messages about drinking from many hundreds of glamorous, friendly, healthy, adventuresome, sexy—and in some cases even famous—people telling them of the joys and benefits of drinking. . . . (It is) well within the jurisdiction of this Subcommittee to ask how this massive barrage of 'information' affects our nation's health.[56]

Commenting on the failure of the Federal Trade Commission to include alcoholic beverages in its rules governing food advertising as it affects health, Senator Hathaway expressed his intention to introduce a specific amendment to the next FTC authorization bill.[57] A sense of the changing emphasis (albeit glacial in pace) can be gleaned from a look backward at former NIAAA Director Chafetz' position:

> Our experience to date indicates that while advertising is a persuasive and highly effective mechanism in our culture, it does not, for the most part, cause people to engage in drinking alcoholic beverages where there is no desire. But advertising can be effective in causing those who are already drinking to switch brands. The simple fact remains that many cultures were misusing alcohol, and experiencing severe problems as a result, centuries before alcoholic beverage advertising existed.[58]

Teaching the ABC's of Prevention

In contrast, one jolt in the status quo which occurred during former Director Chafetz' tenure, concerned alcohol control laws. Although designed ostensibly to promote temperance, Alcoholic Beverage Control laws are concerned primarily with industry regulation and the generation of revenue. Laws governing jurisdiction over hours and condition sale vary greatly from state to state, locality to locality:

> For any specific measure, there is often a lack of clarity about the exact aim and about the connection between the measure and the aim. At different times and places in accordance with different theories, control laws aiming to promote temperance have forbidden drinking sitting down and drinking standing up, drinking so as to be visible from the street and drinking so as to be hidden from the street, selling liquor in small quantities and selling it in large quantities.[59]

Growing in response to varied pressures, the motley "system" of ABC regulation has evolved into an arrangement of industrial protection—as stated earlier, preserving the market of those already in the alcoholic beverage industries, and refereeing between the various competing interests within those industries. This comfortable situation was shaken somewhat by a study contracted by NIAAA, whose principal investigator, Stuart Matlins, pointed to the fifty-one different bodies of ABC law and regulation throughout the states and the District of Columbia, the little understanding of the fact that public health issues might be involved in the ABC system and the little recognition that these issues should be considered.[60] As Matlins told the NIAAA Advisory Council:

> At best, the current ABC laws are a communications media, and one of the most pervasive. And that media sends out conflicting messages about society's view of alcohol use. This may contribute to destructive drinking patterns.[61]

Matlins called for new thinking, new information and a new kind of action in ABC systems in order to make ABC laws an effective contributing part of a more positive concept of prevention. Consequently, a stated goal of NIAAA, as presented to the Advisory Council in 1977, was working with the states to consider the public health consequences of existing ABC laws.

As explained previously, the attempt to merge the California Office of Alcoholism with the state ABC had stemmed in part from a state report that had reached similar conclusions. Out of the agitation over this defunct merger came the appointment of Governor Brown's friend, and minister without portfolio during the merger talks, Baxter Rice, to be Director of California's Department of Alcoholic Beverage Control. Rice immediately demonstrated his departure from previous directors in his first public utterances, quoting the forgotten section of the ABC code to the effect that laws which relate to distribution, sale and service of alcoholic beverages exist for the protection of the welfare, safety, health, peace and morals of the people of the state of California, "and to promote temperance in the use and consumption of alcoholic beverages." As he told me,

> I'm not willing to say that a person who abuses alcohol is necessarily an alcoholic. I'm more interested in the adverse outcome of the abuse or misuse of alcohol beverage, whether that means wrapping himself around a tree, or my wife around a tree, or going home and beating his wife, or a worker becoming involved in an industrial accident, or absenteeism. There is some indiscriminate use of the substance that is not necessarily alcoholism.

Thus, Rice sees the role of the ABC in California expanded to include prevention aspects. For example, his office joined voluntarily in a traffic safety program in Los Angeles County funded by the Department of Transportation, which employed increased manpower to catch the drunk driver. Since licensees are not supposed to serve anyone who is obviously intoxicated, and are expected to exercise judgment over patrons who appear to be reaching that point, Rice's tack was to inform licensees that the Los Angeles project was underway, calling upon their "responsibility to the community" to assure that their patrons were not the ones arrested. His further aim was to see if there is a pattern to certain licensees being a source of such arrests, and if confirmed by observation, bring a charge of "disorderly premise."

Some aspects of the "new era" for California's ABC, such as the moratorium on the transfer of liquor licenses in Los Angeles County and the study (in conjunction with the Los Angeles County Office of NIAAA) attempting to correlate the concentration of licenses in ghetto areas with crime reports, were ambitious, if somewhat misplaced. After all, statistics that can be produced to connect crime with alcohol in ghetto areas, also connect crime to proverty, unemployment, bad housing, bad schools and broken families. Perhaps more appropriate are some modest questions raised by Rice, such as whether the 6 A.M. opening hour of bars relates to worker absenteeism and industrial accidents.[62]

The Impact of Insurance and Legal Imperatives

In another salient intersection of worlds, developments occurring within insurance and legal arenas have had an effect on ABC's nod toward prevention. As a result of personal injury decisions (such as the one involving actor James Stacy, who was awarded $1.9 million in a suit which held liable a Beverly Hills bar) liability insurance premiums have skyrocketed, and the number of carriers offering liquor liability protection has dropped dramatically. Rice has proposed to the Bartenders Association that just as insurance premiums are reduced for drivers who participate in driver education, and for non-smokers in regard to life insurance, participating in a prevention program might bring about a similar reduction. Although the majority of bartenders are not the licensees, Rice suggested that insurance carriers might look kindly on reduction of a licensee's premium if he could show that his employees had participated in some kind of seminar on alcohol abuse or the law and/or social responsibilities.

In a sense this is simply an example of the enlargement of the "social model" beyond responsibility for recovery to responsibility for prevention. And while bar owners may resist some of Rice's proposals, like breath analyzers to help them spot potential drunk drivers, legal and insurance imperatives are forcing the question of responsibility just as they have for gun sellers. The spin-off is yet to be measured—one reputable report claimed that the nature of the restaurant-bar business was changing. "Several on-salers commented that they're eliminating happy hours, drink price specials, pitchers of Margaritas or beer, and other drink promotions. Rather they're going to downplay their bars and push food service more." [63] Furthermore, after one large corporation in California lost a liability judgment, the number of corporation Christmas parties has declined.

Although these are merely scattered indications that responsibility has indeed been enlarged, more can be expected from the legal world. A gradual shift has occurred in court decisions, reflecting the blurred line between the moral-culpability implications of a problem-drinking perspective and the loss-of-control concept of a disease perspective, and also reflecting the mixed thinking inherent in legal moves into uncharted territory. Prior to 1971, California courts had sustained the common-law rule that *consumption* rather than *sale* of liquor was the proximate cause of injuries incurred as a result of intoxication. A significant California Supreme Court decision in 1971 partially abrogated this position, finding that a bar-owner who violates the Business and Professions Code is "presumptively negligent"—that furnishing an alcoholic beverage to an "obviously" intoxicated person may be a proximate cause of injuries inflicted by that individual *on a third person*.[64] Not faced in this decision was the question of whether a person who is served alcoholic beverage in violation of a statute may recover for *his own* injuries suffered as a result of that violation.

In 1976, however, a California court of appeal addressed this precise issue, ultimately denying recovery to the injured patron.[65] In doing so, the court found both the plaintiff-patron and the defendant-bar-owner guilty of willful misconduct. Since the question of whether a party's behavior rises to the level of willful misconduct is ordinarily a factual one, the court by its finding unsurped the jury's role as the arbiter of fact. Nonetheless, having made this determination, the court was able to invoke the doctrine of contributory negligence, which in this case called for the denial of compensation to the plaintiff for the injuries he suffered. The court's somewhat equivocal finding of willful misconduct may be attributed in part to its apparent moral resolve to deny the plaintiff's recovery. In its opinion the court saw fit to make its moral position explicit:

> Nothing is more elementary than that a person becomes intoxicated as a result of his own volition. . . . (T)he drunken patron in reality commits a crime as he sits upon the bar stool. Before imbibing at all, he is fully aware of the debilitating effect of alcohol upon the senses, and of its total effect upon himself. He knows that if he consumes it to excess, his subsequent activities may render him a danger and a menace to himself and others, especially innocent third persons. Yet, despite this prior knowledge, he inexcusably proceeds to consume alcohol in sufficient quantities to bring about the predicted result. This is willful and wanton misconduct as clear as any imaginable.[66]

Even though the bar-owner had served the plaintiff while he was obviously intoxicated, in violation of the Business and Professions Code, the court emphasized the moral blameworthiness of the plaintiff: "To allow monetary recovery to a plaintiff would not only be an improper exercise of government paternalism which would encourage individual irresponsibility, but would, according to the court, be 'morally indefensible.' " [67]

Expressly excluded from the scope of the court's opinion were minors and alcoholics, a policy which in effect is two steps forward and one backward. If, as most disease-adherents claim, early onset is gradual—symptoms are easily rationalized, there is a gradient of difference in susceptibility, potential alcoholics do not differ from non-alcoholics in any initial psychological, social or cultural factors, before symptoms develop they drink for all the reasons other people do—how are the courts to determine whether or not future plaintiffs passed the line from responsibility to loss-of-control while sitting on that bar stool? Furthermore, if restriction on the sale of liquor to obviously intoxicated persons is meant to protect the welfare, safety, health, peace and morals of the people, where does the legal responsibility of the bar-owner begin and end?

In 1978, the California Supreme Court moved in the direction of treating the bar-owner's liability to an intoxicated patron as a question henceforth to turn on the facts of each case. In this decision, the Court disagreed with the finding in *Kindt v. Kauffman* (above) that a patron *necessarily* commits willful misconduct in consuming sufficient liquor to bring about a state of intoxication. The case under review involved a man who, while celebrating his twenty-first birthday, was challenged by a friend to down the stiffest drink in the house. Served ten shots of 151-proof rum within one and one-half hours, plus a vodka collins and two beers, the man passed out and died after being taken home. The lower court, pursuant to the doctrine of contributory negligence, barred the wrongful death action brought by the decedent's sons. Contributory negligence only operates to deny a plaintiff's recovery if both plaintiff and defendant are culpable in the same degree, or if the plaintiff is culpable in a higher degree than the defendant. The state Supreme Court, reversing, ruled that because a reasonable jury could find that the bartender's conduct amounted to willful misconduct, while the patron's conduct was merely negligent, the lower court improperly barred the plaintiff's suit.[68] Such a finding by the jury would render the doctrine of contributory negligence inapplicable, since the defendant's willful misconduct involves a greater degree of culpability than the plaintiff's mere negligence. It became clear that future suits involving liquor law liability would generally constitute questions for a jury to decide on the individual facts of the case. More important, however, this decision signaled the enlargement of responsibility occasioned by the Supreme Court's recognition of a cause of action against a bar owner for the injuries of intoxicated patrons. This avenue of relief had heretofore been blocked by the California lower courts.

Of further significance was a development in tort law which occurred in California in 1975. The California Supreme Court, in yet another case [69], adopted a system of comparative negligence. Briefly, comparative negligence calls for the diminution of a plaintiff's recovery in proportion to his own negligence. While the foregoing cases arose prior to the effective date of *Li,* subsequent cases were to be governed by the comparative negligence principles of shared responsibility. This sharing of responsibility was expected to have the net effect of further increasing the incidence of suits brought against bar owners for intoxication-related injuries. In 1978, the bounds of responsibility stretched to the breaking point with another landmark decision which extended third-person liability to social hosts.[70]

Organized reaction was not long coming. After much jockeying in the legislature, Governor Brown signed a bill absolving bartenders and hosts at private parties from responsibility for damages caused by drunken patrons or guests as of January 1, 1979, effectively wiping out the previous court decisions. The governor's office claimed that the court rulings had resulted in substantial increases in insurance rates for taverns and restaurants, and threatened to increase homeowner insurance premiums. The California Trial Lawyers Association (CTLA) had led the fight against this legislation, and had been supported by the ABC and the California Highway Patrol up until the last hearing in the Assembly Judiciary Committee, at which point they were "called off by the Governor," according to Ralph Drayton, president of the CTLA.[71] Lobbying efforts in favor of the bill had come mainly from the insurance world, aided by restaurant associations. Drayton accounted for CTLA's defeat:

> The insurance companies couldn't even explain why they set their premiums so high. But they managed to get their customers all excited. When social hosts became liable too, the Legislature really overreached, and immunized everyone. They burned down the barn to get rid of the smell.[72]

At this writing, the issue is far from dead. Efforts are underway within the legislature to enact another bill, this time exempting social hosts while re-imposing liability on bartenders.

In Summary

Clearly, the extension of social responsibility for alcohol problems cannot be totally reversed. Accordingly, the alcoholic beverage industries world is feeling somewhat beleaguered if only in contrast to former "previsibility" days. Out of a need to demonstrate good faith, publications from this world stress disapproval of the misuse of alcohol; distilled spirits companies place advertisements in magazines to disseminate the "responsible drinking" message; others combine their efforts with volunteer groups, like the Jaycees, in distributing Know Your Limits cards (information on safe and unsafe alcohol consumption according to the number of drinks per hour and body weight); a larger body like the Distilled Spirits Council of the United States (DISCUS) provides grants for research to signal good faith. Cooperation (critics call it collusion) also comes in the form of participation on boards, and of membership in organizations and coalitions. A representative of the California Wine Institute is on the board of the Bay Area National Council on Alcoholism, another on NCA's national board; Licensed Beverage Industries,

Inc., is a member of the Alcohol Drug Problems Association (ADPA); and the Distilled Spirits Council of the United States (DISCUS) is a member of the National Coalition for Adequate Alcoholism Programs (NCAAP).

Nevertheless, the alcoholic beverage industries world no sooner eliminates one tiger than another comes along—the latest being a proposal for warning labels on alcoholic beverages. An amendment requiring liquor labels reading *"Caution: Consumption of Alcoholic Beverages May Be Hazardous To Your Health"* was attached to the NIAAA renewal bill by Senator Strom Thurmond in 1979. As lines were being drawn for this battle, yet another coalition, the Beverage Alcohol Information Council (BAIC), an *ad hoc* consortium of ten beverage industry organizations, announced an educational campaign aimed at women of childbearing age and based on the following theme:

> You owe it to yourself and your unborn child to be informed about drinking during pregnancy and to avoid excessive or abusive drinking. In addition, all who are pregnant or considering having a baby should follow their physician's advice on drinking, nutrition and other health factors.[72]

Evidently the alcoholic beverage industries world preferred to narrow the warning to a select audience, in the hope that this compromise would stem the tide. Ernest Noble, while director of NIAAA, had entered his discussions with the industries' and media representatives out of his conviction that:

> It is copping out to say the problem is not in the bottle—it is both in the bottle *and* the individual. Alcohol is a drug, not a food, one of the dirtiest drugs we have—it brings much more damage than heroin does to the brain, liver and muscles.[73]

But it would be naive not to realize that his crusade was up against tremendous odds, considering the government's dependence on revenue from the alcoholic beverage industries. (When the American Cancer Society suggested that tax benefits to tobacco growers be withdrawn, and cigarette advertising employing attractive models be banned, the Tobacco Industry responded that the Cancer Society should devote itself exclusively to cancer research.) Faced with immediate opposition to the stabilized consumption goal of NIAAA, Deputy Director John Deering argued (shades of the candy bar) that absolute alcohol consumption can be reduced by lowering the alcohol content of beverages without affecting the volume of sales.[74] Nor can it be expected that Senator Donald Riegle's colleagues (Senator Riegle has succeeded Senator Hathaway as chairman of the Senate Alcoholism and Drug Abuse Committee), or the electorate they represent, will look too kindly on any measures that encroach on their drinking practices. Similarly, one respondent suggested that California ABC Director Rice would, by design, be kept so busy with other matters, such as fair trade or the sale of beer at baseball games, that he would have little time for prevention measures. Nevertheless, as Gusfield has astutely observed, "certain policies may be important, not so much because they have this or that particular or peculiar effect but because they put something on the agenda." [75] A significant illustration is the move by the armed services to "de-glorify" the use of alcohol by ordering an end to "happy hours" (the hours between 5 P.M. and 7 P.M. on Friday when service clubs sell drinks at half price) and to such traditions as awarding "alcoholic prizes" for the most liquor consumed.[76] ABC laws and Rice's mode of persuasion also have a symbolic value, and if even some cultural attitudes toward drinking change, making it comfortable *not* to drink, it would be a service to those recovered alcoholics who have trouble maintaining abstinence. After all, the anti-smoking campaign that has made the most headway deals with rights of non-smokers, and a turn-about in the former image of smoking as a mark of sophistication *has* occurred.

Nonetheless, in assessing the enlargement of responsibility, it should be emphasized that there is a questionable assumption underlying the concept of prevention—that what we seek to prevent is an undesirable state which people wish to avoid:

> This assumption, of course, makes sense in the classical territory for discussions of the prevention of disease; few of us wish to contract smallpox, cholera, or rabies, and it can usually safely be assumed that only ignorance and negligence lie in the path of preventive efforts. . . . But . . . when we are talking about alcohol problems in the general population, we are talking about problems associated with voluntary human behavior—behavior which many people find pleasurable, and which many have ethical, economic, or personal interests in continuing.[77]

Despite evidence of an enlargement of social responsibility, as identified in this chapter, social reform in the guise of "prevention" has a thin line to tread if an anti-temperance backlash is to be avoided.

Notes

1. See Chapter 1.
2. Roizen, "Alcoholism Treatment's Goals and Outcome Measures," NIAAA report, 1976, pp. 85-91.
3. Ibid., p. 89

4. J. Milam, *The Emergent Comprehensive Concept of Alcoholism* (Kirkland, Wash.: ACA Press, 1970), p. 24.
5. Vernelle Fox, "The Controlled Drinking Controversy," *Journal of the American Medical Association*, Vol. 236 (1976), p. 863.
6. Seminar, Berkeley, California, January 12, 1977.
7. M. Taylor, *Alcoholics Anonymous* (Ph.D. dissertation, University of California, 1977), p. 155.
8. *See:* H. Toch, *The Social Psychology of Social Movements* (Indianapolis: Bobbs-Merrill, Co); and Taylor, *Alcoholics Anonymous.*
9. Melvyn Kalb and Morton S. Propper, "The Future of Alcohology: Craft or Science?", *American Journal of Psychiatry*, Vol. 133 (1976), p. 643.
10. Ibid., p. 644.
11. Milam, *The Emergent Comprehensive Concept*, p. 23.
12. Kalb and Propper, "The Future of Alcohology," p. 644.
13. See discussion in Chapter 7.
14. Scottie Hastie, "High and Dry," KQED-FM, February 18, 1977.
15. *Lifeline*, National Council for Alcoholism, Vol. 2 (October, 1977), p. 6.
16. D. Moynihan, *Maximum Feasible Misunderstanding* (New York: The Free Press, 1970).
17. J. McCarthy and M. Zald, *Trends of Social Movements* (Morristown, N.J.: General Learning Press, 1965), p. 24.
18. A. Gouldner, "Taking Sides: The Sociologist as Partisan and Non-Partisan," in *The Relevance of Sociology*, p. 130.
19. Kingsley Davis, "Mental Hygiene and the Class Structure," *Psychiatry*, Vol. 1 (1938), pp. 55-65.
20. David A. Musto, "Whatever Happened to 'Community Mental Health'?", *The Public Interest*, No. 39 (1975), pp. 53-79.
21. Organizing letter from NAPP, February 7, 1977.
22. *Drug Survival News*, Do It Now Foundation, Phoenix, Arizona, Vol. 5 (November-December, 1976), p. 1.
23. Selden Bacon, address to the annual meeting of Alcohol and Drug Problems Association, September 13, 1976, as reported in *The Alcoholism Report*, Vol. 4 (September 24, 1976), p. 4.
24. See page 7.
25. Bacon, Address to the Meeting.
26. D.E. Beauchamp, *Precarious Politics* (Ph.D. dissertation, Johns Hopkins University, 1973), p. 100.
27. *The Alcoholism Report*, Vol. 5 (April 13, 1977), p. 7.
28. R. Room and S. Sheffield (eds.), *The Prevention of Alcohol Problems* (Sacramento: California State Office of Alcoholism, 1976), p. 142.
29. J. Gusfield, "Categories of Ownership and Responsibility," *Journal of Drug Issues* (1975), p. 299.
30. Robin Room and S. Sheffield, *The Prevention of Alcohol Problems*, p. 16.
31. S. Bacon, "Concepts," in *Alcohol, New Thinking and New Directions* (Cambridge: Ballinger, 1976), p. 83.
32. R. Room, *"The Prevention of Alcohol Problems,"* pp. 36-37.
33. M. Sobell and L. Sobell, "Second-Year Treatment Outcome of Alcoholics Treated by Individualized Behavior Therapy," in *Emerging Concepts of Alcohol Dependence* (New York: Springer, 1977).
34. Address before the Annual Meeting of the National Council on Alcohol, San Diego, California, April 30, 1977.

35. Lewis, "Washington Report," *Journal of Studies on Alcohol,* Vol. 37 (1976), p. 1390.
36. Ibid., p. 1391.
37. *The Alcoholism Report,* Vol. 5 (October 22, 1976), p. 1.
38. Remarks at Round-Table Discussion, San Mateo, California, December 8, 1976.
39. Education Commission of the States, Task Force Report on Responsible Decisions About Alcohol (1977).
40. *The Bottom Line,* Vol. 1 (Summer, 1977), p. 24.
41. Ibid.
42. Ibid., p. 28.
43. *The Alcoholism Report,* Vol. 5 (May 23, 1977), p. 5.
44. Proceedings of the Fourth Annual Alcoholism Conference of the National Institute on Alcohol Abuse and Alcoholism, June 12-14, 1974, Washington, D.C., DHEW Public No. (ADM) 76-284, 1975, p. 8.
45. *Public Attitudes and Economic Patterns,* DISCUS Facts Book 1976, Distilled Spirits Council of the United States, Inc., Washington, D.C., p. 13.
46. *The Alcoholism Report,* Vol. 5 (June 10, 1977), p. 3.
47. *See:* Kettil Bruun, Griffith Edwards, Martti Lumio, Klaus Mäkelä, Lynn Pan, Robert E. Popham, Robin Room, Wolfgang Schmidt, Ole-Jørgen Skog, Pekka Sulkunen, and Esa Osterberg, *Alcohol Control Policies in a Public Health Perspective* (Helsinki: The Finnish Foundation for Alcohol Studies, Vol. 24, 1975); and Jan DeLint and Wolfgang Schmidt, "Consumption Averages and Alcohol Prevalence: A Brief Review of Epidemiological Investigations," *British Journal of Addiction,* Vol. 66 (1971), pp. 97-107.
48. Room and Sheffield, eds., *The Prevention of Alcohol Problems,* p. 335.
49. *San Francisco Chronicle* (October 17, 1975), p. 5.
50. *The Alcoholism Report,* Vol. 4 (October 8, 1976), p. 3.
51. *The Alcoholism Report,* Vol. 5 (April 13, 1977), p. 10.
52. *The Alcoholism Report,* Vol. 5 (December 24, 1976), p. 4.
53. *The Alcoholism Report,* Vol. 5 (January 28, 1977), p. 8.
54. *The Alcoholism Report,* Vol. 5 (December 24, 1976), p. 4.
55. *The Alcoholism Report,* Vol. 4 (June 10, 1977), p. 2.
56. *The Alcoholism Report,* Vol. 4. (March 12, 1976), p. 2.
57. *The Alcoholism Report,* Vol. 5 (January 28, 1977), p. 7.
58. Morris Chafetz, guest editorial in *Advertising Age,* an industry trade weekly, as reproduced in *The Alcoholism Report,* Vol. 3 (August 22, 1975), p. 3.
59. Room and Sheffield, *The Prevention of Alcohol Problems,* pp. 31-32.
60. Medicine in the Public Interest, Inc., "A Study in the Actual Effects of Alcoholic Beverage Control Laws," Washington, D.C., 1975.
61. *The Alcoholism Report,* Vol. 5 (October 22, 1976), p. 3.
62. *Beverage Bulletin* (May 1, 1977), p. 4.
63. *Beverage Bulletin* (December 1, 1976), p. 1.
64. *Vesely v. Sager,* 1971.
65. *Kindt v. Kaufman,* 1976.
66. Ibid.
67. For an analysis of decisions around this issue, *see:* Thomas L. Hanavan, "Liquor Law Liability-Comparative Negligence; Drunk Bar Patron Denied Recovery for his Injuries in a Suit Against the Bar," *Santa Clara Law Review,* Vol. 17 (1977), pp. 469-84.

68. *Ewing v. Cloverleaf Bowl*, 1978.
69. *Li v. Yellow Cab Co.*, 1975.
70. *Coulter v. Superior Court*, 1978.
71. *The Recorder*, Vol. 105 (September 21, 1978), p. 1.
72. *The Alcoholism Report*, Vol. 7 (July 13, 1979), p. 4.
73. Remarks at Round-Table Discussion on "Relationship of the National Institute on Alcohol Abuse and Alcoholism and the State-Funded Alcoholism Program"; San Mateo, California, December 8, 1976.
74. *The Alcoholism Report*, Vol. 5 (June 10, 1977), p. 3.
75. Room and Sheffield, *The Prevention of Alcohol Problems*, p. 298.
76. *San Francisco Chronicle* (May 26, 1977), p. 28.
77. Robin Room, "Minimizing Alcohol Problems," *Alcohol, Health and Research World*, (Fall, 1974), p. 13.

14.

Summary and Implications

After leading the reader through animating, legitimizing and demonstrating the problem of alcohol use, perhaps an apology is in order for not offering a section devoted to *solving* the problem. Social problems which appear intractable are so for a variety of reasons: prostitution, because of "human nature"; poverty, because many people do not want to "solve" it. The problem of alcohol use may be intractable for the reasons I have attempted to convey: the ambiguities in problem definition, the varying perspectives bearing on the problem, the very complexities and conflicts that are illuminated by a guiding framework of a social arena of social worlds. Bacon has said that in this arena understanding requires "more than good-bad dichotomies of problem-oriented pressure groups and more than 'borrowings' from conceptual items or patterns which were developed in response to other classes of phenomena"—calling for "an identifiable structure of its own for understanding 'alcohol phenomena,'"[1] by which he means alcohol behavior. By focusing on *problem perception, rather than problem incidence,* I have attempted to provide the structure for that structure!

Summary

We have seen how *an arena built around the social problem* of alcohol use has grown from an invisible to a *visible* state. Each of the *processes* contributing toward that increased visibility has been introduced in a separate chapter to ease the reader's understanding. However, since the action reflected in these processes is in constant interaction with external conditions—and since a wide range of actions and conditions has been covered—perhaps a review would be helpful.

Life has been infused into a diffuse arena: associations have grown in membership and strength, and some associations have experienced a shift in allegiance; constituencies have developed; summer schools and individual courses are being offered; a common pool of knowledge has developed for arena participants; a training constituency has been enlarged. Efforts have been devoted to building the arena's respectability in the eyes of the general public through the publicity emanating from prominent recovered alcoholics; the establishment of a national institute; the softening of language from "drunk" to "alcoholic" to "alcoholic people"; the improved image inherent in the existence of a national clearinghouse for information, an epidemiology division within NIAAA, and of research centers devoted solely to problems of alcohol use. The bounds of responsibility for the problem of alcohol use have been extended as careers in the arena have increased; prevention approaches geared toward community involvement have been suggested, and to a lesser degree, implemented; pressure on the alcoholic beverage industries has been intensified.

We have seen how *external conditions have affected the arena's growth.* We have examined the impact of the history of the arena: the effect of its roots in the mental health arena on the ideological stance of associations, on treatment philosophies, and on the impetus to maintain a separate identity for alcohol problems. We have also looked at the basis for the arena's borrowed treatment approaches: the closely-protected turf rights and intellectual isolation of the early alcohologists, and the disinterest and/or inability of other professional worlds to take on the problem of alcohol use. We have seen what the infusion of money has meant: a competition over funds (such as that between the clearinghouse and the Rutgers Center, or that surrounding care for the public inebriate) but also the enlargement of the constituency through the awarding of grants and contracts; the increase in treatment facilities and recovery homes; the design of new approaches, such as occupational programs and social setting detoxification. *The impact of other conditions* has been examined: the effect of New Deal programming and an ideology of citizen participation on the growth of associations, advisory boards, special minority boards and commissions; the temperance movement's influence on the concept of addiction; the pragmatic impulse in American thought—in combination with the growth of the health professions and institutions, the veneration of scientific thought and the beneficence of foundations—

all contributing to a clinical perspective and its concomitant disease concept; the twentieth-century moral relativism which led to a drinking-problem perspective; the cost-benefit thrust of the 1960s and its consequence for the arena in terms of the configuring of public information; the political reversion to fiscal stringency which marks the 1970s and the resultant increased burden on demonstrating both the problem of alcohol use and the efficacy of programs. The salience of other conditions has been explored: the effect of redevelopment on social setting detoxification and on the issue of the public inebriate; the reflection of the professional reform movement on career growth and prevention efforts; the experience of the recovered alcoholic as it is expressed in career strains between professionals and non-professionals, and in the development of the social model of recovery; the importance of the self-help movement, the women's movement and humanistic medicine in relationship to recovery approaches.

We have looked at a number of other matters. (1)We have examined divisive issues: the disease concept; responsible drinking; controlled drinking; straight alcoholism versus broad brush occupational programs. (2) We have looked at inter-organizational relations, and (3) the uses to which research is put in the formation of "public facts." (4) We have seen how the processes of building an arena have created problems in regard to power relationships between advisory boards and the bureaucracy; evaluation of programs; decriminalization; certification of personnel; accreditation of facilities. (5) We have seen how shifting alliances can halt change, as when the volunteer action world, the recovery service world and the alcoholic beverage industries world combined forces to oppose the consolidation of California's Office of Alcoholism with the Department of Alcoholic Beverage Control; or when the forces were mustered in opposition to the Rand Report's position on alternatives to abstinence as a treatment goal. (6) We have looked at the impact of "outside worlds" such as law and insurance, and the way an intersection of sub-worlds, such as that occurring between civil rights law and a segment of the alcohol arena over decriminalization, can have far-reaching consequences, i.e., the disease concept of alcoholism. (7) Last, *we have examined consequences of the arena processes*—some untoward, such as the building of a dependency through the bestowal of grants, and the confusion regarding the inclusion of alcoholics in affirmative action for the handicapped—but all contributing toward increased visibility.

Implications for the Arena

Some years back, Robinson offered the opinion that the arena had "lost control" over the disease concept of alcoholism and that this "alcohologist's addiction" suggested a need to pare the definition of alcoholism back to Jellinek's classic theory.[2] My research indicates that the growth of this arena—its network of associations, boards, grantees, contractees, constituencies, and the institutionalizing of a wider scope inherent in a national institute mandated to look at alcohol abuse as well as alcoholism—makes that movement backward, though perhaps desirable, highly unlikely. That the definition of what constitutes the social problem of alcohol use should have grown commensurate with the growth of arena participation should not be surprising—just as enlarging the responsibility (as discussed in Chapter 13) was a logical outgrowth of an enlarged arena.

Where I hope to have made a contribution to the arena is in clarifying the linkages to help guide a future course. For example, a direction suggested by the Social Research Group is based on their assessment of the need to "disaggregate" alcohol-related-problems, to move beyond a disease concept and beyond a drinking-problem perspective to a drinking-problems understanding. The goal would be to "focus attention on the particular circumstances and *available* interventions for each specific type of problem"[3] (emphasis added), such as accidents, suicide, drunk driving. This raises questions about the present use of data, as discussed in Chapter 11, and the assessment of outcome measures, as discussed in Chapter 12. As Roizen has summarized the age-old dilemma for those who wish to market a social problem:

> How do we show that things are getting worse and worse (justifying expenditures for a particular social problem) while we are also capable of showing that they are getting better and better (showing the effectiveness of the treatment we are applying)? . . . are they indeed relevant measures of one another, or each other? Will a great track record of treatment successes actually reduce the societal problems which were the original impetus for treatment activities?
>
> . . . how would alcohol problems be diminished in the United States if we took every labeled alcoholic in the United States and shipped him to, say, Finland? Certainly, ostensible treatment and public assistance costs would fall off, but, if our data concerning the general population can be a guide here, a substantial number of alcohol problems would continue to arise— and not just from prodromal alcoholics. Heavy drinking would not disappear and, so, neither would cirrhosis. Drunk driving certainly wouldn't seem to disappear, on the basis of our data and others'. Job problems, role-performance problems would not disappear. The various dimensions of alcohol difficulties that we measure would not be substantially diminished.[4]

Implicit in Roizen's comments is the gap in understanding which still exists regarding the observed quality of (and reasons for) differences between the treatment population and the population at large. Furthermore, Roizen underscores another linkage: the role that alcohol plays in American society, i.e., the positive value placed on drinking alcohol by a sizable portion of the population. Whether "disease" or "disability," the transition into a labeled category is dependent on varying definitions of the situation. To quote Room:

> Obviously, there is room for considerable disagreement over whether a "problem" exists at all; thus, for instance, a respondent may not recognize that a friend has quietly dropped him because of impatience with his drinking, or conversely the survey analyst may impute the existence of the problem where the behaviour was not in fact problematic. [5]

The social acceptability of alcohol use (and the varying *degrees* of acceptability) presents an obstacle to the very concept of "prevention," as does a link to another American value: the democratic tradition that people should not be told what to do unless they seek help or present a problem of "dangerousness" to themselves or society. Some arena participants have suggested a substitution for the concept of "prevention": a goal of "minimization" of alcohol problems by taking small steps and half-measures.[6] This is no doubt what Room wishes to convey (above) when he speaks of "available" intervention. And, indeed, another link demonstrates the restrictions placed on ambitious prevention approaches. NIAAA Director Noble's early "neo-temperance" line was quickly tempered, following the attack which was mounted against one of the goals in the institute's national plan—stabilizing per capita consumption at the present level (through reassessment of control policies).[7] The volunteer action and recovery service worlds long ago saw the need to separate themselves from the temperance world, whose legitimacy had been damaged by the failure of Prohibition. Talk of control measures will not be endorsed so long as there is any threat to the primary goal of the *combined* constituency: getting the long sought services. As explained in Chapter 1, people who were concerned with alcohol-related problems recognized early on that in communicating alcoholism to the public, it was appropriate first to consider what alcoholism was not. There was an astute appreciation of the early movement's political implications—implications no less important today. In his 1947 lecture before the Yale Summer School of Alcohol Studies, Selden Bacon warned against incurring the opposition of groups which may be opposed to alcoholism, but would not support an anti-alcohol drive—moderate drinkers in general, restaurant associations, social work agencies, the legal profession, AA, the medical profession, public health officers.[8]

As Beauchamp points out, Bacon "did not add (but did not need to) the liquor industry among those 'powerful, prestigeful, and organized groups.' " [9] Over the years there has been a tacit truce with the alcoholic beverage industries world regarding the disease concept, and certainly with funding for programs now in the bargain, this is no time to take on such a formidable and unnecessary enemy. Thus, as unexpected as it was to find the Salvation Army representative urging NIAAA to drop its goal of stabilization of per capita consumption—since it is "a little strong and would hurt the cause" [10]—his position was less surprising in view of the linkage of worlds described herein. Pressed by the combined force of this coalition, Noble soon altered his position, suggesting that stabilization of per capita consumption be viewed as "a measure or barometer of the success of NIAAA's treatment and prevention efforts, rather than an objective itself." [11]

Dr. Chafetz, in his testimony before Congress, had reminded his audience that "we are dealing with a painful condition that has plagued people from the earliest moments of history . . . what really remains for us to accomplish is to continue to search for provisional truths." [12] It is the "provisional truths" and their interconnection that I have tried to illuminate. Nonetheless, while attempting to stay above the fray, I would be less than honest if I claimed that after three years of research and analysis I remained completely neutral. My position can be summarized very simply. (1) No more able than anyone else to "prove" whether there is a distinction between "alcoholics" and "alcohol abusers" or whether these groups represent a continuum, my position is closest to that presented by Scott.[13] People seek an altered state of consciousness for a variety of reasons, and an individual becomes "addicted to" or "dependent on" the agent that produces the greatest benefit in attaining that state by employing healthy or unhealthy means. For the alcoholic or alcohol abuser, drinking is an unhealthy method of securing that state; yet it is sought despite the problems on the way to the goal. (2) Government has been called upon to deal with the visible aspects of this situation. What is more, as the arena builds, government is part of the process of increasing the visibility. But, because alcoholism is not a clear-cut syndrome, like diabetes, promoting a disease analogy obfuscates the issues that must be confronted, such as just what constitutes "recovery" and what is a reasonable treatment goal. (3) Competing for the dollar is as intrinsic to an arena built around a social problem as are shifting alliances. But "treatment" has to be based on the understanding that people with problems of drinking have different needs—not only for different levels of care, but for different environments in which to deal with their problems. Drinkwatchers is as good for some people as Alcoholics Anonymous is for others; and for still others, a third alternative may be necessary. Furthermore, skid row residents have as much "right" to available facilities [14] as do any other clients. (4) If a society is to consider itself humanitarian, it will expect government to continue to fund alcohol programs. And if a society is to consider itself responsible, it will expect accountability for those programs. But to cling to figures like "the costs to the nation" is to miss an opportunity to educate the public (and the arena!). The National Institute on Alcohol Abuse and Alcoholism cannot regulate sentiment but it could have a bearing on behavior and attitudes if evaluation of programs were shifted toward discovering what is happening in largely untapped areas such as the process of getting from the general population into treatment, or the process of therapy. And, if NIAAA could signal to its grantees and contractees "the importance of failure, and of studying and learning from it rather than covering it up" [15] a valuable counter-effort would be made to the selecting of data that plagues all government programming. (5) My position on the relationship between care and evaluation is neatly expressed by O'Briant:

> "Alcoholism" does not fit into the "medical model" or traditional "rehabilitation model" of care and therefore cannot be appropriately evaluated with methods and criteria designed for other conditions. An episode of drinking or crisis resulting from long standing alcoholism is not really comparable to other conditions such as fracture or pneumonia. An alcoholic is subject to moral, legal and social sanctions. The condition itself is embedded in a range of social, personal, cultural, and institutional contexts. We cannot overlook the fact that the alcoholic is a person with a particular lifestyle, with or without access to resources or the support of others; with specific past experiences with helping or punishing institutions. He is someone who may have been rejected and degraded as a result of his vulnerability to alcohol. His care and rehabilitation, even if temporary or crisis oriented, must therefore be based on a philosophy and a model of care which is sensitive to all the aforementioned factors.[16]

(6) Obviously "combining for strength" is less destructive for the arena than "competing for attention"; hence, including the alcoholic beverage industries world in a Task Force on Responsible Decisions About Alcohol appears to be a felicitous move. However, it should not come as a surprise when the report of such a task force is "compromising in tone" and more of a "political" than a "scientific" document.[17] The Education Commission of the States document says little that had not already been said by the Cooperative Commission on the Study of Alcoholism [18] and reflects nothing of the changes that have occurred in the arena in the intervening ten years. So long as powerful elements within the recovery service and volunteer action worlds feel it is in their interests to avoid a

confrontation with the alcoholic beverage industries, it cannot be expected that task force recommendations (even when based on a $2 million investment) will be more concrete than a call for an interdisciplinary effort "to help Americans develop rational attitudes about the use and nonuse of beverage alcohol," i.e. "responsible-decision-making." (7) Minimization of alcohol-related problems is a reasonable goal, but if it is to be effective a more painstaking analysis of whether, and how, each problem is indeed related to alcohol will be required. Under the present conditions of a wide variety of attitudes about drinking alcohol; industries that promote its use; and a disease concept which conveniently narrows the definition of an alcoholic to "someone else," *prevention* will make little headway. Here a bit of personal experience in germane. From the time I started my research, I encountered curious reactions among my friends. Already feeling the impact of the "public facts" I have delineated in this study, they either nervously asked me if their one (or two, or whatever) drinks a night meant they were alcoholic; or they assumed I was passing judgment on their drinking patterns; or they retreated into joke-lines, such as "I'll drink to that." Also significant, I found contradictory impulses within myself. When I became aware of how much I had been influenced by social pressure to drink, I discovered I gradually was decreasing my own (already moderate) drinking pattern. On the other hand, when in the company of friends who were outspoken about the self-doubt my research subject was evoking, I drank with them to put them at ease! If this "slice of data" is a reflection of present American attitudes—and here I must emphasize that I am merely relaying personal observation since *drinking* was not my study-problem—then communities could benefit from an exploration of attitudes toward drinking such as that suggested in the original format of the State Prevention Coordinator Program, described in Chapter 5. A newspaper account regarding drinking in Alaska, contains a pertinent quotation from District Court Judge Ethan Windhal:

> Some glibly say a breakdown in the Eskimo culture causes people to resort to alcohol. Maybe I'm a dimestore anthropologist, but it seems to me we have so many people raising a ruckus because so often here a person is not deemed drunk until he has passed out. If there is no violence, people just tend to get out of the way. If I behaved that way at a cocktail party in Southern California, everybody would be appalled at my behavior.[19]

Not only, as O'Briant suggests, is the alcoholic condition embedded in a range of social, personal, cultural and institutional contexts—so, too, the general human condition. Perhaps if NIAAA conscientiously fostered some hard thinking among communities about the conditions which influence drinking behavior, a reduction of drinking problems would occur.

Sociological Implications

Again I must stress, it is crucial to understand that continual segmenting occurs within all social worlds. As stated in Chapter 2, most social worlds seem to dissolve, when scrutinized, into sub-worlds. I have demonstrated this with many examples: The Council of State and Territorial Alcoholism Authorities (CSTAA) splitting off from the Alcohol and Drug Problems Association (ADPA) and returning under changed conditions; the formation of new groups, like Drinkwatchers and Women for Sobriety; the short-lived California Association of Alcoholism Advisory Boards. At times I have specified I was referring to a sub-world, as with the civil liberties sub-world of the legal world. But it is obvious that to say "a sub-world of the alcoholic beverage industries world" would be cumbersome indeed. However, as a guiding perspective, social worlds in a social arena was far from cumbersome. I shall discuss three of its contributions to the sociological pursuit: the transcending of organizational theory; the balancing of "macro" and "microsociology," i.e., of structure and process; the insight provided regarding the unplanned nature of human action.

Much theorizing on organizations still suffers from the deficiencies analyzed in Gouldner's 1959 critique [20] and updated in a more detailed account by Perrow.[21] When organization theory follows the "rational" model, the emphasis is on logic and cognition, the focus on conscious planning, goal seeking and decision making.[22] Departures from rationality are attributed to random mistakes, ignorance or error in calculation. But non-rational elements are central to organizations: "within an organization ends may vary, are not necessarily identical, and may in fact be contradictory." [23] The organizational oscillations of the Council of State and Territorial Alcoholism Administrators (CSTAA), discussed in Chapter 4, present a case in point; so too the conflicting views within NIAAA regarding a national credentialing body, discussed in Chapter 8. As Perrow remonstrates, intergroup conflict is a fact of organizational life but is not built into the work of rational theorists, except as evidence of a failure to utilize the model. Group conflict is studied only in anecdotal or descriptive case studies. Quite the opposite occurs within the general frame of reference of social worlds in a social arena. Implicit in this approach is an expectation of problems of consensus, communication and coordination among the tremendous variety of sub-worlds.

Another scheme in organization theory, the "natural-system" or "organic" model also has limitations. This scheme reflects the sociology of the 1950s and 1960s, drawing on the conceptual framework of structural functionalism which holds that functions determine the structure of organizations and that structures can be understood by analyzing their functions.[24] As Perrow explains, specific processes (leadership, communication) are analyzed in detail, but it is the nesting of these processes into the whole that gives them meaning. Gouldner draws attention to a basic limitation of the natural-system model which stems from the very notion of "system": the emphasis on the interdependence of the parts within an organization. (By "parts" Gouldner refers both to its group structures or roles and to the socialized individuals who are its members.) "The natural-system model tends to focus on the organization as a whole, to take the 'interdependence' of the parts as a given, and therefore fails to explore systematically the significance of variation in the *degrees* of interdependence." [25] A social worlds/social arena frame of reference, on the other hand, highlights the manner in which various parts of whole organizations proceed at a different pace, and possibly in a different direction—for instance, how a segment of the recovery service world, as represented in the leadership of the California Association of Alcoholic Recovery Homes (CAARH), has moved in the direction of a social model of recovery, while other segments of the membership of CAARH remain tied to the philosophy of the older organization, The Association of Halfway-House Alcoholism Programs (AHHAP).

Much of the organizational literature presents organizations as closed, isolated systems, with no attention to the effect of inter-organizational relationships, change over time, or the influence of the environment on organizations.[26] It is in this respect that the social worlds/social arena perspective makes a significant contribution. Inter-organizational relationships—in the credentialing and accreditation drive, in the conflict over "controlled drinking," on the issues of straight alcoholism/broad brush occupational programs—have been demonstrated to be vital to the flow of events within the arena. Equally important, the search for inter-relationships between organizations has drawn attention to the uses to which alcohol research is put—as in the selecting of supportive data (Chapter 11). Change over time has been, of course, at the core of my narrative, and the influence of the environment on organizations sufficiently highlighted as the macrosociological conditions affecting the arena's growth to require no further amplification here. One further criticism of organization theory is raised, however, in Perrow's discussion of the "institutional school," the label by which he designates natural-history theorists who concentrate on carefully documented and analyzed case studies of single organizations:

That school's view of organizations and society fails to connect the two. Parts
of the "environment" are seen as affecting organizations, but the organization is not seen as defining, creating and shaping its environment.[27]

To demonstrate the manner in which "society" is adaptive to organizations—that is, the manner in which alcohol use as a social problem has
been defined, created and shaped—has been the central thesis of this
book.

This ties in to the second contribution of a social worlds/social arena
approach—the balancing of structure and process. A brief contrast with
another sociological framework, conflict theory, is in order. Conflict theory conceives of social structure as held together by latent force and
constraint—conflict over belief systems is inevitable. Coercion of some by
others is the basis for society; stable coordination is achieved because
some groups have dominance over others, not because of society-wide
consensus on values. Where structural-functionalism looks for stability,
conflict theory, like interactionism, assumes change. But since conflict
theory stresses the need to understand the structural forms that institu-
tionalize the positioning of the powerful and the powerless, there is an
overconcentration on structure at the expense of equally important processes of human action.

A social worlds/social arena perspective has allowed me to transcend
the rigidity of conflict theory and discover not only the differentiation of
power (as. say between the Rutgers Center of Alcohol Studies and the
National Clearinghouse for Alcohol Information, or between the alcoholic beverage industries world and NIAAA over the issue of prevention
of alcohol problems) but the processes of interaction and the patterning
of events resulting therefrom. Both of these cases demonstrate the sliding
nature of "power"—and all the negotiating, maneuvering, constraining,
and exchanging brought into play as power shifts. Deterministic schemes
like conflict theory, in their fascination with "social forces" do not acknowledge that "the lines of impact" between social conditions and
human action "can run *either* way." [28] Consider the advent of a social
model of recovery. This development has been influenced by structural
conditions—the introduction of redevelopment and its effect on detoxification services—as discussed in Chapters 7 and 10. But the social model
has also been influenced by sentiments (antipathy toward medical and
psychiatric care) and by concurrent movements (Alcoholics Anonymous,
the self-help movement). Reciprocally, social model advocates have
made *their* impact on the social structure. As part of the process of
building respectability by buying into the health insurance institution
(see Chapter 8), social model advocates have been active in developing

state standards for recovery homes in California. As part of the process of combining for strength with other organizations (see Chapter 10), these actors have affected the shape of the alcohol-problem constituency and its potential political muscle.

Strauss has offered a proviso for the practicing social researcher:

> Structure is not "out there"; it should not be reified. When we talk about *structure* we are, or should be, referring to the structural *conditions* that pertain to the phenomena under study. Those conditions surely do obtain but they just as surely need to be discovered and analytically linked with their consequences.[29]

The fluidity of a social worlds/social arena framework—the image of intersecting sub-worlds, each with its own biography, *influencing* and *being influenced*—forces the researcher's attention to the reciprocal nature of structure and process.

A third contribution of this perspective is the light it casts on the unplanned nature of human action. I have discovered that crucial action in an arena occurs where sub-worlds intersect—and, most important, much that happens is not by design. This has been demonstrated in the checkered history of the credentialing of alcohol counselors. The extensive stretch-out in obtaining credentialing has been tied up with cross-cuts of personalities and conflicting agendas of organizations. But it has also been marked by untoward timing, as exemplified in the effort to get a nationally funded certification board just when Congress had become exercised over NIAAA grants to voluntary organizations, or the coinciding of publication of cost estimates with the appointment of a new NIAAA director, bent on watching the letter of the law, as discussed in Chapter 8. Many people view history as a ruthless series of plots, ignoring that "history is their master, not their servant, and that its course is determined more by accident than by human direction."[30] I am not proposing that a totally fateful view of history is any more reasonable than the proposition that all is fashioned by human design. It is simply that a social worlds/social arena perspective has helped me discover, and I hope convey, the "accidental intersections."

Formal Theory

In Appendix A, explaining that my own theory was developed for a *substantive* area of sociological inquiry—the social problem of alcohol use—I also state that *formal* theory could be derived from substantive theory. Formal theory means that developed for a formal, or conceptual, area of sociological inquiry, such as stigma, deviant behavior, formal organization, socialization, status congruency, authority and power, reward systems or social mobility. I must emphasize that I have *not* set about to devise a formal theory of social worlds. Rather, I have viewed the phenomena I studied against a combined action frame of reference and social worlds/social arena framework (see Chapter 2), using a constant-comparative process analysis method (see Appendix A), to develop a substantive theory: building an arena around the social problem of alcohol use entails increasing its visibility by animating the problem, legitimizing it, and demonstrating it.

Nevertheless, I will admit aspiring to the formal application of my findings. I have written about alcohol use, but I have also analyzed the emergence, organization, construction, legitimation, demonstration of a social problem—based on a summary of conditions, dimensions, concepts and relationships, apart from the subject of alcohol use. What I have "discovered" is a formal theory of the *collective definition of a social problem,* a possible prototype that could be applied to other arenas. One can look at an emerging social problem (stuttering, for instance, which shares with this arena varying perspectives as to cause and cure) [31] and predict that it will go through changes—differing from my summary in substance—but exhibiting the same processes of animating, legitimizing and demonstrating, as well as the component sub-processes I have designated. One could apply my theory, and ask why other "problems" are not "social problems"—loneliness, for instance—or conversely, how has "aging" *become* a social problem (or child abuse, wife abuse, and most recently, husband abuse)?

Despite the pretentiousness surrounding the words "substantive and formal theory," what I have modestly suggested is a hypothesis which can be read on two levels: for its applicability to the arena of alcohol use and for its applicability to the sociological interest in collective definitions. To those, both within and outside the arena, who are concerned with validity and replicability, my answer can only be: use your own design to test my conclusions. In the sociological pursuit, well-grounded refutation is as valuable as substantiation. [32]

Notes

1. S. Bacon, "Concepts," in W. J. Filstead et al. (eds.), *Alcohol, New Thinking and New Directions* (Cambridge: Ballinger, 1976), p. 125.
2. D. Robinson, "The Alcohologist's Addiction," *Quarterly Journal of Studies on Alcohol,* Vol. 33 (1972), pp. 1028-42.
3. Robin Room, "The Scope and Definition of Alcohol-Related Problems," prepared for the Task Group on Problem Definition, President's Commis-

sion on Mental Health, May, 1977, Social Research Group Working Paper F-58, 1977, p. 9.

4. R. Room and S. Sheffield, *The Prevention of Alcohol Problems* (Sacramento: California State Office of Alcoholism, 1976), pp. 242-43.

5. R. Room, "Measurement and Distribution of Drinking Patterns and Problems in General Populations," in *Alcohol-Related Disabilities* (Geneva: WHO, 1977), p. 77.

6. *See:* K. Bruun, "The Minimization of Alcohol Damage," *Drinking and Drug Practices Surveyor,* Vol. 8 (1973), p. 47; abstracted from: Alko-holihaitat Mahdollisimman Vahalsikski, *Alkolipolitukka,* Vol. 35 (1970), pp. 185-91; Robin Room, "Minimizing Alcohol Problems," *Alcohol Health and Research World,* (Fall, 1974), pp. 12-17.

7. See Chapter 13. For summary of the criticism, *see: The Alcoholism Report,* Vol. 5 (October 14, 1977), p. 2. *The Alcoholism Report,* Vol. 6 (October 28, 1977), pp. 2-3. *DISCUS Newsletter,* No. 368 (October, 1977), p. 1. *DISCUS Newsletter,* No. 369 (November, 1977), p. 1.

8. Selden Bacon, "The Mobilization of Community Resources for the Attack on Alcoholism, *Quarterly Journal of Studies on Alcohol,* Vol. 9 (1948), pp. 374-497.

9. D. Beaucamp, *Precarious Politics,* Ph.D. dissertation, Johns Hopkins (1973), p. 51.

10. *The Alcoholism Report,* Vol. 5 (June 10, 1977), p. 3.

11. *The Alcoholism Report,* Vol. 6 (November 25, 1977), p. 1.

12. Testimony before the Subcommittee on Alcoholism and Narcotics of the Senate Labor and Public Welfare Committee, 1976, p. 18.

13. See page 101.

14. See Chapter 10.

15. R. Room, "Policy Initiatives in Alcohol Problems Prevention," p. 56.

16. O'Briant, "Some Thoughts on Evaluation," *The Hearth* (January, 1976).

17. See Chapter 13.

18. *See:* T. Plaut, *Alcohol Problems: A Report to the Nation* (London: Oxford University Press, 1967).

19. *San Francisco Chronicle and Examiner* (December 26, 1976), Section B, p. 7.

20. Alvin Gouldner, "Organizational Analysis," in Robert K. Merton, Leonard Broom and Leonard S. Cottrell, Jr. (eds.), *Sociology Today* (New York: Basic Books, 1959), pp. 400-28.

21. Charles Perrow, *Complex Organizations* (Illinois: Scott, Foresman and Company, 2nd ed. 1978). The models discussed here are ideal types. The point is not that *all* theorists fall within one school or another, but rather that *some* theorists tend towards one model or the other. Occasionally both models are drawn upon by an author, as, for example, Victor A. Thompson, *Bureaucracy and the Modern World* (Morristown, New Jersey: General Learning Press, 1976). Also, it should be noted, another theoretical frame-work, the "human relations school" which Perrow includes in his criticism, is not relevant to our discussion since it is focused on psychological explanations (behavior, attitudes) rather than sociological, or organiza-tional, explanations.

22. *See, for example:* Herbert Simon, *Administrative Behavior,* 2nd ed. (New York: The Macmillan Company, 1957). James G. March and Herbert Simon, *Organizations* (New York: John Wiley & Sons, 1958). Amitai

Etzioni, *Modern Organizations* (Englewood Cliffs, N.J.: Prentice-Hall, Inc., 1964).

23. Gouldner, "Organizational Analysis," p. 420.
24. *See:* Robert Merton, *Social Theory and Social Structure* (New York: The Free Press, 1968). As applied to organizational theory, *see:* Victor A. Thompson, *Modern Organizations* (New York: Alfred A. Knopf, 1961).
25. Gouldner, "Organizational Analysis," p. 419.
26. This is not meant as a blanket indictment. Perrow cites examples from the perspective he has termed the "institutional school" where attention is paid to the interaction between organizations and their environments. He also singles out for special notice, and rightly so, Arthur Stinchcombe's essay, "Social Structure and Environment," in James March (ed.), *Handbook of Organizations* (Chicago: Rand McNally, 1965). Other notable exceptions are: David Silverman, *The Theory of Organisations* (New York: Basic Books Inc., 1971); Peter M. Blau and W. Richard Scott, *Formal Organizations* (San Francisco: Chandler Publishing Co., 1962), Chapter 8; Roland Warren, Stephen Rose, and Ann Bergunder, *The Structure of Urban Reform* (Lexington, Mass.: Heath & Co., 1974); Jeffrey Pressman and Aaron B. Wildavsky, *Implementation* (Berkeley: University of California Press, 1973).
27. Perrow, *Complex Organizations*, p. 199.
28. Anselm Strauss, *Negotiations* (San Francisco: Jossey-Bass, 1978), p. 101.
29. Ibid., p. 257.
30. Richard Harris, "The New Justice," *The New Yorker*, (March 25, 1972), p. 57.
31. A newspaper account of the National Stuttering Project calls for organizing the parents and spouses of stutterers and of speech therapists; demanding health insurance coverage "on the same basis as coverage for the alcoholic, the person with psychiatric problems"; and fighting job discrimination. *San Francisco Examiner and Chronicle* (February 27, 1977) Scene Section, p. 6.
32. Martindale, *The Nature of Sociological Theory*, p. vii, discusses the comparative candlepower of any theory:

> The power and reliability of a theory are not always evident all at once. A theory may have a power to explain what was not originally anticipated; it may also disclose the existence of problems it cannot explain. The inevitable process begins of attempting to improve the theory and of searching for alternatives to it.

APPENDIX A

Method

Peter Berger has offered some common sense on the esoteric subject of "sociology as a science," explaining that the statements of sociologists must be arrived at through the observation of certain rules of evidence that allow others to check on or to repeat or to develop the findings further. "It is this scientific discipline that often supplies the motive for reading a sociological work as against, say, a novel on the same topic that might describe matters in much more impressive and convincing language." [1] Nevertheless, he cautions that some sociologists have become so preoccupied with methodological questions that they have ceased to be interested in society at all, adding: ". . . in science as in love a concentration on technique is quite likely to lead to impotence." [2] With Berger's sound warning in mind, I shall present in this Appendix an explanation of the techniques I employed in the collection and analysis of my research data.

An Inductive Mode of Process Analysis

I have used a method which Glaser and Strauss call "grounded theory," [3] a formidable term, which, when parsed, is not nearly so awesome. Grounded theory is an inductive mode by which data are coded, such codes then guiding further data collection. Such further collection generates further codes, which are then developed in respect to their properties and dimensions, and the whole then integrated into a theory. It is perhaps the connotation surrounding the word "theory," evoking an image of the natural sciences, that is misleading. Deriving a theory simply means identifying the interrelationship between concepts, and presenting a systematic view of the phenomena being examined, in order to explain "what is going on."

The Glaser/Strauss method is a hypothesis-seeking strategy for generating substantive and formal theory. By substantive theory, they mean "that developed for a substantive, or empirical area of sociological inquiry, such as patient care, race relations, professional education, delinquency, or research organizations." [4] In this instance, my substantive theory deals with building an arena around the social problem of alcohol use. Formal theory means "that developed for a formal, or conceptual, area of sociological inquiry, such as stigma, deviant behavior, formal organization, socialization, status congruency, authority and power, reward systems or social mobility." [5] In this instance, formal theory may be derived from my data regarding the collective definition of social problems. Both substantive and formal theory are considered "middle-range" theories, i.e., as Merton specifies, theories that "fall between the 'minor working hypotheses' of everyday life and the 'all-inclusive' grand theories." [6]

The term "grounded," meaning "grounded in data" is also often misunderstood. As a colleague has argued, *anyone* claiming to be a scientist would be seeking empirical grounding, at least in his own estimation. The point is rather that Glaser and Strauss are challenging the conventional approach by which extant theory is regarded as the *beginning* of research activity and imposed on the data. Under the Glaser/Strauss method, the explanation and interpetation of the "discovered" concepts derive from the subjects themselves. Discovery lies in picking up the categories which participants themselves use to order their own experience.

This approach looks for the core social/psychological processes which account for, or explain, *most* of the variation in behavior within the social life under investigation—processes meaning phenomena which show continuous change in time. Fundamental to this approach is the position that there are ways to find explanations of social/psychological processes other than the traditional canons of theory verification, and, in fact, that an approach borrowed from the natural sciences is not ideally suited to the study of human behavior. As Taylor explains the distinctions:

> It (grounded theory) is not a useful technique for theoretical verification, for which hypotheses must be developed prior to the research, and fre-

quently quantitative data are necessary. But it is a particularly organized and focused model for dealing with qualitative data, for conducting relatively inexpensive research involving relatively small samples, and for generating an understanding of social processes, rather than social units.[7]

Thus, the title of the Glaser/Strauss book, *The Discovery of Grounded Theory,* is more a reflection of the *goal* of their technique than it is of the method itself. The technique is more accurately one of process analysis through the use of a constant comparative method. Bigus' comments are helpful:

> The aim of process analysis is to develop the dimensions, properties, conditions, and so forth of the particular process under scrutiny, within the particular context(s) within which the research is being conducted. In this manner, process analysis is distinguishable from "unit" analysis. The focus of unit analysis is a particular unit, whether it be a population unit, cultural unit (e.g. skid row), or defined social unit (e.g. alcoholics). The aim of unit analysis is to develop a description of the particular unit under scrutiny, through qualitative description, the construction of statistical rates, or whatever. . . . in contrast, the results of process analysis are not generalized to a unit, but to the generic process itself. Thus, if one were to conduct a study of upgrading in reference to home purchases in America, the results of that study could be generalized to the generic process of upgrading. The properties and so forth of upgrading which were discovered are just that, properties of upgrading, not properties of a unit.[8]

Mullen, too, has captured the distinguishing properties of unit versus process analysis. As she specified, the grounded theory approach uses social units to study the movement of social life through time:

> Rather than one or two snapshots, one gets a motion picture. And, social processes have greater generality because they transcend specific identities of particular units. The unit only provides the *social conditions* under which the process varies.[9]

In my research, units were being examined: a treatment center within the recovery service world, or a laboratory within the research world, or an office within the bureaucratic world. The goal was not to describe those units, but rather to unearth the processes by which those units are mobilized.

Coding Through the Constant Comparative Method

How, then, are these processes discovered? Coding and analysis begin with the earliest data collection since, as Glaser and Strauss suggest, the researcher cannot be confined to the practice of coding first and then analyzing the data. In generating theory, the researcher is constantly redesigning and reintegrating theoretical notions as the material is received. Coding is done using the constant comparative method. The analyst starts coding each incident in the data into as many categories as possible. For example, early in my interviews a pattern of comments emerged such as "alcoholism is a step-child—you have to wear somebody else's clothes," or "in this Center we offer a potpourri of treatment." Since I was coding not only interviews and field notes but also the literature, I found many statements such as "the cure has easily been adapted to fit institutional requirements, the personal training of the therapist and faddish influences from other treatment sectors." [10] All such incidents in the data, I began to code as "using," until I came across Selden Bacon's comments on "special purpose borrowing." [11] Changing the code to "borrowing," I began to employ Glaser and Strauss' basic, defining rule for the constant comparative method: "while coding an incident for a category, compare it with the previous incidents in the same and different groups coded in the same category." [12] This procedure soon starts to generate theoretical properties of the category—for example, in some cases prestige is being borrowed, in others expertise is being borrowed. Further analysis of my notes revealed that an important dimension running throughout the accounts was "mutual borrowing," a concept which I developed in Chapter 6.

At various points, I followed the second rule for the constant comparative method: "stop coding and record a memo on your ideas." [13] Memo writing allows the analyst to think through a category and its properties freely and expansively, unconstrained by the restrictions of formal writing, and to search for the interrelationship with other emerging categories. To cite another example, early in my interviewing and literature search I began coding comments such as:

> While the success of Alcoholics Anonymous (AA) should have been sufficient to persuade NIAAA to reject obfuscation in favor of clarity, it did just the opposite.

> An alcoholic worker became a "troubled employee," an alcoholism program in industry became an "employee assistance program" and all of it was swept under with "a broad brush." [14]

The above quotation was a protest against the blurring of programs, which I coded as "maintaining a separate identity." Upon further exploration, I found that there was a difference between separating alcohol problems from mental health problems as opposed to separating them from drug problems. While both of these separations concerned avoiding further stigma, also operating was an antipathy toward the mental health professions. Additional analysis clarified my understanding that this issue had connections to the history of the arena (as I developed in Chapters 3 and 6). And further analysis revealed that the separate identity issue is also tied to the dollar (as explained in Chapter 9).

Another fruitful use of the constant comparative method was comparing the alcohol arena to other arenas: drugs, mental health, aging, sensory disabilities, and even the arena currently building around stuttering. I pursued this avenue both by directed conversations with representatives of comparative arenas, and by a literature search. This technique aided the teasing-out of dimensions in the alcohol arena, as, for instance, the unique properties inherent in the role played by recovered alcoholics.

Theoretical Sampling

Since the analyst is jointly collecting, coding, and analyzing the data, a question often posed is: "how do you decide what data to collect next and where to find them?" Glaser and Strauss call this joint procedure "theoretical sampling," pointing out that beyond initial collection of data, further collection cannot be planned in advance of the emerging theory (as is done in research designed for verification and description). "The emerging theory points to the next steps—the sociologist does not know them until he is guided by emerging gaps in his theory and by research questions suggested by previous answers." [15] Or, as Mullen paraphrases: "The analytical memoranda which were continually being produced from the coding in turn pointed to directions for further data collection—either questions for new interviews or comparative groups or subgroups which should be sampled. The conceptual categories, therefore, introduced a new point of view and made possible certain deductions leading to further data collection—theoretical sampling." [16] Perhaps a short trip through my own application of this method will clarify this procedure.

Sources of Data

My research problem was roughly formulated after I attended the North American Congress on Alcohol and Drug Problems in San Francisco in 1974. My first memo was an attempt to discern the properties of the arena as it appeared to me at the conference. Commencing what was to become my practice, I was also coding the literature I had been reading as part of a three-quarter course on "Alcohol and Other Drugs" at the University of California, Berkeley. This early memo identifies some of the properties of the arena I had observed: many associations; much contention; a linkage to government; an infusion of money; various professions; conflicting perspectives; industry involvement; conflicting terminology. Also, I had started with a dual analytical scheme: an action frame of reference (symbolic interactionism/phenomenology), which meant that I would want to interview arena participants in order to get the varying "definitions of the situation"; and the framework of social worlds in a social arena, which gave me a larger perspective against which to view the thicket before me.

Since this theoretical stance suggests that all social reality is problematic, rather than given and static, my early questions—in seeking respondents who would represent the multiple points of view—were an enlargement of the questions I have already indicated in Chapter 2:

- which are the important groups?
- why are they there?
- how long have they been around?
- where did they come from?
- what kind of claims do they make?
- what kind of places are they building?
- do they go after the same or different clients?
- are some going out of business/are some amalgamating with others/have some applied different cosmetics but not changed much?
- what are the interests, strategies, resources, stakes, of each group?
- who listens to whom?
- who has a stake in which social policy?
- what happens in the competition over funding?

I started interviewing representatives of the recovery service world and the volunteer action world, using an open-ended style which more closely resembles conversation—*roughly* guided by the above questions, but more often proceeding along lines directed by the responses. I also interviewed veterans of the arena, who, by looking backward, provided the sharp contrast needed to bring the present arena into focus—areas of strain and conflict, most salient issues, where to find alliances, trends observed. (It should be noted that such historical comparison is yet one more facet of the constant comparative method.) In some instances respondents referred me to new respondents; in others, I discovered representative arena-participants at public meetings; in still others, I sought leaders of organizations, or people engaged in research, employed in agencies, running recovery programs, serving on boards. This type of sampling differs from that conducted around one specific site. My goal was to get as wide a representation as possible of many different organizations, styles, points of view, segments of worlds. I must emphasize that

I did not take anything said at face value. Contrarily, my theoretical framework (as described in Chapter 2) allowed me to order whatever point of view came across. Some interviews were taped; others were not. All were recorded as field notes would be.[17] As patterns began to emerge, coding commenced, followed by memo writing, as described above.

At this point, I was fortunate to be able to combine a trip to Washington, D.C. with some intensive, and directed, interviews, due to the good offices of Don Cahalan of the Social Research Group in Berkeley, whose introductory letters brought fourteen positive replies out of fifteen requests. In Washington, I spoke with high level officials in the National Institute on Alcohol Abuse and Alcoholism, representatives of national organizations and the National Center on Alcohol Education and the National Clearinghouse for Alcohol Information, a legislative consultant to the arena, and the editor of *The Alcoholism Report*. Returning to the San Francisco Bay Area, I continued with the procedure described above—seeking representatives of as yet untapped worlds, refining my codes, identifying processes and their relationships through memoranda—in short, developing my theory. In all, I conducted fifty highly selected interviews. In addition, after I was well along in my analysis, I did some checking of concepts through both follow-up phone conversations and on-site interviews. In this way, theoretical sampling among initial respondents was proceeding at the same pace as interviews with new respondents.

Simultaneously, I was employing the same method to record and code notes from observation at public meetings, congressional hearings, sessions of summer schools, advisory board meetings, conferences. Data from the literature were also being utilized and coded as described in Chapter 2.

For further practical assistance in ways to systematically relate categories into theory following this method, the reader is referred to Glaser's monograph directed toward the development of theoretical sensitivity.[18]

Notes

1. Peter L. Berger, *Invitation to Sociology* (Garden City, New York: Doubleday Anchor, 1963), p. 13.
2. Ibid.
3. Barney G. Glaser and Anselm L. Strauss, *The Discovery of Grounded Theory* (Chicago: Aldine Publishing Company, 1967).
4. Ibid., p. 32.
5. Ibid.
6. Ibid.

7. Mary Catherine Taylor, *Alcoholics Anonymous: How It Works; Recovery Processes in a Self-Help Group* (Ph.D. dissertation, University of California, San Francisco, 1977), p. 23.

8. Odis Bigus, *Becoming "Alcoholic": A Study of Social Transformation* (Ph.D. dissertation, University of California, San Francisco, 1974), p. 34.

9. Patricia Dolan Mullen, *Cutting Back: Life After A Heart Attack* (Ph.D. dissertation, University of California, Berkeley, 1975), p. 210.

10. Norman Geisbrecht, Kai Pernanen, Carol Corlis, Frances Tolnai, and Sharon Beaverstone, "Sociological Trends in the Treatment of Alcoholics," paper presented at the 21st International Institute on the Prevention and Treatment of Alcoholism, Helsinki, Finland, 1975, p. 6.

11. S.D. Bacon, "Concepts," in *Alcohol, New Thinking and New Directions* (Cambridge: Ballinger, 1976), pp. 64-67.

12. Glaser and Strauss, *Discovery of Grounded Theory*, p. 106.

13. Ibid., p. 107.

14. Leo Perlis, "The Broad Brush, Employee Assistance, Troubled Employee Program - or WHAT HAPPENED TO ALCOHOLISM?" *The Labor-Management Alcoholism Journal*, National Council on Alcoholism, N.Y., Vol. 5 (1975), pp. 19-20.

15. Glaser and Strauss, *Discovery of Grounded Theory*, p. 47.

16. Mullen, *Cutting Back*, p. 55.

17. *See* Leonard Schatzman and Anselm Strauss, *Field Research: Strategies for a Natural Sociology* (Englewood Cliffs, N.J.: Prentice-Hall, Inc., 1973).

18. Barney G. Glaser, *Theoretical Sensitivity* (Mill Valley, California: The Sociology Press, 1978).

APPENDIX B

Classification of Sources of Data

Types of Respondents
  Officials of:
    National Institute on Alcohol Abuse and Alcoholism
    California Office of Alcoholism
    California Alcoholic Beverage Control
    County Alcoholism Programs
  Directors of:
    Training Programs
    Outreach Programs
    Treatment Programs (out-patient, and in-patient)
    Recovery Home Programs
    Social Setting Detoxification Programs
  Physicians
  Researchers (social science and biochemical)
  Board members:
    County Advisory Board
    Area Alcohol Education and Training Program
  Members of grant review committees
  Representatives of:
    Alcoholic beverage industries
    Alcoholics Anonymous

Women for Sobriety
California Women's Commission on Alcoholism
Organizational Representatives:
Alcohol and Drug Problems Association of North America
National Council on Alcoholism
County Alcohol Administrators Association of California
California Association of Alcoholic Recovery Homes
Salvation Army
Bay Area Council on Co-Alcoholism
California Citizens Action on Alcoholism Public Policy
Council of State and Territorial Alcoholism Authorities
National Center on Alcohol Education
National Clearinghouse for Alcohol Information
Police
Occupational counselors
Lawyer for public inebriates
Legislative consultant
Editor of periodical on alcohol arena

Types of Literature
Books and theses concerned with the alcohol arena
Journals devoted to subject of alcoholism:
Journal of Studies on Alcohol
British Journal of Addiction
Professional journals of:
Nursing
Medicine
Occupational Counseling
Social Work
Sociology
Psychology
Psychiatry

Newsletters:
The DISCUS Newsletter (Publ. Distilled Spirits Council of U.S.)
The Hearth (Publ. Calif. Assoc. of Alcoholic Recovery Homes)
The Drinkwatchers Newsletter
Lifeline (Publ. Bay Area National Council on Alcoholism)
Newsletter of Council on Alcohol Problems (Temperance Org.)
The Alcoholism Information Distiller

Periodicals:
  The Alcoholism Report
  Alcohol, Health and Research World (Publ. NIAAA)
  Drinking and Drug Problems Surveyor (Publ. Social Research
    Group)
  Beverage Bulletin
  The Labor-Management Alcoholism Journal (Publ. National Coun-
    cil on Alcoholism)

Documents:
  Proceedings of:
      International Congresses
      Commissions
      Task Forces
      North American Congress on Alcohol Problems
      Expert Conference on the Prevention of Alcohol Problems

  Organizational Position Papers

  Reports to:
      California State Legislature
      National Institute on Alcohol Abuse and Alcoholism
      Congress of the United States
      World Health Organization

Transcriptions of: Congressional testimony

Types of Meetings Attended
  North American Congress Alcohol and Drug Problems

  Discussions of the Rand Report

  Congressional Hearings

  Monthly luncheons and discussions of the Association of Labor
  Management Administrators and Counselors on Alcoholism

  Round Table discussion on "Relationship of the NIAAA to the State-
    funded Alcoholism Program"

  Summer School Sessions

Guest Seminars, School of Public Health, University of California, Berkeley

County Advisory Board Meetings

Miscellaneous
Weekly Radio Program: "High and Dry," KQED, FM, San Francisco.

Appendix C

Glossary of Acronyms

AA   Alcoholics Anonymous
AAETP   Area Alcohol Education and Training Program
ABC   Alcoholic Beverage Control
ACCEPT   Alcohol Counseling Center For Early & Preventive
            Training
AC/PF   Accreditation Council for Psychiatric Facilities
ADPA   Alcohol and Drug Problems Association of North America
            (formerly NAAAP)
AFL/CIO   American Federation of Labor/Congress of Industrial
            Organizations
AHHAP   Association of Halfway House Alcoholism Programs
ALMACA   Association of Labor Management Administrators and
            Counselors on Alcoholism
AMA   American Medical Association
ATC   Alcohol Treatment Center
BACA   Bay Area Council on Co-Alcoholism
BAIC   Beverage Alcohol Information Council
CAAB   California Alcoholism Advisory Board
CAAAC   County Alcohol Administrators Association of California
CAARH   California Association of Alcoholic Recovery Homes
CAAAL   Classified Abstract Archive of the Alcohol Literature

CAP	California Council on Alcohol Problems
CARD	Counselors on Alcoholism and Related Disorders (Subsequently changed to Counselors on Alcoholism, Addictions and Related Dependencies, CAARD)
CCAAPP	California Citizens Action on Alcoholism Public Policy
COAC	County Occupational Alcoholism Consultants
CSTAA	Council of State and Territorial Alcoholism Authorities
CTLA	California Trial Lawyers Association
DAR	Department of Alcoholic Rehabilitation
DISCUS	Distilled Spirits Council of the United States
ECS	Education Commission of the States
FBI	Federal Bureau of Investigation
FTC	Federal Trade Commission
HEW	Department of Health, Education and Welfare
JCAH	Joint Commission on Accreditation of Hospitals
NAAAP	North American Association of Alcoholism Programs (precursor to ADPA)
NAACT	National Association of Alcoholism Counselors and Trainers
NAATP	National Association of Alcoholism Treatment Programs
NAPA	Network Against Psychiatric Assault
NAPP	National Association of Prevention Professionals
NASDAPC	National Association of State Drug Abuse Program Coordinators
NCA	National Council on Alcoholism
NCAAP	National Coalition for Adequate Alcoholism Programs
NCAE	National Center on Alcohol Education
NCALI	National Clearinghouse for Alcohol Information
NCCAC	National Commission on Credentialing of Alcoholism Counselors
NCWAP	National Coalition for Women's Alcoholism Programs
NHTSA	National Highway Traffic Safety Administration
NIAAA	National Institute on Alcohol Abuse and Alcoholism
NIDA	National Institute on Drug Abuse
NIH	National Institutes of Health
NIMH	National Institute of Mental Health
OA	Office of Alcoholism (California)
OAPM	Office of Alcohol Program Management (precursor to OA)
OMB	Office of Management and Budget
PTA	Parent Teachers Association
RFPs	Requests for Proposals
SPC	State Prevention Coordinator (Program)

SRG	Social Research Group
SRI	Stanford Research Institute
TOVA	The Other Victims of Alcoholism, Inc.
WCTU	Women's Christian Temperance Union
WHO	World Health Organization
WSWAA	Wine and Spirits Wholesalers Association of America
YMCA	Young Men's Christian Association

Bibliography

Aarens, Marc, Tracy Cameron, Judy Roizen, Ron Roizen, Robin Room, Dan Schneberk, Deborah Wingard. (1977) "Alcohol, Casualties and Crime," Report prepared for the National Institute on Alcohol Abuse and Alcoholism.

Alcoholics Anonymous. (1952) *Twelve Steps and Twelve Traditions.* New York: Alcoholics Anonymous Publishing Company.

Armor, David J., Michael Polich and Harriet Stambul. (1975) *Evaluating Alcoholism Treatment.* Santa Monica, California: The Rand Corp.

Asher, Nancy Day. (1978) *Alcohol and Mortality: Separating The Drink From The Drinker.* Ph.D. dissertation, University of California, Berkeley.

Bacon, Selden D. (1943) "Sociology and the Problems of Alcohol: Foundations for a Sociologic Study of Drinking Behavior," *Quarterly Journal of Studies on Alcohol.* Vol. 4, pp. 402-45.

(1948) "The Mobilization of Community Resources for the Attack on Alcoholism," *Quarterly Journal of Studies on Alcohol.* Vol. 9, pp. 473-97.

(1949) "The Administration of Alcoholism Rehabilitation Programs," *Quarterly Journal of Studies on Alcohol.* Vol. 10, pp. 1-47.

(1967) "The Classic Temperance Movement of the U.S.A.: Impact Today on Attitudes, Action and Research," *British Journal of Addiction.* Vol. 62, pp. 5-18.

(1971) "Fragmentation of Alcohol Problem Research." Paper delivered to the Congress on Alcoholism and Drug Dependence, in L.B. Kiloh and D.S. Bell (eds.), *29th International Congress on Alcoholism and Drug Dependence.* Australia: Butterworths, pp. 481-98.

(1976) "Concepts" in W.J. Filstead, J.J. Rossi, and M. Keller (eds.), *Alcohol, New Thinking and New Directions.* Cambridge, Mass.: Ballinger, pp. 57-134.

Bahr, H.M. (1967) "The Gradual Disappearance of Skid Row," *Social Problems.* Vol. 15, pp. 41-45.

Bailey, Margaret B. and Barry Leach. (1965) *Alcoholics Anonymous: Pathway to Recovery.* New York: The National Council on Alcoholism, Inc.

Baker, Keith. (1975) "A New Grantsmanship," *The American Sociologist.* Vol. 10, pp. 206-19.

Bales, Freed. (1942) "Types of Social Structure as Factors in 'Cures' for Alcohol Addiction," *Applied Anthropology.* Vol. 1, pp. 1-13.

Bales, Robert F. (1944) "The Therapeutic Role of Alcoholics Anonymous as Seen by a Sociologist," *Quarterly Journal of Studies on Alcohol.* Vol. 5, pp. 267-78.

(1946) "Cultural Differences in Rates of Alcoholism," *Quarterly Journal of Studies on Alcohol.* Vol. 16, pp. 482-98.

Beauchamp, Dan Edward. (1973) *Precarious Politics: Alcoholism and Public Policy.* Ph.D. dissertation, Johns Hopkins University, Maryland.

(1976) "Comment on 'The Uniform Alcoholism and Intoxication Treatment Act,'" *Journal of Studies on Alcohol.* Vol. 37, p. 1112.

Becker, Howard S. (1963) *Outsiders: Studies in the Sociology of Deviance.* New York: The Free Press.

Berger, Bennett. (1960) "How Long is A Generation?" *British Journal of Sociology.* Vol. 11, pp. 10-23.

Berger, Peter L. (1963) *Invitation To Sociology.* Garden City, New York: Doubleday Anchor.

Berger, Peter and Thomas Luckmann. (1968) *The Social Construction of Reality.* Garden City, New York: Doubleday Anchor.

Biderman, Albert D. and Laure M. Sharp. (1974) "The Evaluation Research Community: RFP Readers, Bidders and Winners," *Evaluation.* Vol. 2, pp. 36-40.

Bigus, Odis. (1974) *Becoming "Alcoholic": A Study of Social Transformation.* Ph.D. dissertation, University of California, San Francisco.

Blau, Peter M. and W. Richard Scott. (1962) *Formal Organizations.* San Francisco: Chandler Publishing Co.

Blum, Eva Maria and H. Richard Blum. (1967) *Alcoholism: Modern Psychological Approaches to Treatment.* San Francisco: Jossey-Bass, Inc.

Blum, Sheila. (1977) "Comment on the 'Rand Report,'" *Journal of Studies on Alcohol.* Vol. 38, pp. 163-68.

Blumberg, Leonard, Thomas E. Shipley, Jr., and Irving W. Shander. (1973) *Skid Row and Its Alternatives.* Philadelphia: Temple University Press.

Blumer, Herbert. (1954) "What Is Wrong With Social Theory?", *American Sociological Review.* Vol. 19, pp. 3-7.

(1966) "Sociological Implications of the Thought of George Herbert Mead," *The American Journal of Sociology.* Vol. 71, pp. 535-44.

(1969) "Sociological Analysis and the Variable," in H. Blumer (ed.), *Symbolic Interactionism: Perspective and Method.* Englewood Cliffs, N.J.: Prentice-Hall, pp. 127-39.

(1971) "Social Problems as Collective Behavior," *Social Problems.* Vol. 18, pp. 298-306.

Bogue, D.J. (1963) *Skid Row in American Cities.* Chicago: Community and Family Study Center, University of Chicago.

Brenner, M. Harvey. (1976) "Estimating the Social Costs of National Economic Policy: Implications for Mental and Physical Health and Criminal Aggression." A study prepared for the use of the Joint Economic Committee, Congress of the United States.

Bruun, K. (1973) "The Minimization of Alcohol Damage." *Drinking and Drug Practices Surveyor.* Vol. 8, p. 47; abstracted from: Alkoholihaitat Mahdollisimman Vahalsikski. *Alkolipolitukka* (1970) Vol. 35, pp. 185-91.

Bruun, Kettil, Griffith Edwards, Martti Lumio, Klaus Mäkelä, Lynn Pan, Robert E. Popham, Robin Room, Wolfgang Schmidt, Ole-Jørgen Skog, Pekka Sulkunen, and Esa Österbert. (1975) *Alcohol Control Policies in a Public Health Perspective.* Helsinki: The Finnish Foundation for Alcohol Studies, Vol. 25.

Bunce, Richard. (1974) "An Overview of California and Alcohol: Products, Problems, Programs, Policies." Paper prepared for Participants in the Expert Conference on the Prevention of Alcohol Problems, Berkeley, California, December 9-11, 1974.

Burt, Daniel W. (1974) "A Behaviorist Looks at Alcoholics Anonymous." Paper presented to the North American Congress on Alcohol and Drug Problems, San Francisco, December, 1974.

Cahalan, Don. (1970) *Problem Drinkers.* San Francisco: Jossey-Bass.

Cahalan, Don and Ira Cisin. (1976) "Drinking Behavior and Drinking Problems in the United States," in Benjamin Kissin and Henri Begleiter (eds.), *The Biology of Alcoholism: Vol. 4; Social Biology.* New York: Plenum Press, pp. 77-115.

Cahalan, Don and Robin Room. (1974) *Problem Drinking Among American Men.* New Brunswick, N.J.: Rutgers Center of Alcohol Studies.

Cahn, Sidney. (1969) "Alcoholism Halfway Houses: Relationships to Other Programs and Facilities," *Social Work.* Vol. 14, pp. 50-60.

California State Assembly Office of Research. (1970) "Alcohol Programs: A Need for Reform." Report prepared for the California Legislature.

Chafetz, Morris. (1965) *Liquor: The Servant of Man.* Boston: Little Brown & Co.

(1966) "Alcohol Excess," *Annals of the New York Academy of Sciences.* Vol. 133, pp. 808-13.

(1974) "Monitoring and Evaluation at NIAAA." *Evaluation.* Vol. 2, pp. 49-52.

(1976) "How To Drink Without Becoming A Drunk." *The National Observer* (August 7, 1976), p. 18.

(1977) *Why Drinking Can Be Good For You.* New York: Stein & Day.

Cherrington, Ernest H. (1st ed. 1920; 2nd ed. 1969) *The Evolution of Prohibition in the United States of America.* Montclair, N.J.: Patterson Smith.

Christie, Nils and Kettil Bruun. (1969) "Alcohol Problems: The Conceptual Framework," in M. Keller and T. G. Coffey (eds). *Proceedings of the 28th International Congress on Alcohol and Alcoholism,* Vol. 2. Highland Park, N.J.: Hillhouse Press, pp. 65-73.

Clark, Mark E. and Larry L. Owsley. (1975) "Alcohol and the State: A Reappraisal of California's Alcohol Control Policies." Report prepared for the Department of Finance, State of California.

Clark, W.B. (1966) "Operational Definitions of Drinking Problems and Associated Prevalence Rates." *Quarterly Journal of Studies on Alcohol.* Vol. 27, pp. 648-68.

Clark, W.B. and Don Cahalan. (1973) "Changes in Problem Drinking Over a Four-Year Span." Paper presented at the annual meeting of the American Public Health Association, San Francisco, November, 1973.

Collins, Randall. (1968) "A Comparative Approach to Political Sociology," in R. Bendix (ed.), *State and Society.* Boston: Little, Brown and Co., pp. 42-67.

Collins, Randall and Michael Makowsky. (1972) *The Discovery of Society.* New York: Random House.

Conn, J.H. (1974) "The Decline of Psychoanalysis—Commentary." *Journal of the American Medical Association.* Vol. 228, pp. 711-12.

Cooper, David. (1967) *Psychiatry and Anti-Psychiatry.* New York: Ballantine Books.

Corwin, E.H.L. and E.V. Cunningham. (1944) "History of Special Institutions for the Treatment of Alcohol Addiction" in *Institutional Facilities for the Treatment of Alcoholism.* New York: Research Council on Problems of Alcohol, Research Report No. 7, pp. 12-19.

Davis, Kingsley. (1938) "Mental Hygiene and the Class Structure," *Psychiatry.* Vol. 1, pp. 55-65.

DeLint, Jan and Wolfgang Schmidt. (1971) "Consumption Averages and Alcohol Prevalence: A Brief Review of Epidemiological Investigations," *British Journal of Addiction.* Vol. 66, pp. 97-107.

Department of Health, Education and Welfare. (1975) Proceedings of the Fourth Annual Alcoholism Conference of the National Institute on Alcohol Abuse and Alcoholism, June 12-14, 1974, Washington, D.C. DHEW Public. No. (ADM) 76-284.

Distilled Spirits Council of the United States, Inc. (1976) *Public Attitudes and Economic Patterns.* DISCUS Facts Book. Washington, D.C.

Dodd, Martin. (January, 1976) "How Big is a Recovery Home?" *The Hearth.*

Durkheim, Emile. (1st ed. 1915; 1st paperback ed. 1965) *The Elementary Forms of the Religious Life.* New York: The Free Press.

(1962) *The Rules of Sociological Method.* New York: The Free Press.

Education Commission of the States. (1977) "Task Force Report on Responsible Decisions About Alcohol."

Edwards, Griffith, Milton M. Gross, Mark Keller, and Joy Moser. (1976) "Alcohol-Related Problems in the Disability Perspective." A Summary of the Consensus of the WHO Group of Investigators on Criteria for Identifying and Classifying Disabilities Related to Alcohol Consumption, *Journal of Studies on Alcohol.* Vol. 37, pp. 1360-82.

Emrick, C.D. (1974) "A Review of Psychologically Oriented Treatment of Alcoholism: The Use and Interrelationships of Outcome Criteria and Drinking Behavior Following Treatment," *Quarterly Journal of Studies on Alcohol.* Vol. 35, pp. 523-49.

(1975) "A Review of Psychologically Oriented Treatment of Alcoholism. II. The Relative Effectiveness of Different Treatment Approaches and the Effectiveness of Treatment vs. No Treatment," *Journal of Studies on Alcohol.* Vol. 36, pp. 88-108.

Emrick, Chad D. and Donald W. Stilson. (1977) "Comment on the 'Rand Report,'" *Journal of Studies on Alcohol.* Vol. 38, pp. 152-63.

Erikson, Kai T. (1962) "Notes on the Sociology of Deviance," *Social Problems.* Vol. 9, pp. 307-14.

Estes, Carroll L. (1975) "New Federalism and Aging," *Developments in Aging,* U.S. Senate, June 24, 1975, pp. 150-57.

Etzioni, Amitai. (1964) *Modern Organizations.* Englewood Cliffs, N.J.: Prentice-Hall, Inc.

Fagan, Ronald W. Jr. and Armand L. Mauss. (1978) "Padding the Revolving Door: An Initial Assessment of the Uniform Alcoholism and Intoxication Treatment Act in Practice," *Social Problems.* Vol. 26, pp. 232-46.

Fisher, Berenice and Anselm Strauss. (1978) "The Chicago Tradition: Thomas, Park and Their Successors," *Symbolic Interaction.* Vol. 1, pp. 5-23.

Fox, R. (1965) "Treatment of Chronic Alcoholism" in Jules H. Masserman (ed.), *Current Psychiatric Therapies.* Vol. 5, pp. 107-11.

Fox, Vernelle. (1976) "The Controlled Drinking Controversy," *Journal of the American Medical Association.* Vol. 236, p. 863.

Fuller, Richard C. and Richard R. Myers. (1941) "Some Aspects of a Theory of Social Problems," *American Sociological Review.* Vol. 6, pp. 24-32.

(1941) "The Natural History of a Social Problem," *American Sociological Review.* Vol. 6, pp. 320-28.

Giesbrecht, Norman, Kai Pernanen, Carol Corlis, Frances Tolnai and Sharon Beaverstone. (1975) "Sociological Trends in the Treatment of Alcoholics." Paper presented at the 21st International Institute on the Prevention and Treatment of Alcoholism; Helsinki, Finland, p. 6.

Glaser, Barney G. (1978) *Theoretical Sensitivity.* Mill Valley, California: The Sociology Press.

Glaser, Barney G. and Anselm L. Strauss. (1967) *The Discovery of Grounded Theory.* Chicago: Aldine Publishing Company.

Glatt, M.M. (1967) "The Question of Moderate Drinking Despite 'Loss of Control,' " *British Journal of Addiction.* Vol. 62, pp. 267-74.

Goethe, Wayne. (1975) "The Death of a Philosophy." Paper presented to the Association of Halfway House Alcoholism Programs of North America.

Goodwin, D. (1976) *Is Alcoholism Hereditary?* New York: Oxford University Press.

Gordon, Jack D., Robert I. Levy, and Charles B. Perrow. (1958) "Open Ward Management of Acute Alcoholism," *California Medicine.* Vol. 89, pp. 397-99.

(1970) "The Alcoholic Patient," *Hospitals.* Vol. 44, p. 63.

Gouldner, Alvin. (1959) "Organizational Analysis," in Robert K. Merton, Leonard Broom, and Leonard S. Cottrell, Jr. (eds.), *Sociology Today.* New York: Basic Books, pp. 400-28.

(1970) *The Coming Crisis of Western Sociology.* New York: Basic Books, Inc.

(1970) "Taking Sides: The Sociologist as Partisan and Non-Partisan," in Jack D. Douglas (ed.), *The Relevance of Sociology.* New York: Appleton-Century-Crofts, pp. 112-48.

Guerrero Street Program. (1976) "A Medical Evaluation of the Safety of Non-Hospital Detoxification." Report prepared for the National Institute on Alcohol Abuse and Alcoholism.

Gusfield, Joseph. (1963) *Symbolic Crusade: Status Politics and the American Temperance Movement.* Urbana: University of Illinois Press.

(1967) "Moral Passage: The Symbolic Process in Public Designations of Deviance," *Social Problems.* Vol. 15, pp. 175-88.

(1975) "Categories of Ownership and Responsibility in Social Issues: Alcohol Abuse and Automobile Use," *Journal of Drug Issues.* Vol. 5, pp. 285-303.

(1975) "The (F)Utility of Knowledge?: The Relation of Social Science to Public Policy Toward Drugs," *The Annals of the American Academy of Social Science and Drug Policy.* Vol. 417, pp. 1-15.

(1976) "The Prevention of Drinking Problems," in W. J. Filstead, J.J. Rossi and M. Keller (eds.), *Alcohol, New Thinking and New Directions.* Cambridge, Mass.: Ballinger, pp. 267-92.

Hall, Peter. (1976) "A Symbolic Interactionist Analysis of Politics," in Andrew Effrat (ed.), *Perspectives in Political Sociology.* New York: Bobbs-Merrill, pp. 35-75.

Hanavan, Thomas L. (1977) "Liquor Law Liability-Comparative Negligence: Drunk Bar Patron Denied Recovery for his Injuries in a Suit Against the Bar," *Santa Clara Law Review.* Vol. 17, pp. 469-84.

Harris, Richard. (March 25, 1972) "The New Justice," *The New Yorker,* pp. 44-105.

Havemann, Joel. (August 7, 1976) "When Uncle Sam Pays the Way for State and Local Lobbyists," *National Journal.* pp. 1116-21.

Helfgot, Joseph. (1974) "Professional Reform Organizations and the Symbolic Representation of the Poor," *American Sociological Review.* Vol. 39, pp. 475-91.

Hofstadter, Richard. (1955, revised) *Social Darwinism in American Thought.* New York: Alfred A. Knopf.

(1955) *The Age of Reform.* New York: Alfred A. Knopf.

Hollister, D.B. (1970) "Alcoholics and Public Drunkenness: The Emerging Retreat from Punishment," *Crime and Delinquency.* Vol. 16, pp. 238-54.

Hughes, Everett C. (1963) "Professions," *Daedalus.* Vol. 92, pp. 665-68.

Jellinek, E.M. (1946) "Phases in the Drinking History of Alcoholics," *Quarterly Journal of Studies on Alcohol.* Vol. 7, pp. 1-88.

(1952) "Phases of Alcohol Addiction," *Quarterly Journal of Studies on Alcohol.* Vol. 13, pp. 673-784.

(1960) *The Disease Concept of Alcoholism.* New Haven: College and University Press.

Jonas, Gerald. (November 15, 1976) "The Disorder of Many Theories," *The New Yorker,* pp. 119-61.

Jones, Thomas L. (1976) "Drop-In and Referral Centers for Public Inebriates." Discussion paper prepared for the California Office of Alcoholism.

Kaij, L. and J. Dock. (1975) "Grandsons of Alcoholics," *Archives of General Psychiatry.* Vol. 32, pp. 1379-81.

Kalb, Melvyn and Morton S. Propper. (1976) "The Future of Alcohology: Craft or Science?", *American Journal of Psychiatry.* Vol. 133, pp. 641-45.

Kaufman, Herbert. (1976) *Are Government Organizations Immortal?* Washington, D.C.: The Brookings Institute.

Keller, Mark. (1969) "Some Views on the Nature of Addiction." Paper presented at the 15th International Institute on Prevention and Treatment of Alcoholism, June 9-18, 1969; Budapest, Hungary.

(1972) "The Oddities of Alcoholics," *Quarterly Journal of Studies on Alcohol.* Vol. 33, pp. 1147-48.

(1975) "Multidisciplinary Perspectives on Alcoholism and the Need for Integration," *Journal of Studies on Alcohol.* Vol. 36, pp. 136-38.

(1976) "Problems with Alcohol: An Historical Perspective," in W.J. Filstead, J.J. Rossi and M. Keller (eds.), *Alcohol, New Thinking and New Directions.* Cambridge, Mass.: Ballinger, pp. 5-28.

(1977) "A Lexicon of Disablements Related to Alcohol Consumption," in G. Edwards, M.M. Gross, M. Keller, J. Moser, and R. Room (eds.), *Alcohol Related Disabilities.* Geneva: World Health Organization, Offset Publication #32, pp. 23-60.

Kessel, Neil, Ann Hawker, and Herbert Chalke (eds), (1974) *Alcoholism: A Med-*

ical Profile. Proceedings of the First International Medical Conference on Alcoholism, London, September 10-14, 1973. London: B. Edsell & Company, Ltd.

Kitsuse, John I. (1970) "Societal Reaction to Deviant Behavior," in Earl Rubington and Martin S. Weinberg (eds.), *Deviance/The Interactionist Perspective.* New York: The MacMillan Co., pp. 19-29.

Kitsuse, John I. and Malcolm Spector. (1975) "Social Problems and Deviance: Some Parallel Issues," *Social Problems.* Vol. 22, pp. 584-94.

Knupfer, Genevieve. (1967) "The Epidemiology of Problem Drinking," *American Journal of Public Health.* Vol. 57, pp. 973-86.

(1972) "Ex-Problem Drinkers," in Merrill Roff, Lee Robins, and Max Pollack (eds.), *Life History Research in Psychopathology,* Vol. 2. Minneapolis, Minn.: University of Minnesota Press, pp. 256-80.

Kobler, John. (1973) *Ardent Spirits: The Rise and Fall of Prohibition.* New York: G.P. Putnam's Sons.

Korn, Richard. (1973) "The Autoplastic Self Changing Solution and Its Treatment: Medical Models of Deviance and Therapy," in National Commission on Marihuana and Drug Abuse, *Drug Use in America: Problem in Perspective,* the technical papers of the 2nd Report, Vol. 4, Treatment and Rehabilitation. Washington, D.C.: U.S. Government Printing Office.

Krause, Elliott A. (1968) "Functions of a Bureaucratic Ideology: 'Citizen Participation,' " *Social Problems.* Vol. 16, pp. 129-43.

Kristol, Irving. (1974) "Taxes, Poverty and Equality," *The Public Interest.* No. 37, pp. 3-28.

Kurtz, Norman R. and Marilyn Regier. (1975) "The Uniform Alcoholism and Intoxication Treatment Act: The Compromising Process of Social Policy Formulation," *Journal of Studies on Alcohol.* Vol. 36, pp. 1421-41.

Laing, Ronald D. (1968) *The Politics of Experience.* New York: Ballantine Books.

Lemert, Edwin M. (1951) *Social Pathology.* New York: McGraw-Hill.

(1967) "The Concept of Secondary Deviation," *Human Deviance, Social Problems and Social Control.* Englewood Cliffs, N.J.: Prentice-Hall.

Levine, Harry Gene. (1975) "The Curse of the Middle Class: Social Problems and the Anti-Alcohol Movement." Unpublished dissertation prospectus, University of California, Berkeley.

(1978) "The Discovery of Addiction: Changing Conceptions of Habitual Drunkenness in America," *Journal of Studies on Alcohol,* Vol. 39, pp. 143-74.

(1978) *Demon of the Middle Class: Self-Control, Liquor and the Ideology of Temperance in 19th Century America.* Ph.D. dissertation, University of California, Berkeley.

Lewis, Jay. (1976) Interview with Ernest P. Noble, "Washington Report," *Journal of Studies on Alcohol.* Vol. 37, p. 1390.

Light, Donald. (1975) "Costs and Benefits of Alcohol Consumption," *Society*. Vol. 12, pp. 13-24.

Lockhart, D. and M. Desrys (1975) "Detoxification Center Evaluation Report: Sacramento County: June 1973–April 1974." Sacramento: State of California, Office of Alcohol Program Management.

Luckmann, Benita. (1970) "The Small Life-Worlds of Modern Man," *Social Research*. Vol. 37, pp. 580-96.

March, James G. and Herbert Simon. (1958) *Organizations*. New York: John Wiley & Sons.

Markowitz, Gerald E. and David Karl Rosner. (1973) "Doctors in Crisis: A Study of the Use of Medical Education Reform to Establish Modern Professional Elitism in Medicine," *American Quarterly*. Vol. 45, pp. 84-107.

Marshall, Eliot. (July 23, 1977) "Fair Play for Drunks," *The New Republic*. Vol. 177, pp. 7-8.

Marshall, T.H. (1964) *Class, Citizenship, and Social Development*. Garden City, N.Y.: Doubleday & Co., Inc.

Martindale, Don. (1960) *The Nature of Sociological Theory*. Boston: Houghton Mifflin.

Marx, Gary T. and James L. Wood. (1975) "Strands of Theory and Research in Collective Behavior," in Alex Inkeles, James Coleman, and Neil Smelser (eds.), *Annual Review of Sociology*. Palo Alto, California: Annual Reviews Inc., pp. 363-428.

Mauss, Armand. (1975) *Social Problems As Social Movements*. Philadelphia: J. B. Lippincott Co.

Maxwell, Milton A. (1962) "Alcoholics Anonymous: An Interpretation," in David Pittman and Charles R. Snyder (eds.), *Society, Culture and Drinking Patterns*. New York: John Wiley & Sons, pp. 577-85.

McCarthy, John D. and Mayer N. Zald. (1965) *The Trend of Social Movements in America: Professionalization and Resource Mobilization*. Morristown, N.J: General Learning Press.

Mead, George Herbert. (1956) *The Social Psychology of George Herbert Mead*, A.L. Strauss (ed.). Chicago: University of Chicago Press.

Medicine in the Public Interest, Inc. (1976) "A Study in the Actual Effects of Alcoholic Beverage Control Laws," Washington, D.C.

Merton, Robert. (1968 enlarged ed.) *Social Theory and Social Structure*. New York: The Free Press.

Milam, James R. (1970) *The Emergent Comprehensive Concept of Alcoholism*. Kirkland, Washington: ACA Press.

Mills, C. Wright. (1959) *The Sociological Imagination*. London: Oxford University Press.

Moynihan, Daniel P. (1970) *Maximum Feasible Misunderstanding*. New York: The Free Press.

Mueller, J.F. and Terrie Schwerdtfeger. (1974) "The Role of the Nurse in Counseling the Alcoholic," *Journal of Psychiatric Nursing and Mental Health Services.* Vol. 12, pp. 26-32.

Mulford, Harold and Ronald Wilson. (1966) *Identifying Problem Drinkers in a Household Health Survey,* Public Health Service Publication No. 1000, Series 2, No. 16, Washington, D.C.: U.S. Government Printing Office.

Mullen, Patricia Dolan. (1975) *Cutting Back; Life After A Heart Attack.* Ph.D. dissertation, University of California, Berkeley.

Musto, David A. (1975) "Whatever Happened to 'Community Mental Health'?", *The Public Interest.* No. 39, pp. 53-79.

National Council on Alcoholism. (1972) "Criteria for the Diagnosis of Alcoholism," *American Journal of Psychiatry.* Vol. 129, pp. 127-216.

National Institute of Mental Health. (1974) "From Program To People." Research on Alcoholism, Task Force Report #6; DHEW Publication No. (ADM) 75-155.

National Institute on Alcohol Abuse and Alcoholism. (1971) *First Special Report to the U.S. Congress on Alcohol and Health,* from the Secretary of Health, Education and Welfare. Washington, D.C.: U.S. Government Printing Office.

(1974) *Second Report to the U.S. Congress on Alcohol and Health New Knowledge,* from the Secretary of Health, Education and Welfare. Washington, D.C.; U.S. Government Printing Office.

(1976) Division of Prevention. "Report of a Study of Overlap and Duplication Between Rutgers Center of Alcohol Studies and the National Clearinghouse for Alcohol Information."

(1976) "Report on Grants and Contracts to National Organizations."

(1978) *Third Special Report to the U.S. Congress on Alcohol and Health,* from the Secretary of Health, Education and Welfare. Washington, D.C.: U.S. Government Printing Office.

O'Briant, Robert G. (Winter 1974/75) "Social Setting Detoxification," *Alcohol Health and Research World.* pp. 12-18.

(January, 1976) "Some Thoughts on Evaluation," *The Hearth.*

O'Briant, Robert G., Henry L. Lennard, Steven D. Allen, and Donald C. Ransom. (Fall 1973) "Recovery from Alcoholism: A Social Treatment Model," *Alcohol Health and Research World,* pp. 27-28.

(1973) *Recovery From Alcoholism.* Springfield, Ill.: Charles C. Thomas.

O'Briant, Robert, N. William Petersen, and Dana Heacock. (Winter 1976/77) "How Safe is Social Setting Detoxification?", *Alcohol Health and Research World,* pp. 22-27.

Odegard, Peter H. (1928) *Pressure Politics: The Story of the Anti-Saloon League.* New York: Columbia University Press.

Pattison, E. Mansell. (1976) "A Conceptual Approach to Alcoholism Treatment Goals," *Addictive Behaviors.* Vol. 1, pp. 177-92.

Pattison, E.M., E.G. Headley, G.C. Gleser, and L.A. Gottschalk. (1968) "Abstinence and Normal Drinking; An Assessment of Changes in Drinking Patterns in Alcoholics After Treatment," *Quarterly Journal of Studies on Alcohol.* Vol. 29, pp. 610-33.

Perlis, Leo. (1975) "The Broad Brush, Employee Assistance, Troubled Employee Program—or WHAT HAPPENED TO ALCOHOLISM?" *The Labor-Management Alcoholism Journal,* National Council on Alcoholism, N.Y. Vol. 5, pp. 19-20.

Perrow, Charles. (1972) *Complex Organizations.* Illinois: Scott Foresman and Company. 2nd ed. 1978.

Pittman, David J. (1967) "The Rush To Combine," *British Journal of Addiction.* Vol. 62, pp. 337-43.

Pittman, David and C. Wayne Gordon. (1958) *The Revolving Door: A Study of the Chronical Police Case Inebriate.* Glencoe, Ill.: The Free Press.

Plaut, Thomas F.A. (1967) *Alcohol Problems: A Report to the Nation.* London: Oxford University Press.

Policy Analysis Inc.. (1971) *The Economic Cost of Alcoholic Abuse and Alcoholism.* Boston, Mass.

Popham, Robert E., Jan E.E. DeLint, and Wolfgang Schmidt. (1968) "Some Comments on Pittman's 'Rush To Combine.'" *British Journal of Addiction.* Vol. 63, pp. 25-27.

Pressman, Jeffrey and Aaron B. Wildavsky. (1973) *Implementation.* Berkeley: University of California Press.

Rayack, Elton. (1967) *Professional Power and American Medicine.* Cleveland: World.

Reynolds, Janice M. and Larry T., Reynolds. (1973) "Interactionism, Complicity and the Astructural Bias," *Catalyst.* Vol. 7, pp. 76-85.

Reynolds, Lynn M. (1974) *The California Office of Alcohol Program Management: A Development in the Formal Control of a Social Problem.* Ph.D. dissertation, University of California, Berkeley.

Robins, Lee N. (1975) "Alcoholism and Labeling Theory," in Walter R. Gove (ed.), *The Labelling of Deviance.* New York: Sage Publications, pp. 21-33.

Robinson, D. (1972) "The Alcohologist's Addiction," *Quarterly Journal of Studies on Alcohol.* Vol. 33, pp. 1028-42.

Roizen, Ronald. (1975) "Drinking and Drinking Problems: Some Notes on the Ascription of Problems to Drinking." Paper presented at the Epidemiology Section meeting, 21st International Institute on the Prevention and Treatment of Alcoholism; Helsinki, Finland, June, 1975.

(1977) "Comment on the 'Rand Report,' " *Journal of Studies on Alcohol.* Vol. 38, pp. 170-78.

(1977) "Alcoholism Treatment's Goals and Outcome Measures," Social Research Group Working Paper F61. Report prepared for the National Institute on Alcohol Abuse and Alcoholism.

Roizen, Ronald, Don Cahalan and Patricia Shanks. (1978) " 'Spontaneous Remission' Among Untreated Problem Drinkers," in Denise Kandel (ed.), *Longitudinal Research on Drug Use: Empirical Findings and Methodological Issues.* Washington, D.C.: Hemisphere Press.

Roman, Paul M. and H.M. Trice. (1968) "The Sick Role, Labelling Theory, and the Deviant Drinker," *International Journal of Social Psychology.* Vol. 14, pp. 245-51.

Room, Robin. (1968) "Amount of Drinking and Alcoholism." Paper presented at the 28th International Congress on Alcohol and Alcoholism, Washington, D.C.

(1971) "The Effects of Drinking Laws on Drinking Behavior." Paper presented at the annual meetings of the Society for the Study of Social Problems. Denver, Colorado; August, 1971.

(1972) "Comment on 'The Alcohologist's Addiction.' " *Quarterly Journal of Studies on Alcohol.* Vol. 33, pp. 1049-59.

(1973) "Regulating Trade Relations and the Minimization of Alcohol Problems." Statement to the California Senate Committee on Governmental Organization Hearing on the Tied-House Provisions of the California Alcoholic Beverage Control Act. San Francisco. November 26, 1973.

(1973) "Saving Money Vs. Reducing Suffering." *Surveyor.* No. 7.

(1973) "The Social Psychology of Drug Dependence," in *The Epidemiology of Drug Dependence.* Report on a conference organized under the auspices of the Regional Office for Europe of the World Health Organization and the United Kingdom Department of Health and Social Security. Copenhagen. September, 1972.

(Fall, 1974) "Minimizing Alcohol Problems." *Alcohol Health and Research World*, pp. 12-17.

(1976) "Comment on 'The Uniform Alcoholism and Intoxication Treatment Act,' " *Journal of Studies on Alcohol.* Vol. 37, pp. 113-44.

(1977) "Measurement and Distribution of Drinking Patterns and Problems in General Populations," in G. Edwards, M.M. Gross, M. Keller, J. Moser and R. Room (eds.), *Alcohol-Related Disabilities.* Geneva: World Health Organization offset publication #32. pp. 61-87.

(1977) "Priorities in Alcohol Social Science Research." Paper prepared for presentation at the Symposium on Research Priorities, Rutgers Center of Alcohol Studies. New Brunswick, N.J., October 7-9, 1977.

(1977) "The Scope and Definition of Alcohol-Related Problems." Prepared for the Task Group on Problem Definition, President's Commission on Mental Health, May, 1977. Social Research Group Working Paper F-58.

(1978) "Draft Position Paper: Policy Initiatives in Alcohol Problems Prevention." Social Research Group Working Paper F48, prepared for National Institute on Alcohol Abuse and Alcoholism Division of Prevention.

(1978) *Governing Images of Alcohol and Drug Problems: The Structure,*

Sources and Sequels of Conceptualizations of Intractable Problems. Ph.D. dissertation, University of California, Berkeley.

Room, R. and N. Day. (1974) "Alcohol and Mortality." Special Report to the National Institute on Alcohol Abuse and Alcoholism.

Room, R. and S. Sheffield (eds.). (1976) *The Prevention of Alcohol Problems.* Sacramento: California State Office of Alcoholism.

Ropers, Richard. (1973) "Mead, Marx and Social Psychology," *Catalyst.* Vol. 7, pp. 42-61.

Ross, Robert and Graham L. Staines. (1972) "The Politics of Analyzing Social Problems," *Social Problems.* Vol. 20, pp. 18-40.

Rothman, David. (1971) *The Discovery of the Asylum: Social Order and Disorder In The New Republic.* Boston: Little Brown.

Rubington, E. (1958) *What To Do Before Skid Row Is Demolished.* Philadelphia: The Greater Philadelphia Movement.

Rusco, Elmer. (1960) *Machine Politics, California Model: Arthur H. Samish and the Alcoholic Beverage Industry.* Ph.D. dissertation, University of California, Berkeley.

Sagarin, Edward. (1972) *Odd Man In.* Chicago: Quadrangle Books.

Schatzman, Leonard and Anselm Strauss. (1966) "A Sociology of Psychiatry: A Perspective and Some Organizing Foci," *Social Problems.* Vol. 14, pp. 3-17.

(1973) *Field Research: Strategies for a Natural Sociology.* Englewood Cliffs, N.J.: Prentice-Hall, Inc.

Scott, Edward M. (1974) "An Attempt at Reworking the Definition and Dynamics of Alcoholism." Paper presented to the North American Congress on Alcohol and Drug Problems, San Francisco, December, 1974.

Seeley, John. (1962) "Alcoholism Is A Disease: Implications for Social Policy," in Pittman, D. and C. Snyder (eds.), *Society, Culture and Drinking Patterns.* New York: John Wiley & Sons, pp. 588-93.

Shibutani, Tamotsu. (1961) *Society and Personality.* Englewood Cliffs, N.J.: Prentice-Hall.

Shore, Richard S. and John M. Luce. (1976) *To Your Health.* New York: The Seabury Press.

Silber, A. (1970) "An Addendum to the Technique of Psychotherapy With Alcoholics," *Journal of Nervous and Mental Disease.* Vol. 150, pp. 423-37.

Silverman, David. (1971) *The Theory of Organisations.* New York: Basic Books Inc.

Simmel, Georg. (1955) *Conflict and the Web of Group Affiliations,* tr. by Kurt H. Wolff and Reinhard Bendix. Glencoe, Ill.: The Free Press.

Simon, Herbert. (1957) *Administrative Behavior.* 2nd ed. New York: The Macmillan Company.

Simonton, O. Carl and Stephanie S. Simonton. (1975) "Belief Systems and Management of the Emotional Aspects of Malignancy," *Journal of Transpersonal Psychology.* Vol. 7, pp. 29-47.

Sinclair, Andrew. (1964) *Era of Excess: A Social History of the Prohibition Movement.* New York: Harper.

Singer, Max. (1971) "The Vitality of Mythical Numbers," *The Public Interest.* No. 23, pp. 3-9.

Smart, Reginald. (1978) "Do Some Alcoholics Do Better in Some Types of Treatment?", *Drug and Alcohol Dependence.* Vol. 3, pp. 65-75.

Smithers Foundation. (1968) *Understanding Alcoholism: For the Patient, The Family, and The Employer.* New York: Scribners.

Sobell, Mark B. and Linda C. Sobell (1977) "Second-year Treatment Outcome of Alcoholics Treated by Individualized Behavior Therapy: Results," in Sobell and Sobbel (eds.), *Emerging Concepts of Alcohol Dependence.* New York: Springer Publishing Company, pp. 300-335.

Spradley, J.P. (1970) *You Owe Yourself a Drunk: An Ethnography of Urban Nomads.* Boston: Little, Brown.

Stevens, Rosemary. (1971) *American Medicine and the Public Interest.* New Haven: Yale University Press.

Stinchcombe, Arthur. (1965) "Social Structure and Environment," in James March (ed.), *Handbook of Organizations.* Chicago: Rand McNally.

Straus, Robert. (1976) "Problem Drinking in the Perspective of Social Change 1940-1973," in W.J. Filstead, J.J. Rossi and M. Keller (eds.), *Alcohol, New Thinking and New Directions.* Cambridge, Mass.: Ballinger, pp. 29-56.

Straus, Robert and Selden Bacon. (1951) "Alcoholism and Social Stability: A Study of Occupational Integration in 2,023 Male Clinic Patients," *Quarterly Journal of Studies on Alcohol.* Vol. 12, pp. 231-60.

(1953) *Drinking in College.* New Haven: Yale University Press.

Strauss, Anselm L. (1978) "Social Worlds," in Norman Denzin (ed.), *Studies In Symbolic Interaction.* New York: J.A.I. Press.

(1978) *Negotiations.* San Francisco: Jossey Bass.

Strauss, Anselm, Leonard Schatzman, Rue Bucher, Danuta Ehrlich, and Melvin Sabshin. (1964) *Psychiatric Ideologies and Institutions.* Glencoe, Ill.: The Free Press, reprinted 1980, Transaction Books.

Sumner, William Graham. (1961) *Folkways.* New York: Mentor.

Szasz, Thomas. (1966-67) "Alcoholism: A Socio-Ethical Perspective," *Washburn Law Journal.* Vol. 6, pp. 258-68.

(1972) "Bad Habits Are Not Diseases: A Refutation of the Claim That Alcoholism is a Disease," *The Lancet.* Vol. 2, pp. 83-84.

Taylor, Mary Catherine. (1977) *Alcoholics Anonymous: How It Works; Recovery Processes in a Self-Help Group.* Ph.D. dissertation, University of California, San Francisco.

Thompson, Steve and associates. (1975) "Drunk on the Street: An Evaluation of Services to the Public Inebriate in Sacramento County." Report to the Sacramento County, California Department of Health.

(1975) "An Overview of State Alcoholism Services." Report submitted to the Senate Health and Welfare Committee, State of California.

Thompson, Victor A. (1961) *Modern Organizations.* New York: Alfred A. Knopf.

Tiebout, H.M. (1951) "The Role of Psychiatry in the Field of Alcoholism; with Comment on the Concept of Alcoholism as Symptom and as Disease," *Quarterly Journal of Studies on Alcohol.* Vol. 12, pp. 52-59.

Timberlake, James H. (1970) *Prohibition and the Progressive Movement 1900-1920.* New York: Atheneum.

Toch, H. (1965) *The Social Psychology of Social Movements.* Indianapolis: Bobbs-Merrill, Co.

Tocqueville, Alexis de. (1835) *Democracy in America,* Phillips Bradley (ed.) (1945) New York: Vintage Books, Vol. II.

Torrey, Edwin Fuller. (1974) *The Death of Psychiatry.* Radnor, Pa.: Chilton Book Company.

Ullman, Albert D. (1958) "Sociocultural Backgrounds of Alcoholism," *Annals of the American Academy of Political and Social Science.* Vol. 315, pp. 48-54.

Wallace, S.E. (1965) *Skid Row as a Way of Life.* Totowa, N.J.: Bedminster Press. Reprinted as a Harper Torchbook, New York: Harper & Row (1968).

Wallach, Lawrence M. (1977) "Analysis of State Prevention Coordinator Reports for the Period April through June, 1977." Report prepared for the Division of Prevention, National Institute of Alcohol Abuse and Alcoholism.

Waller, Willard. (1936) "Social Problems and the Mores," *American Sociological Review.* Vol. 1, pp. 922-32.

Wallgren, Henrik and Herbert Barry. (1970) *Actions of Alcohol.* Amsterdam, N.Y.: Elsevier Publ.

Warren, Roland, Stephen Rose, and Ann Bergunder. (1974) *The Structure of Urban Reform.* Lexington, Mass.: Heath & Co.

Weber, Max. (1941) *The Methodology of the Social Sciences.* Glencoe, Ill.: The Free Press.

Weil, Maurice. (1974) "Social Setting Alcohol Withdrawal Leading to Referral." Paper researched under a Special Services Contract from the National Institute on Alcohol Abuse and Alcoholism, Yale University.

White, Morton. (1947) *Social Thought in America.* Boston: Beacon Press.

Wilkinson, Rupert. (1970) *The Prevention of Drinking Problems.* New York: Oxford University Press.

Wilson, Holly S. (1974) *Infra-Controlling: Social Order Under Conditions of Freedom in an Anti-Psychiatric Community.* Ph.D. dissertation, University of California, Berkeley.

Wiseman, Jacqueline P. (1970) *Stations of the Lost.* Englewood Cliffs, N.J.: Prentice-Hall.

Wittman, Friedner D. (1971) "Alcoholism and Architecture: The Myth of Specialized Treatment Facilities." Paper presented at the American Institute of Architects Meeting, Los Angeles, January, 1971.

World Health Organization. (1952) Expert Committee on Mental Health, Alcoholism Subcommittee Second Report. Annex 2, "The Phases of Alcohol Addiction," World Health Organization Techn. Rep. Ser. No. 48.

(1975) Working Document for the United Nations Ad Hoc Inter-Agency Meeting on Rehabilitation of the Disabled, Annex 1. Geneva 16-22.

Young, Arthur and company. (1975) "Final Report Evaluation of the Santa Clara County Alcohol Facility (Evaluation and Referral Unit)," Sacramento, California.

Zola, Irving Kenneth. (1975) "In the Name of Health and Illness: On Some Socio-Political Consequences of Medical Influence," *Social Science and Medicine.* Vol. 2, pp. 83-87.

Citations from *The Alcoholism Report* and various newspapers and newsletters are included in the reference list at the end of each chapter.

Index

Abstinence, 82, 201ff, 220, 223, 232, 233, 235, 247, 253

Accreditation Council for Psychiatric Facilities (AC/PF), 128

Accreditation of alcoholism programs and facilities, 128, 158, 224, 253, 260

Action frame of reference, 12, 263, 272

Addiction concept of alcoholism, *see* Disease concept of alcoholism

Addiction Research Foundation (Canada), 212

Advisory boards, 20, 40, 44ff, 162, 170, 178, 252, 253, 273; Area Alcohol Education and Training, 62; California, 172, 209-10, 213; Mental Health, 46, 47; Minority, 49, 58; National Council on Alcoholism, 48. *See also* National Advisory Council to the National Institute on Alcohol Abuse and Alcoholism

Air Line Pilots Association, 53-54

Alcohol and Drug Problems Association (ADPA) [formerly the North

American Association of Alcoholism Programs (NAAAP)], 32, 33, 34, 40, 53, 54, 55, 57, 58, 64, 68, 96, 99, 126, 128, 141, 144, 150, 161, 170, 172, 236-37, 246, 259

Alcohol Counseling Center for Early and Preventive Training (AC-CEPT), 228

Alcohol, Drug Abuse and Mental Health Administration (ADA-MHA), 126, 141, 180, 194

Alcohol Health and Research World, 69

Alcoholics Anonymous (AA), 19, 30, 34, 35, 40, 75, 79, 80, 82-85, 93-94, 97, 98, 107, 110, 119, 120, 173, 183, 206, 211, 214, 221-22, 224-25, 255, 256, 261, 270; Al-Anon, 224-25; Al-Ateen, 224; Burt on comparison to behavioral psychology, 84; Twelve Steps in, 83, 221-22

Alcoholic Beverage Control, Department of (ABC), 21, 146-49, 151, 169, 239-41, 247, 253

Alcoholic beverage industries world, 5, 18, 38, 142, 146-49, 169, 188,